ATTACHMENT BEHAVIOUR
AND THE SCHOOLCHILD

All teachers will recognise those children who, in spite of normal intelligence, 'just can't get started' on learning basic skills; those who later lose their capacity for learning; and those who are resistant to learning, seeming deliberately to 'get it wrong' and to rubbish their work. These children are apparently unable to make use of the opportunities offered to them in school. This can result in teachers becoming distressed and frustrated, leaving them in doubt about their own skills.

The authors, who are both experienced teachers and clinically trained educational therapists, take a fresh look at children who have lost their capacity to learn. They explore the relationship between emotional development and cognitive learning processes, believing that understanding this helps to make sense of, and resolve, the problems confronting learning-disabled children.

The idea of educational therapists becoming 'educational attachment figures' for school children is introduced. The concept of attachment behaviour is taken from the work *Attachment and Loss* by John Bowlby, and has considerable relevance to children today, increasing numbers of whom experience separation and loss in their family lives. It is possible for schools to offer these children an emotional, as well as educational, continuity. Understanding the close relationship between attachment behaviour and interactional learning processes both at home and at school is becoming ever more important for all class teachers.

There is an increasing need for educational therapy as a cost-effective intervention and resource for learning-disabled children and their families. Educational therapists are qualified and experienced teachers who have received a specialist clinical training and there is an increasing need for the work they do. This is the first detailed account of that work, illustrated by many moving and vivid stories of children who have benefited from it.

Muriel Barrett is an Educational Therapy Consultant and Supervisor in Educational Therapy Training. **Jane Trevitt** is an Educational Therapist and Teacher-in-Charge of a children's psychiatric unit, and a member of the Cambridge Area Special Education Team.

ATTACHMENT BEHAVIOUR AND THE SCHOOLCHILD

An introduction to educational therapy

Muriel Barrett and Jane Trevitt

TAVISTOCK/ROUTLEDGE
London and New York

First published in 1991
by Routledge
11 New Fetter Lane, London EC4P 4EE

Simultaneously published in the USA and Canada
by Routledge
a division of Routledge, Chapman and Hall Inc.
29 West 35th Street, New York, NY 10001

© 1991 Muriel Barrett and Jane Trevitt

Typeset by
NWL Editorial Services, Langport, Somerset

Printed and bound in Great Britain by
Mackays of Chatham PLC, Chatham, Kent

British Library Cataloguing in Publication Data
Barrett, Muriel
Attachment behaviour and the schoolchild: an introduction to
educational therapy.
1. Learning disordered students. Therapy
I. Title.   II. Trevitt, Jane, 371.9043

Library of Congress Cataloging in Publication Data
Barrett, Muriel, 1926–
Attachment behaviour and the schoolchild: an introduction to
educational therapy/by Muriel Barrett and Jane Trevitt.
p.   cm.
Includes bibliographical references and index.
1. Learning disabled children – Education – Case studies.
2. Attachment behaviour in children – Case studies.   3. Remedial teaching.
I. Trevitt, Jane, 1934–   .   II. Title.
LC4704.5.B37   1991   90–39714
371.9 – dc20   CIP

ISBN 0-415-04797-8
0-415-04798-6 (pbk)

To our children, stepchildren and grandchildren

Experience is never at fault; it is only your judgement that is in error in promising itself such results from experience as are not caused by our experiments. For having given a beginning, what follows from it must necessarily be a natural development of such a beginning, unless it has been subject to a contrary influence, while, if it is affected by any contrary influence, the result which ought to follow from the aforesaid beginning will be found to partake of this contrary influence in a greater or lesser degree in proportion as the said influence is more or less powerful than the aforesaid beginning.

Leonardo da Vinci, *Philosophy*, Codice Atlantico 154r.b
(translated by MacCurdy 1938)

CONTENTS

CONTENTS

ACKNOWLEDGEMENTS

We extend our gratitude to John Bowlby for the generous gift of his time and for his encouragement. His acceptance of our application of some of his concepts, presented in *Attachment and Loss*, to our work as educational therapists inspired us to take a closer look at our interaction with learning-disabled children and their families.

We also thank Margaret Walker at the Tavistock Joint Library for her unfailing interest and help in clarifying many details, and Mary-Sue Moore for being our 'sounding board'.

Contributing authors:

Sister Janet (Barr), Director, Notre Dame Child Guidance Clinic, Glasgow.

Mia Beaumont, Educational Therapist, Hornsey Rise Child Guidance Unit, Hornsey Rise Health Centre, London.

Ann Casimir, Educational Therapist in London Schools.

Argelia Franco, Director, Faculty of Psychology, Bogota University, Colombia.

Gill Salmon, Educational Psychologist, Bromley, Kent.

We greatly appreciate their considerable contributions to this book, and we acknowledge the help afforded by many other colleagues during our discussions on the practice of educational therapy, both here and overseas. Finally, we pay tribute to the support of our husbands, Harry Barrett and John Trevitt, who did much to bring our work to fruition.

INTRODUCTION

All teachers will recognise those children who 'just can't get started' on learning basic skills, those who 'get stuck', and those who seem deliberately to 'get it wrong' and rubbish their work. These children are apparently unable to come to terms with what is required of them in school. This can result in teachers becoming distressed and frustrated, leaving them in doubt about their own skills.

In this book we describe our work with some of the learning-disabled children who are referred to us for educational therapy. John Bowlby's work on attachment and loss provides the basis of our thinking about these children. (We give full references for our discussion of the work of Bowlby and other authorities at the appropriate points in the main text.)

The children we see have a wide range of ability, and are aged between 5 and 16. All of them have lost their capacity for learning (and sometimes for play). In this context the work of Barkley (1981) is relevant:

> The disorders referred to herein as specific learning disabilities do not in any sense imply that the child *cannot* learn academic material. Rather, they refer to children showing various *degrees* of difficulty in acquiring academic skills compared to normal children of similar age and intelligence.

We realise as experienced teachers and clinically trained educational therapists that there is a considerable overlap between those who don't learn, those who stop learning and those who try not to learn. The effect that their emotional development appears to have on their cognitive learning and acquisition of social skills is the most significant common factor.

Our examination of the parallel categories of emotional development and cognitive learning has helped us to understand the children's problems. Patterns of learning in school have their foundations in the child's first interactional learning experiences in the home. When all the growing infant's energy is directed towards gaining or maintaining proximity to his mother he is unable to explore his environment. (In order to avoid unnecessary confusion we refer to all infants and children as 'he' [in practice more boys than girls are referred for educational therapy]. Whenever we refer to

1

'mother' we mean the child's primary care-giver, and educational therapists are referred to as 'she' [the majority in this country are in fact women].) This exploration of people, places and things forms the key to learning. At times of stress the child needs to be confident that his mother is available to comfort and reassure him, and in her absence the secure child will seek an alternative. (A small boy starting school for the first time reassured his mother that if he needed something he would 'cry to Miss'.) Initially we look in detail at the two-way process that involves adaptability in both mother and child, interacting within a family system.

The ability to tolerate and manage change is essential for healthy development, and it is easy to overlook the complex adjustment that this involves. For example, the arrival of the first baby brings about major changes in the family dynamic. All subsequent changes and transitions, such as starting school or moving house, have similar implications.

The majority of the children referred to us for educational therapy have experienced separations which have proved traumatic (e.g. illness, hospitalisation or the break-up of the family by divorce or death), and there is frequently a history of unresolved grief within a family which directly or indirectly affects the child.

In this introduction to the intervention of educational therapy we have not given detailed accounts of our work with families and schools. Instead we have chosen to focus on the learning of individual children and the significance of their attachment behaviour. Our interaction with these children enables us to understand how they perceive themselves as members of their peer, family and school systems.

Irrespective of their ability, some children seem to be particularly vulnerable to life's vicissitudes, while others seem better equipped and survive apparently unsurmountable odds. The majority of children manage the first major transition into school well enough. They adapt to this new experience, confidently expecting that their teachers will provide a continuation for the learning that began at home with mothers, family members and friends. Any anxiety that they may suffer is only temporary. Some of these children will inevitably have learning difficulties, but they are likely to be able to make use of the help that is available within their mainstream school. Parents and teachers become increasingly anxious about the minority of children who are unable to manage their learning. We believe that this anxiety reflects the anxiety of the children themselves, who have never felt secure enough to direct their energies towards exploratory behaviour, except in as much as it involves seeking attention from adults often by inappropriate behaviour. Even more worrying are those children who have given up trying to get attention, who withdraw and direct their energy towards remaining invisible.

The range of 'therapeutic' interventions for these troubled children depends on local provision and may include psychotherapy, play therapy, family therapy or educational therapy. The majority of referrals are made to a clinic, where psychologists, psychiatrists and social workers are core members of the team. Some clinics also employ teachers, most of whom are clinically trained educational therapists.

The intervention of educational therapy stands as a therapy in its own right. Its focus on the examination (through the use of the metaphor) of feelings about learning using educational material differentiates it from, for example, remedial teaching or child psychotherapy. The educational therapist seeks to reawaken the child's capacity for play and learning and to rediscover the skills he does possess.

In addition to the family work already mentioned the educational therapist has three roles: teacher, educational attachment figure (a concept introduced in the main text) and consultant to teachers in schools. Each child is helped on a sessional basis, which allows him to remain within his mainstream school.

In Britain children start school when they are 5 years old. Some primary schools offer continuous provision for children until they make the transition at 11 to secondary school; in other areas the primary stage is divided and children start in infant schools, changing to junior schools when they are 7. (Some local authorities and fee-paying schools vary this pattern.) The 'bulge' in the number of referrals for educational therapy appears to be associated with impending school transfer or to be a result of it. This trend is reflected in our book.

The Education Act 1981 introduced a policy of positive integration for virtually all children within mainstream school provision, in line with international trends. This Act emphasised the need to provide support for the teacher and the individual child in the classroom. The implementation of the 1988 Education Reform Act with its National Curriculum and assessment of attainments may well help to highlight and clarify the needs of those children who are underachieving for complex emotional reasons and who, in spite of their ability, fail to achieve what is expected of them.

We believe that anxious, and often distressed, children need a space of their own to work with a trusted adult either individually or in a small group in order to make better use of the classroom situation. If they are referred to an educational therapist they can be offered a shared space within which feelings about loss and learning can be explored. They can then move towards age-appropriate autonomy.

The main purpose of this book is to demonstrate how a schoolchild's experience of attachment behaviour can facilitate or inhibit his learning, and to introduce the practice of educational therapy.

In addition to an improvement in the children's scholastic skills we observe changes in their appearance and in their interactive behaviour with us. We have no hard evidence to quantify the success of this intervention and base our observations on clinical inference. Research is urgently required to evaluate our claims for the effectiveness of educational therapy, which should be more widely available.

(All names and personal details have been changed to ensure confidentiality.)

Part I

THE IMPORTANCE OF ATTACHMENT AND LOSS IN LEARNING

1

THE LEARNING EXPERIENCE OF CHILDREN REFERRED FOR EDUCATIONAL THERAPY

Educational therapy provides a second-chance learning opportunity for children who are unable to make constructive use of their school learning experiences. Their feelings of insecurity appear to be excessive and detrimental to their learning. Their states of mind seem to override their willingness to acquire, retain and extend their cognitive and/or social skills. Their innate ability is not in doubt, whether they are 'gifted' or 'slow learners'; their formal intellectual assessments give them scores ranging from 58 to 130 + (measured on the Weschler Intelligence Scale for Children [Revised] 1976). Most of our work is with children whose chronological ages range from 5 to 16 years, but when working with families we naturally include infants and pre-schoolers in our interactions.

These 'learning-disabled' children have frequently caused their teachers (and often their parents) considerable anxiety, distress and frustration. This is not only because of their slow academic progress, but also because of their behaviour, which ranges from extremely disruptive acting out to a total withdrawal. The attention-seeking behaviour cannot be ignored since it tends to make it impossible for peers or teachers to work effectively. The responses that this behaviour elicits rarely satisfy the child and only seem to exacerbate the situation. The behaviour of the child who seems determined to make himself invisible is even more problematic, and it is difficult to find ways of communicating with him. Obviously there are many other children between these two extreme groups who also have difficulty with their learning.

We examine the links that we see between the first experience of interactional learning that takes place between an infant and mother in the home and the 'second-chance' learning experience between a schoolchild and an educational therapist. Some of the children with whom we work have lost their capacity to play as well as to learn, and one of the most important tasks of the educational therapist is to bring the children into a state of readiness for play as a prerequisite for learning.

SECURE CHILDREN

Before attempting to describe the children referred to us we look briefly at those who feel secure enough about their attachments within their family system to accept the transition into school without undue anxiety. The concept of attachment behaviour is taken from John Bowlby's theory of attachment and loss (1969, 1973, 1980). In Chapter 2 we give a detailed description of certain concepts of this theory, which are central to our work.

It is easy to recognise the children who appear confident and who can relate positively to their teachers and their peers. They expect responses to be equally positive, are able to wait for attention, and are not overwhelmed by apparent rejection. This same flexibility can be seen where interactions within the peer group are concerned. Secure children can be observed finding solutions to problems independently or in cooperation with their peers. They show a responsive interest and a lively curiosity in a school environment that is initially unfamiliar to them. Most of them come from families where their parents have prepared them appropriately for entry into school. They have learned to tolerate separations from those who are important to them (attachment figures), secure in the knowledge that reunion will follow.

With the help of Figures 1.1–1.4 we outline the basic stages in the interactional process between an infant and his mother that facilitate reciprocal attachment behaviour and offer a foundation for subsequent play and first learning experiences, which the majority of the secure children described above will have known.

Observation: mother and infant's first interaction

Figure 1.1 Observation: mother and infant's first interaction

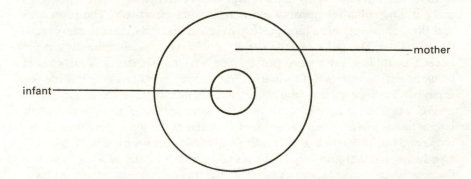

However well the mother has prepared herself, at the birth both she and her infant find themselves entering an unknown relationship, albeit usually within an established family system. If all goes well the mother will be supported by her partner in her new role. Initially the infant is dependent

upon his mother to meet his needs. The sensitivity with which she is able to recognise and respond to her infant's gradually emerging ability to communicate his feelings sets the pattern for interactional learning.

Separation: mother and infant exploring first separations/reunions

Figure 1.2 Separation: mother and infant exploring first separations/reunions

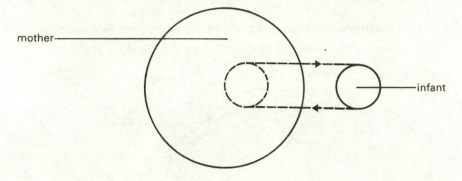

Slowly the infant becomes aware that he is an individual, separate from his mother. He is dependent on her ability to allow this to happen as this is a two-way process. He is then free to develop his relationship with other family members.

He is encouraged to explore by playing sometimes within sound but not necessarily sight of her. The confident child becomes increasingly adventurous and can tolerate brief separations, because he can carry a picture of himself interacting with his mother inside his head.

Individuation: playing and learning in the shared space

Figure 1.3 Individuation: playing and learning in the shared space

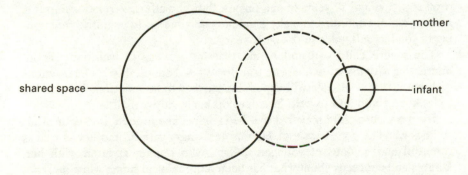

9

The infant's increasing mobility allows him to explore a wider environment which necessitates the acceptance of limits being set. He experiences the idea that his wishes may not match those of others.

He begins to plan ahead, struggling with the things he finds difficult and learning ways of managing himself and his world. The interactions of the mother and her infant take place within the shared space where they can relate without impinging on one another.

Transition: sharing a teacher with the peer group in school

Figure 1.4 Transition: sharing a teacher with the peer group in school

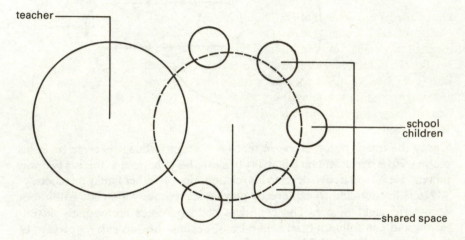

The positive responses that the infant receives confirm his sense of self-worth. The notion that new situations and people can be encountered without undue anxiety is promoted. Estrada *et al.* (1987) in their longitudinal study of children at 4, 5, 6 and 12 years of age suggest that 'the affective relationship (i.e. mother/child) continues to make a unique contribution to cognitive functioning beyond its influence in the early years'.

The secure child will understand that his feelings of well-being about interacting with his mother can be transferred and adapted to his interactions with his first teacher. He will expect his teacher to be emotionally available to look after him and to help him develop his cognitive skills.

Even a secure child may feel that he is being 'abandoned' in favour of his siblings when he goes to school. He may feel angry with his mother as well as resentful and envious of younger siblings who remain at home with her. Doubts and concerns about what has been happening at home while he is not there can become quite intolerable for a few children, and could eventually lead to school refusal or 'phobia'.

Some parents are unable to support their child's entry into school because their own capacity to modify their entrenched mode of thinking apparently becomes temporarily suspended on the occasion of change. Other parents feel uncertain about the experience that is so different from their own schooling; some even envy their children. Elizur states:

School entrance is a stressful situation for the child and family. During a relatively short period of time many changes occur. The child has to adjust to the new rules of the school environment and to develop the emotional, cognitive and social skills needed for coping with the new demands.

[Elizur 1986]

He confirms our view that the 'problems' of the majority disappear after a period of adjustment, but that a 'significant' number of children do not manage this transition that affects the whole family.

Having said that securely attached children approach the advent of school with a feeling of positive anticipation, we now consider those who are anxiously awaiting school entry. The children referred to us for educational therapy have formed anxious attachments (as defined by Ainsworth and Wittig 1969).

ANXIOUS CHILDREN

When the development of attachment behaviour between an infant and mother has been distorted in some way problems may arise. These can affect not only first learning but also future learning patterns. Again we make use of simple diagrams to illustrate three examples of early mismatched interactive behaviour in Figures 1.5, 1.6 and 1.7.

Rejection

When a mother is unable to tolerate the infant within her space, this may result in her rejection of him. It is difficult for him to develop an idea of self as a valued individual, unless he experiences a more positive interaction with an alternative attachment figure.

This mother is unable to be emotionally available for her child, and he is unable to gain the reassurance, support and encouragement that are essential to him. His basic needs are met without reference to his feelings and he is therefore deprived of meaningful interactions. All the energy of such a child may be directed towards trying to attract his mother's attention, though if this fails he may develop his own rejecting responses. His ability to explore and learn constructively can be seriously affected. If he adopts attention-seeking strategies to ensure that he is noticed (particularly if these demands become excessive) his mother's rejecting behaviour may be exacerbated.

11

Figure 1.5 Rejection

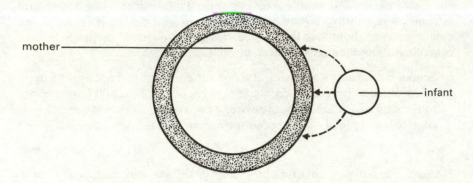

Alternatively, the child may withdraw, making fewer and fewer demands; some of these children continue to avoid personal interaction and channel their energies into intensive scholastic learning.

Overprotection

Figure 1.6 Overprotection

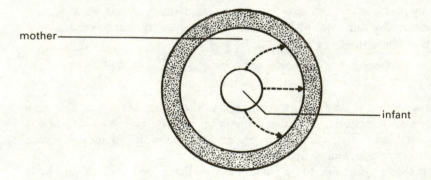

When a mother is unable to allow her infant to explore independently, he has few opportunities to learn that he and she can survive separately. The resulting relationship is sometimes referred to as symbiotic or 'smothering mothering'. The interaction of the pair is further complicated by mistiming which leads to a mismatch of their approaches to one another. A child with an over-protective mother is rarely allowed to experience frustration, all his needs being met almost before he has become aware of them for himself. He has therefore had no chance to develop problem-solving strategies nor to discover that frustration and anger can be survived. This can result in omnipotent behaviour with the child never discovering that his wishes are not commands. Without any experience of individuation the child cannot develop a realistic sense of self.

Confusion

Figure 1.7 Confusion

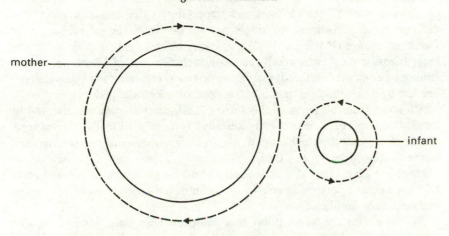

Where neither mother nor infant discover a shared, fixed point of reference they give the impression of spinning within an uncontained space. No contact seems possible. There is no apparent opportunity for the formation of any attachment since the mother's emotional availability is inconsistent. The infant's behaviour appears to be excessively anxious. Because he receives few responses, he is unable to learn any meaningful strategies for interacting with others. He may be offered tantalising glimpses of closeness by his mother only to have them instantly withdrawn. Both mother and infant seem to alternate between perpetual motion, often frantically searching for each other, or sinking into despair. While excessive activity can defend against feelings of depression for some children, others may attempt to take control for themselves by adopting a parenting role.

The effects of anxious attachment are felt by all vulnerable children at any age or level of ability, and there are some infants who are less energetic than others at overcoming it or seeking ways of making their needs known. It is also important to note that there is another group of children whose early

13

learning is thought to be affected by some degree of neurological damage, which further complicates their acquisition of the basic '3R' skills. Children labelled 'dyslexic' (a controversial label that we shall not concern ourselves with here) often fall into this category.

We believe that children who have not participated in a 'good-enough' relationship with an 'attachment figure' are less likely to learn effectively in school. Our experience has shown that clear links can be made between the loss by death or separation of family members and the loss of a child's capacity for learning. Losses associated with miscarriages, stillbirths or cot deaths are seldom recognised as contributing to a child's learning disability. Increasing numbers of children are experiencing the trauma of their parents' separation or divorce, with all the changes and uncertainties that this can bring. The difficulties of adjustment to single-parent family status or reconstituted family groupings (Robinson 1982) can easily be overlooked as they become increasingly a part of 'normal' life. Although the loss of house or teacher cannot be equated with family losses, nevertheless the effects of these changes are felt by more children than is recognised or acknowledged.

Children from all parts of the socio-economic spectrum are affected by loss. Their parents may be materially and educationally advantaged, 'successful' by most people's standards, in their careers and in pursuing their interests (Dowling *et al.* 1985). Conversely, others are seriously disadvantaged. A single parent may look to a child for parenting or expect him to take on an adult partnering role (a situation which can, of course, also occur in two-parent families).

We work on the assumption that children who have formed anxious attachments to people whose behaviour has been unpredictable, inconsistent or punitive are at risk. The circumstances that lead to adverse situations developing in any family are diverse, often dictated by factors outside the family's immediate control, and again sometimes cross-generational in origin.

In our experience and that of our educational therapy colleagues, many anxious learning-disabled children have been unable to separate from their mothers when first entering school. Many of them seem preoccupied with their longing to return to an infantile state of dependency, thus precluding age-appropriate scholastic learning.

Many parents cannot anticipate the developing needs of their children. A few may not be able to provide the play materials that could make the difference to a child's later development and learning (Gottfried 1984). The learning of the parents themselves often appears to have been inhibited, and the way they communicate with others is frequently misinterpreted. Their memory of interacting with their own parents influences the way they treat their children; and their recall of their own schooling can affect their attitude to their child's school and teachers. Some parents may present the advent of school in a negative manner, or, if their children are misbehaving in the family system, even as a threat.

We need to remember that many of the learning-disabled children about whom we are writing have experienced unpredicted separation from, or loss of, adults with whom they have formed a close relationship, in addition to suffering the loss of their learning skills.

Each family is as unique as the individual child. If they have a common characteristic it is a pattern of erratic care-giving that is often repeated from earlier generations. Frequently their behaviour toward the referred child contrasts with that shown to siblings. One brief example is the behaviour of Mrs Andrews. When she arrived at the clinic waiting room she was carrying several large bags of food. Her weekly ritual was to offer her two sons a cake. The 'good' boy was allowed to eat his immediately, but her 'bad' boy was told he must wait until after his session. The educational therapist working with the latter noted that on their return to the waiting room the 'bad' boy's cake had invariably been eaten. Is there something about one child's behaviour that elicits a different response from the parents, and does the position in the family contribute towards this? Dunn (1988) in her discussion of 'normative life events as risk factors' emphasised the importance of taking into account the 'individual differences in children's responses to stressful events', which in turn might well affect a parent's treatment of a child.

Family interviews have helped us to understand the family dynamic from the referred child's point of view, and in what way family interactions may contribute to his learning disability. Certain pre-school behaviours, such as excessive clinging or untoward aggression, are often readily acknowledged. Masturbation or bed-wetting may be considered too embarrassing to discuss. Milestones such as delayed speech, walking or toilet-training are more likely to be remembered than slowness in the acquisition of cognitive skills such as counting or learning colours. Some parents may feel there is no need for concern when a child is 'no trouble'. This is similar to a complacent description of an infant who makes no demands and is called a 'good baby who never cries'.

The question of parental disagreement about bed times, television or choice of schools may lead to open discussion within the safe boundary of a family interview. Facts about family history may have been hitherto unknown to the children, although serious marital discord is seldom revealed openly. The families with whom we have worked usually make it clear whether they wish the focus to remain on the educational 'problem', or are willing to accept that certain events might have contributed to the child's loss or change of learning; while others show a willingness to explore how they individually or collectively feel ready to acknowledge and re-assess any responsibility for one member's difficulties.

Many families take a long time to recall and reveal events which they have chosen (consciously or unconsciously) to 'forget'. In an effort to conceal more serious family secrets, such as abuse (with its many variations), all knowledge of them may be denied.

15

Frequently the children referred do not come up to their parents' expectations or reach the achievement level in school that they hoped for; their efforts tend to be denigrated. They often say that the child is 'just like I was at that age, *I've* made out all right', with the implication that there is no real need for change. Indeed, they find the prospect of any change threatening because it is interpreted as personal criticism of them as parents or individuals. An underlying envy is occasionally revealed in statements such as 'no one offered *me* any help'. Like Mrs A with her bags of food (see p. 15), parents may express dislike of the referred child and show overt preference for a sibling. Others express ambivalence; denigration followed immediately by praise. A large proportion of parents are unable to accept responsibility for a child's failure at school, or his 'bad' behaviour. Blame is apportioned to the child for being stupid or lazy, both common accusations; to another member of the immediate family for causing the 'problem' either from inherited genes or behaviourally; to the grandparents for their 'failure' in parenting the parents, which often includes undervaluing education; and lastly to authority figures, especially members of the educational system, for example head teachers and educational psychologists (Heard and Barrett 1982).

There are parents who have been able to care for their children only on an intermittent basis, either by force of circumstance or to meet their own needs. An example of some work undertaken with Mark, a boy of 8 who came from such a background, is given in Chapter 9. D.W. Winnicott (1965) described children similar to those we know as coming from what he called 'unsatisfactory' homes (a rather judgemental term we are unlikely to use nowadays). But he was making the point that the less advantaged children, emotionally speaking, arrive at school with an expectation that the school and its teachers could provide the very qualities missing from their home life. They hope to find what he calls a 'home from home', a stable emotional climate in a new setting/context/system that can replace, or act as a substitute for, their earlier insecure family life.

We have found that the over-anxious behaviour of parents when facing new situations is made manifest in various ways: confusion about appointment times or which family members should attend an interview are common examples. A referral can trigger a repeat of earlier parental reaction. At the beginning of our work with one family, mother was surprised to discover that she had 'forgotten' to bring her daughter, aged 9, to the clinic, although she had brought her other two children, who were not causing concern. She then recalled how she had 'forgotten' this daughter when she had to be placed in intensive care, following a difficult birth. A father chose to work several hundred miles away from home because he could not tolerate the behaviour of his infant son. This father could not tolerate his now 7-year-old son's low attainment in school and was once again seriously contemplating working far from home.

Very often the parents perceive themselves in a similar light to the child about whom they are most worried. The fact that their own needs may override their capacity to meet those of their children means they have little energy left to support them. Without intervention a pervasive atmosphere of hopelessness is likely to continue.

We are left with the impression that many of the children referred to us feel lost. Is this because they do not truly understand who they are, or what their role in the family or surrogate family should be? This seems to apply particularly to children who are members of more than one family. When they become members of a much larger and even more complex system, a school, are their feelings of being lost, *un*attached as it were to any one person, likely to be even more painful to manage?

THE TRANSITION INTO A SCHOOL SYSTEM

The interdependence of the two systems, family and school, may be denied by either, but attachment behaviour continues within both, and we, as educational therapists, are concerned about the impact of the dual systems on the children we see.

The children whose manner in the new setting is anxious do not necessarily recognise the attempts of their class teacher to help them. The very fact that the teacher and the school environment represent yet one more bewildering experience in their chain of disruptive life events is likely to negate their capacity to function age-appropriately. Children who adopt a defensive mode of behaviour, either vociferous or aggressive, are likely to be noticed, albeit not often in the way they would wish; for the quiet, withdrawn children who cause no trouble, there is a danger that they will be overlooked. We feel that these behaviours are especially prevalent among children who have been cared for by too many child-minders, have suffered neglect, or have been placed in and out of care (Berridge 1985).

It has long been understood that there are mothers who find it intolerable to bear the 'loss' of the youngest member of the family when it is time for him to start school. Not all are able to find a balance between the conflicting feelings that are engendered when it is time to relinquish any of their children to a teacher. The fact that young children in particular frequently say to a parent, 'But my teacher says ...', can elicit some resentment in that parent. They may feel their parenthood is being undermined. As children progress through their school years this can lead to serious confrontations which are frequently based on misunderstandings over the authority of parents versus that of teachers. The feelings of conflict that remain are often left to reside in the child, perhaps more particularly in adolescents. When a child's behaviour is reported to be markedly different at home and in school, a conflict may arise between the two systems, thus exacerbating the child's anger and distress.

Teachers sensitive to each child's needs seem able to find ways of responding to 'their' children as individuals, even when they have the responsibility of a large class. Quite often teachers will have had the experience of being called 'Mum' – less frequently 'Dad' – by one or more of the children they are teaching. The fact that the teacher concerned does not share the gender of the parent appears to be irrelevant to the children who, for whatever reason, seem momentarily to forget that they are in school. Understandably, this is more likely to occur in a reception class in the child's first year at school, although it has been observed and reported at other times of transition, notably what for the majority is the final one into secondary school. This may well evoke memories of their first entry into school. The change always entails meeting many different peers transferring from several local schools, and frequently involves a journey. In addition, these children have to adjust to complex timetables, and are expected to relate to many more teachers than they encountered in their primary schools. Most schools now prepare children for the entry into secondary school but a few children cannot manage the change. The following observation demonstrates the need for this minority to have one teacher as a reference point, a 'specific attachment person' as defined by Sroufe (1983). Although he uses this term when examining different attachment behaviour patterns of pre-schoolers, we think it equally applicable when describing the role of a teacher who can represent a secure base in the initial confusion and constant changes that occur in a secondary school.

In a large, co-educational inner city school, Mrs Jones, teacher-in-charge of a special needs department had been allocated four boys as the result of an intake procedure assessing the attainment of all children entering the school. The boys, aged 11 and 12 years, were considered to be in need of additional support due to their severe reading problems, which precluded their attendance at mainstream English lessons. There was an expectation, however, that they would attend all other mainstream lessons, entailing a considerable amount of movement around the school, which had over a thousand pupils on roll. Towards the end of their second term Mrs Jones commented to the educational therapist with whom she was working that she could not understand why the four boys kept returning to her room outside the times scheduled for their extra English lessons. During breaks in their timetable one came to ask the way to another much-frequented part of the school, a second needed help to find lost property(!), the third asked permission to eat his sandwiches in the room while the fourth wished to do his homework there at lunch-time. Each boy sought her attention and engaged her in conversation far beyond the ostensible 'reason' for his visit. She reported that this was a daily occurrence. The first two boys' behaviour showed a clear need for quite close proximity to this teacher. The other two needed less direct attention from her and were satisfied with minimal interaction with her. One put his head around the door *en passant* and called

18

out, 'Hi, Miss!' while the other gave a slight wave in her direction, which she acknowledged. Occasional contact with their 'specific attachment person' was enough to reassure these last two boys. This behaviour is similar to the younger child's ability to function within sound of mother but only occasional sight of her, for example when playing in another room. The 'idea' of themselves and a caring figure had become part of a growing memory which allowed the boys to move towards behaving more age-appropriately in school. The four boys above could be said to be behaving in a manner that, for part of their school day at least, was reminiscent of a much earlier stage of their development.

Whenever we have worked with teachers individually, sub-systems (Barrett 1985), or staff groups, it seems to us that very few of them are aware of the importance of their role and their potential to become a 'specific attachment person' especially for children who are anxious. Most teachers see themselves as skilful practitioners, working creatively and earnestly but under great pressure from society to maintain high academic and behavioural standards for the children placed in their care. They have chosen to work with children in particular age groups, encompassing varying intelligence levels, states of mind and ranges of behaviour. Our work with teachers gives a clear indication that they are only too well aware of the needs of individual children and at the same time recognise that not all children can make use of the interactive process with an adult. There are those however who have difficulty in maintaining their professional role. Occasionally teachers may respond inappropriately to anxious children. They may react by showing overt hostility to and rejection of a child who defends against anxiety by aggressive behaviour or rudeness, or conversely may adopt a 'motherly' or 'fatherly' role resulting in over-protection or over-indulgence towards a withdrawn or helpless child. It may well be that the child's manner tends to elicit these responses. If he has previously experienced rejection or smothering mothering as previously outlined (see pp. 11–13) his expectation is likely to be that it will be perpetuated. When a teacher appears to be 'spinning', like our third group of mothers, only the more secure children will be able to manage.

While readily acknowledging the fundamental importance of families to all children it is worth remembering that Michael Rutter and colleagues, in the title of one of his many books on education, *Fifteen Thousand Hours: Secondary Schools and their Effects on Children* (1979), reminds us of the length of time that children spend together with their teachers as members of the educational system in Britain.

THE CHILDREN THEMSELVES

We have already suggested that certain behaviours indicate a child's state of mind in school. Certain behaviours can also be used to express feelings about classroom skills. When these do not match those of their peers, a way of showing their discomfort or anxiety lies in untoward behaviour: incapable of concentration, cannot sit still, uneasy or non-existent peer relationships, or a combination of all three. Feelings about their learning may also be expressed by withdrawal, aggression and/or clowning, or by more anti-social behaviours such as stealing. A teacher's concern about the children's behaviour cannot necessarily be shared with colleagues, from fear either of seeming incompetent or of being misunderstood. Wittenberg-Salzberger, Henry and Osborne examined these dilemmas and concerns (1983).

How then do we interpret what appears to be the misleading behaviour of these children? Bryan and Bryan (1976) called children with learning disabilities 'poor people readers'. We would like to suggest that the coping behaviour they use to compensate for inner fears often makes it difficult for us to 'read' them. Frequently the situation is further complicated by the children presenting their teachers and peers with facial expressions and body language that show the opposite of what they are feeling. Figures 1.8 to 1.13 explore this further.

Figure 1.8 The individual child

as he may seem   *as he may feel*

This child may have become partially or completely withdrawn in school because he is afraid that he will not be able to handle the explosive feelings inside him. Part of the fear may be that he will elicit reciprocal feelings of anger from others towards himself if he reveals his inner state of mind.

Figure 1.9 The individual child

as he appears

and really feels

Aggressive behaviour can be an overt expression of internal despair relating to the child's inability to elicit the kind of response that he needs. He may in fact wish that his behaviour could be controlled or he may set out to be as bad (and sad) as everyone has told him he is.

Figure 1.10 The individual child

as she looks

but is feeling

It is well known that fewer girls are referred for major learning problems. Low achievers often present a happy face that belies their inner feelings of confusion and inadequacy about themselves and their role in school.

21

Figure 1.11 The individual child

he may be shown   *but see*

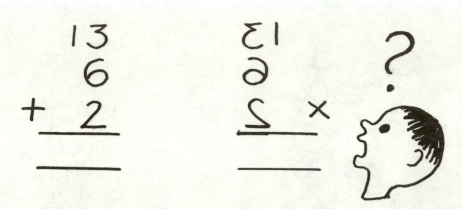

Quite a number of learning-disabled children have specific visual and auditory problems in addition to emotional problems. When this is not recognised their coping mechanisms can mislead their teachers. They sometimes get labelled the class 'clown' or are accused of being lazy or 'stupid'. The children in Figure 5 also belong in this group.

Figure 1.12 The individual child

he is told   *but what can he hear?*

Figure 1.13 The individual child

he is given specific help

This illustration is based on a real event. A caring learning-support teacher was teaching an 8-year-old 'e' for egg, because she knew his father kept hens. Her mental picture was maternal – a mother hen sitting on a nest of eggs. The child did not 'see' this picture. It contrasted starkly with his own. On the morning that he was struggling to master the sound 'e' for egg his father had shouted at him in temper 'eat up your bloody egg now your mother's cooked it for you'.

Numerous learning-disabled children feel that they have little hope of modifying their behaviour or understanding how their state of mind could be affecting their learning.

Most of the children referred to us for educational therapy feel that they have no control over circumstances concerning themselves and their families. They do not perceive themselves as individuals who have a choice, either in small matters, for example choosing a comic or sweets, or concerning more important issues, such as bedtimes or playing with friends versus doing the shopping. An adult seeking their opinion, or taking their often quite reasonable wishes into account, rarely forms part of their experience, even in adolescence. A boy of 14 could not convince either of his parents that he would like to have a later bedtime than his 5-year-old brother; the request was received as 'outrageous'. Some children continue to fight or argue against the decisions of parental figures and older siblings, while others give up and become compliant or passive. A few withdraw by watching television or becoming silent; others into self-cosseting such as over-eating; some opt out and acquire streetwise skills, where at least in fantasy they are able to exercise autonomy; others present a cynical facade that convinces no one, least of all themselves. Yet another minority retreat into academic pursuits to the exclusion of developing close personal relationships.

The state of mind of an increasing number of children reveals a different kind of fear and despair, with little hope of change. We are referring to those children, who cannot give their attention to learning because they come from homes where behaviour is violent and they suffer or observe physical, verbal or sexual abuse. A statement made by Maher (1987) that 'teachers have a very significant role to play in child-abuse cases', is one which we would like to see given prominence in all training courses. In their studies of the effects of maltreatment on the development of young children Pianta *et al.* found it was children who had been neglected that presented the most severe and varied problems at ages 5 and 6 years. 'In the classroom they were anxious, inattentive, failed to comprehend their academic work, lacked initiative, and relied heavily on the teacher for help, approval, and encouragement .... These neglected children were not cooperative with adults, nor were they sensitive or empathic with peers' (Pianta *et al.* 1989). These children were well below the other children in the total sample on academic achievement. It seems likely that they had learned to expect that they were not worthy of being treated with respect. It also emerged from the study by Pianta *et al.* that many of the children had little opportunity to establish long-term relationships with any teachers or even peers because they changed schools so frequently. In summarising their findings they comment that 'The consequences of psychologically unavailable parenting were dramatic in the early years as children showed a decline in cognitive functioning and presented a wide range of behaviour problems.' Again these findings match the empirical evidence that we have on the importance of consistent adult availability (attachment figures) for anxious children, especially at times of transition or change.

The majority of children referred to an educational therapist have been unable to make use of the educational continuum provided for them, even when this has been special. In a classroom the teacher appears to be inaccessible to them: they are too anxious to make any use of skills to attract her attention. Again Sroufe (1983) found in his research into adaptive patterns of attachment behaviour of pre-schoolers that 'since children interact with the environment in terms of their previous adaptation, a self-perpetuating cycle is maintained'. If they have never felt they had the 'right' to adult attention, how can they develop skills to reach the person they hope will take note of their anxious feelings? In his summing up, he presents an hypothesis that certain children 'elicit reactions from teachers which are most congruent with their history of maladaption'. Many of the children in this study were observed to be 'attention-seeking in negative ways', thus perpetuating the response that confirmed their feelings.

There is now a move away from small group provision towards learning support in the classroom, but the teacher within the small group is undoubtedly more accessible to a child. For the anxious child, however, the experience can be too reminiscent of life in his family, where he has to compete with siblings for mother's attention. The next move for a child may well be a transfer to a unit with a specialist teacher, where he will receive individual teaching, learn to recognise the needs of peers and understand how feelings contribute to the group dynamic. Even this specialised input fails to engage a very small group of anxious children. If their learning-disability 'symptom' or difficult behaviour is their way of drawing attention to a troubled family, family therapy may be advocated. For others exhibiting extremely disturbed behaviour psychotherapy may be available.

The ostensible reason for a child's referral to an educational therapist is usually some form of scholastic 'failure'. This may mean that he has never acquired basic skills, his learning has become suspended, or he resists learning altogether. The underlying feelings that eventually come to light, either in individual sessions, family interviews or group work reveal the depth of pain and despair of all the learning-disabled children with whom we work.

One of our tasks as educational therapists is to put the children in touch with this pain, particularly that relating to loss, until they are ready to contemplate the future and the renewal of their appetite for learning. The use of the metaphor in creative work and the use of educational materials enable them to express some of their feelings within the safe boundary of the materials.

In this chapter we have introduced the concept of the attachment behaviour of infants within their family systems and how we feel this can affect the attachment behaviour of children within their educational systems. Those who feel secure can negotiate transitions and tolerate stressful experiences without long-term disruption to their general development and scholastic progress. Children who are emotionally insecure and anxious are less able to overcome these difficulties and, in the extreme, become overwhelmed and lose their capacity for play and learning.

Our understanding of Bowlby's theory of attachment behaviour has led us to feel confident enough to to offer this second-chance learning experience to anxiously attached children. Each session offers an opportunity to explore interactive behaviour and to discover self in the here and now. Once a memory of this experience is internalised lost scholastic skills can be rediscovered.

25

2

THE EDUCATIONAL THERAPIST'S
USE OF ATTACHMENT THEORY
AND OTHER CONCEPTS

While working with children and families we began to recognise the importance of attachment behaviour and how this affected patterns of learning. We also noted, within this context, that parents often misinterpreted the behaviour of their children, and seemed unable to respond appropriately to the actions of those in the family for whom they cared so much. Attachment theory held some answers for us.

ATTACHMENT THEORY

The development of attachment theory by John Bowlby (1969, 1973, 1980) and others has made a major contribution to our understanding of the emotional development of infants. For the purpose of this book we have employed only those broad concepts of the theory that will clarify this introduction to the process of educational therapy and the practice of the intervention. Bowlby reminds us that infants are members of a family system, and, as far back as 1953, he stated that the majority of children are best provided for by their parents at home, even when the quality of infant care proffered by mothers (or other attachment figures) falls short of the ideal.

What is attachment behaviour?

The concept of attachment is of a control system intended to achieve certain goals. The primary aim of an infant is to seek the presence of an attachment figure, usually his mother, when feelings of alarm, upset, or anxiety are dominant. When these anxious feelings are assuaged by a responsive mother, other behaviour such as the exploration of the environment becomes possible; the child can tolerate separation from this available attachment figure when his memory of self interacting with her is secure. Other people and situations can be explored and, as emotional and cognitive learning develop, it becomes possible to extend and reconstruct the control systems which have been built on past experience so that future experience can be safely anticipated.

Secure base

The term 'secure base' was used by Mary Ainsworth (1967) to describe an infant's use of mother 'as a secure base from which to explore'. Her study suggests that an infant's anxious feelings about the absence of an attachment figure override his willingness to explore. Bowlby put forward the view that an infant's behavioural system is activated towards seeking the proximity of mother (or other primary care-giver), particularly at times when he is feeling afraid. He stated:

> At some stage in the development of the behavioural systems responsible for attachment, proximity to mother becomes a set goal. The wish to maintain closeness can be observed when an infant, at the stage when his smiles and actions denote a distinct preference for his mother's presence, cries if she leaves him momentarily to move to another room.

(Bowlby 1969)

The degree of intensity of feeling will vary between different infants, and will be also influenced both by the age of the infants and by adults' response to their behaviour. Infants rely on active responses which, of course, include care-giving and the provision of food. When attachment figures are more or less consistently able to provide love and care for their infants, the infants learn to trust this reciprocal adult behaviour. The infant's experience of being able to rely on comfort when he is feeling anxious or fretful is an essential part of his early learning. Mother is learning too. Bowlby (1969) noted that 'the way a mother is herself behaving towards her child can affect the intensity with which his attachment behaviour is shown'. He suggested that mothers who 'discourage proximity' or behave in a threatening manner elicit intense attachment behaviour: 'When a mother rebuffs her child for wishing to be near her, or sit on her knee, it not infrequently has an effect exactly the opposite of what is intended – he becomes more clinging than ever.' This may also occur when a mother attempts to leave her child without preparing him for any separation, be it just to move away into another room for a moment or to be apart from her child for a longer period.

A mother who is able to accept her child's wish for proximity, and can maintain it, enables that child to behave in a more relaxed manner. The child does not need to be watchful or to expend energy in finding ways of staying close to mother. This experience of interaction with a mother attuned to her child's attachment behaviour establishes a 'secure base'. The child is safe in the knowledge that mother recognises, respects and responds to her infant's behaviour, especially when anxious feelings are aroused.

'Separation: anxiety and anger'

The meaning of attachment behaviour is most easily understood through the effect of separation from an attachment figure, and to emphasise the nature of the concept we have used as a sub-heading the title of Bowlby's second volume about attachment theory (1973). The shifting feelings in a normal secure-attachment relationship can be observed in the behaviour of children who have spent a brief period in hospital, and whose mothers, because of family commitments, are unable to remain with them. (The Platt Report (1959) encouraged those responsible for the care of young children to stay with them in hospital for long or short stays.) The secure child is likely to exhibit anxiety when it is time for mother to leave, and will protest with cries when she departs as a way of showing his distress at being abandoned. The memory of an affectionate relationship and the belief that mother will return however, enables most secure children to accept the fact that they are separated. Hopkins (1983) described the reaction of three anxious children to this experience, and contrasts their behaviour to that of a more secure child and her 'emotional recovery'. Once a child leaves hospital and returns to his family, Hopkins suggests that the 'gradual process of mastering the conflicts aroused by hospitalization' begins. The reaction is likely to include the expression of anger towards mother for 'allowing' him to be sent away to hospital; for the separation; and for the anxiety experienced. The children who feel secure enough to express their anger openly believe that mother will understand it. Not only do they feel she will respond in a manner that alleviates their continuing anxiety, but also that she will recognise their fear of being separated from the family again. A series of five films made by James and Joyce Robertson between 1967 and 1975 vividly portray a small child's feelings about separation.

Exploratory behaviour

This behaviour is inextricably linked to attachment behaviour; put very simply, infants are unable to explore unless they feel secure. Anxious feelings need to be assuaged and terminated before exploratory behaviour can take place. At a very early stage infants begin to discover their own control systems. They attempt to elicit certain responses from those who care for them and to influence or 'control' the responses of their attachment figures. Does exploratory behaviour begin at a very early age through touch by fingers, tongue, mouth and nipple (or bottle teat) when feeding, and developing eye contact with mother? Or discovery of self by later body awareness, such as thumb or finger sucking, touching genitals and grasping toes and toys? Bowlby (1969) regarded exploration as 'a class of behaviour in its own right'.

As infants mature and their experience widens, they become more responsive: a smiling response emerges, and they begin to make sounds in speech-related patterns. Grasping and watching behaviour indicate the growing wish to explore further. Other behaviours, such as turning the head, crying, wriggling or sleeping, will show that they wish to cease their exploratory behaviour; they no longer wish to explore, they have lost interest in or cannot accommodate any further stimuli. When the infant can rely on his mother's emotional availability and consistent responsive behaviour, and he becomes increasingly mobile, crawling and later walking, exploration of the immediate environment takes place. Relationships with other members of the family are developed and enjoyed. If this behaviour is encouraged, and these earlier facilitating experiences are confirmed, the process actively continues. (When we use the word 'encourage' we include helping an infant or toddler to accept the setting of limits, not only to avoid danger but also as a tentative introduction to being able to encompass the idea that another person's goal-directed system may be different from his own.)

The acquisition of sounds and later words is part of exploratory behaviour. When talking and conversational skills are developing, children still like to explore the construction and meaning of words when they are playing or when they are interacting with adults who know them well. For secure children the process is carried forward into school. Sroufe working with pre-schoolers (1983) and Main et al. (1985) in her study with 6-year-olds both found that securely based children are better able to manage and explore new situations such as playgroup and school than their anxious peers.

Bowlby (1969) regarded secure attachment behaviour as having 'two sets of influences'. The first of these is an external one, like the one described above: the 'set-goal' that is aimed at bringing about the actual presence of an attachment figure. The second set of influences is an internal one. Bowlby regarded 'developments of organisation' which provide a 'structure', or plan, as part of our behavioural systems. We begin by seeking proximity; when we are upset we expect our anxious feelings to be assuaged so that we can return to our former feeling of well-being; later our goal-directed behaviour becomes more sophisticated and consciously demanding; much later we are able to recognise that others too have set-goals and feelings that may differ from our own. External and internal 'influences' might be considered a circular process, each moving in two directions, the external influencing the internal which becomes integrated to form an 'internal working model', thus influencing the experience of the external.

Internal working model

This concept from Bowlby (1969) enables us to understand how an infant begins to build a picture of himself as a worthwhile individual interacting with a preferred attachment figure. His worth has been validated in interaction with this person by numerous gestures, tone of voice and eye contact, in addition to more concrete provision. It is unlikely that these feelings are consciously recognised by an infant until later in his first year of life, but these two important aspects of an internal working model – the infant's active seeking of attention from his mother and mother's active response to this – affirm a secure base. Then, if all goes well, the infant can extend his goal-seeking beyond the immediate presence of his mother; he has built up an internal picture or memory of his attachment figure, which he can retain even when she is not actually close by. This is a gradual process: in the early months eye contact will suffice as reassurance, but later it becomes possible to tolerate actual short separations, safe in the knowledge that this figure will return.

For an infant who develops more than one internal working model of the same attachment figure, the situation is more complex. Bowlby (1973) relates this to defensive processes that may result in later life in behaviour that is not age-appropriate. The early experience is defended against and a second model develops that may be 'incompatible' with the more primitive one, as a defence against the probably unbearable memory of it. Bretherton and Waters (1985) gives an example of this process described as 'defensively disassociated. Such disassociations are especially likely when the child cannot cope with viewing rejecting parents in an unfavourable light or when parents attempt to persuade the child to interpret their rejecting behaviour as loving.'

Main *et al.* (1985) in their 'reconceptualization of individual differences in attachment organization' provided a 12-point definition of internal working models. This longitudinal study compared the patterns of attachment behaviour of twenty-four 6-year-old boys with their parents, to their patterns of attachment in infancy.

New 'structures' are added to our internal working models to accommodate the differences or similarities between internal and external experiences. Not only are we adjusting the map of self interacting with others, but we are also developing skills for creative play and cognitive learning. Bowlby (1973, 1980) refers to this experience as 'updating'.

Updating

When we think of ourselves learning a new skill, such as riding a bicycle or driving a car, we approach the task with a picture of ourselves as inept if we have been told since childhood that our co-ordination is poor. This is a message we have received from people who we know to care for us and who can admire our other skills. When our internal working model of ourselves interacting with these caring people becomes a different one we feel hurt or think that we have been misunderstood. The picture we have in our minds of ourselves as loved and being capable of certain skills alters to one of doubt: this doubt includes a momentary change in the internal working model we have of those very same people with whom we interact. If we consider for a moment the experience of children, we can recall from our own childhood the enormous effort required for re-adjusting or updating the view of self interacting with others.

Loss

To address the question of 'loss' from Bowlby's Attachment Theory in a few sentences risks underrating the importance of this concept and the meaning of attachment behaviour. In his third volume of *Attachment and Loss*, Bowlby's title of 'Sadness and depression' (1980) addresses two concepts that epitomise the experience of so many of the children referred for educational therapy. It does so in two ways, although not necessarily on a conscious level. The children themselves feel sadness or depression arising from their own loss, or they have become sad and depressed as a result of their parents' past unresolved mourning or current reaction to loss. We have found that to express sadness relating to loss of self-worth, family member or learning skill can be inordinately difficult. In addition to actual losses of attachment figures or other familiar people (referred to in Chapter 1), losses can be associated with having to give up the familiar, and face the unknown, without due preparation by the adult figures for whom an anxious attachment had been formed. The children, and many of the parents with whom we have worked, have lost sight of (or never experienced) a secure base. The losses and separations they have had to manage have frequently been intolerable – misunderstood or simply thrust upon them without warning. The result, very often, has meant having to deny their meaning or, alternatively, to accept being in touch with the feelings of pain and anger appertaining to the losses. We can never know, but feel that the processes of mourning described by Bowlby have not been recognised, acknowledged or understood by the parents of these children.

Bowlby (1980) put forward the view that the process of mourning includes four phases, though it may well move over time from one to another:

1 Phase of numbing that usually lasts from a few hours to a week and may be interrupted by outbursts of extremely intense distress and/or anger.
2 Phase of yearning and searching for the lost figure lasting some months and sometimes for years.
3 Phase of disorganisation and despair.
4 Phase of greater or less degree of reorganisation.

These phases refer to an adult's response to the loss of a spouse, but in this volume Bowlby examined the similarities of mourning in early childhood, adolescence and adulthood, and three areas of influence that contribute to the management of mourning in childhood. He considered the circumstances relating to the loss, how much the child had been told, and what time and space he had been offered subsequently to talk about the 'lost' person; he referred to the possible changes in family relationships, and where the child would be placed (with surviving parent, or elsewhere); and he considered the family relationships before the loss between the parents and between each of them and the bereaved child.

Attachment, loss and the learning-disabled child: anxious attachments

The term 'anxious attachment' is taken from the work of Ainsworth and Wittig, which explored the attachment and exploratory behaviour of 1-year-olds with mother and a stranger in what has become known as the Strange Situation Study (1969). We have chosen this study in our attempt to make some specific links between a child's emotional development and his cognitive learning. By clinical inference we are suggesting that certain attachment behaviours in early childhood have affected the first learning of children referred to us. A similar pattern of attachment behaviour can be discerned when these anxious children are interacting with us (second-chance learning), either individually or as members of their families. We believe that the continuation of their anxious attachment behaviour is still affecting their scholastic skills. (This is examined in more detail in our introduction to Chapters 9, 10 and 11.)

The anxiously-attached children are those who remain in a state of uncertainty about their relationship with their attachment figures. We believe that the majority of children who are referred to us for educational therapy have formed 'anxious attachments' to their parents, and that this is what has prevented them from being able to make full use of the education offered to them in school. Their capacity for updating exists in negative form: the term 'backdating' seems a more appropriate one. Some of the feelings they have about themselves interacting with attachment figures are transferred to their teachers.

A second secure base?

We recognise that it is not possible to make much progress when working with a single child, a peer group or a family group until a 'secure base' can be established, one that can somehow be felt and understood by those concerned. To achieve this we must aim as educational therapists to clarify our intentions; to demonstrate our capacity for thinking; to be empathic and open to a different way of perceiving the world; to be able to listen; to avoid collusion or being judgemental; to show a belief in the child's, his family's, and the therapist's own willingness to explore change; and to behave in a consistent manner that gives a message of accessibility. It is essential that the educational therapist maintains her psychological health and acknowledges unconscious phenomena in order to establish a second secure base for the child.

Exploratory behaviour

When children are feeling insecure it becomes increasingly difficult for them to explore. Much of their emotional energy will be taken up in frequently seeking proximity to a primary care-giver, either by clinging excessively or, paradoxically, by rejecting that figure. Any brief attempts by anxiously-attached children to play and explore may be thwarted by a parent who feels anxious, angry or upset, or one who is 'smothering' and inhibiting. Some children may be physically at risk if the adult responsible for their safety cannot protect them from inappropriate exploratory behaviour. The child does not have a secure base under these circumstances.

We indicated in Chapter 1 what happens when anxiously-attached children are exposed to a new environment, such as school: they are disadvantaged when compared to their securely-attached peers. The securely-attached child's care-givers will have provided a stable environment for play and learning which will have included a flexibility that can encompass change, tolerate and support differing moods, and value an interest in numerous activities. The less secure are unable to predict either their own behaviour or that of others.

Internal working models

The picture of themselves that anxiously-attached children carry around inside their heads appears to be one of a person who is at worst 'bad' and, at best, of little use or value. Their early interactive behaviour with primary care-givers has, we think, contributed to low self-esteem and difficulties in managing their feelings and behaviour. Their internalised view of parental figures is one of adults who are emotionally unavailable, inconsistent in behaviour, and ambivalent in attitude, sometimes seeking parenting for themselves. The model of self and parental figures that many of these children have constructed in their minds seems to be based on numerous earlier experiences of uncertainty. Whenever these experiences are repeated, it appears that the child's inner representations of self interacting with others are being confirmed.

Updating

These anxious children feel that their behaviour towards others determines, to a greater or lesser degree, how they, in turn, will be treated. They may set out to prove that this is true each time they encounter new people. Strangely, this may be the only 'structure' available to them, thus preventing any change in their updating capacity. If our inner pictures carry serious doubts about who we are, then we need a great number of different, positive messages from those who are important to us to countermand these perceptions.

It is easy to identify attachment behaviour with early childhood, but in fact it continues into adulthood (Weiss 1982). Whether as adults we seek the actual presence of someone close to us, or make use of our internal working models of them, Bowlby's definition of the behaviour is relevant to us at any age. The modification of its structure continues until death.

CONCEPTS FROM THE WORK OF D.W. WINNICOTT

Some of the concepts from Winnicott's work (1965, 1971, 1986) are similar in essence to some of those from Bowlby's. In the very early stages of interaction between mother and infant, both emphasise the reciprocity of the experience. Bowlby's description of attachment behaviour (1969) includes Ainsworth and Wittig's concept of a secure base (1969); Winnicott refers to a 'nursing couple' (1965), neither mother nor child being differentiated in this relationship. The infant makes a contribution as well as the mother. Early learning about each other takes place within the interaction. Many years ago both Winnicott and Bowlby acknowledged the significance of a child's environment to his feeling of well-being.

The facilitating environment

Winnicott (1965) tells us that 'the environment does not make the infant grow, nor does it determine the direction of growth'. When it is right it 'facilitates the maturational process' in the presence of a person who is able to 'offer subtle adaptation to changing need'. Winnicott uses the psycho-analytic term 'object relating' when describing a mother and her infant interacting. We prefer Bowlby's term 'attachment behaviour' to describe what is happening during interactions between a mother and her infant, or indeed between any other two people who have formed a relationship.

Good-enough mothering

This concept of Winnicott's (1965) is perhaps the most widely known, and is closely linked with his 'facilitating environment'. He says 'only if there is a good-enough mother does the infant start on a process of development that is personal and real', and that an infant will survive and manage a state of 'going on being' even if the mothering being received is not perfect but is 'good-enough'. (Sadly there are mothers who feel that they must be perfect.) Here the view of Bowlby differs. In his opinion many infants not only survive but continue to strive to maintain their attachment to mother even when her mothering is not 'good-enough', for example rejecting.

Holding

Winnicott's interpretation (1965) of this concept implies that a child's primary care-giver is not only physically holding an infant but holding him in mind. His attachment figure takes responsibility for his well-being and ensures that his feelings too are in safe-keeping. He is thought about, even in his absence. Once a child has understood that he too can hold another in mind, similar to Bowlby's internal working model, he is more likely to be able to tolerate separation. Heard (1978) linked the concept of holding by Winnicott to the concept of attachment behaviour by Bowlby – 'The attachment dynamic'. She suggests that 'good-enough parental holding maintains for a child a state in which creative exploration and reality testing are possible' and is part of that dynamic. If the words 'parental holding' could be substituted by 'educational therapist's holding', this statement would seem to describe one important role of the educational therapist.

Transitional objects

Even if this term is not in common usage, most parents, or those who have an interest in small children, would recognise it. A transitional object is a toy or an old piece of blanket that a 'child takes to bed to help the transition from waking to dream life' (Winnicott 1965); he may use his thumb or fingers in a similar way. Children seek comfort from transitional objects when they are tired, distressed or missing their attachment figure. They may treat the object in a brutal or a loving manner, demonstrating their ambivalent feelings towards it. Winnicott says 'It is not the object, of course, that is transitional. The object represents the infant's transition from being merged with the mother to a state of being in relation with the mother as something outside and separate ....' The idea that the transitional object in some sense symbolises the experience and memory of self interacting with mother over time is, like 'holding in mind', closely allied to Bowlby's concept of an internal working model. (The possibility of a story becoming a transitional object has been explored by the author, Trevitt 1989.)

'Not-me'

The concept of holding (Winnicott 1971), that is being held, and the transitional phenomena are for Winnicott experiences that lead an infant to a state of mind that can tolerate weaning. Through this 'separation' from mother he slowly learns to understand that he is no longer merged with her; she is 'not-me' but another person.

The capacity to be alone

Winnicott (1965) wrote of the importance of a child's 'capacity to be alone'. For him the use of the word 'I' implies emotional growth because the individual has become 'established': the strength of his ego exists. He said that when a child can say 'I am' this is a statement of further growth, which has been reached by the provision of a 'facilitating environment', which for Winnicott includes good-enough mothering. He stated further that 'I am alone' is related to a child's unconscious awareness of the existence of an emotionally available mother, and wrote of the 'paradox that the capacity to be alone is based on the experience of being alone in the presence of someone'. He suggested that unless an infant is allowed this experience, his capacity to be alone will be unlikely to develop. (This pre-supposed the capacity of the mother to tolerate *inactive* participation.) Children who are anxiously attached to their mothers may not have had this experience, and we try to ensure that they are helped to discover their capacity to be alone in the presence of their educational therapist.

Working space

One of us (Barrett) developed the concept of a working space, based on Winnicott's view of a shared playing space, for psychotherapeutic work with children. Winnicott (1965) stressed the importance of the therapist's capacity for play and defined her task as 'where playing is not possible then the work done by the therapist is directed towards bringing the patient from a state of not being able to play into a state of being able to play'. We have already stated the necessity of integrating the concept of play into our work, but define the shared space primarily as a working one, because it is here that work is undertaken on tasks and feelings. It is worth remembering also that the children who come for help expect that they will be working both to improve their scholastic and social skills and also to understand how their feelings and behaviour may be affecting those skills. The working space is understood by children once they have experienced it. They quickly recognise it conceptually by learning that their thoughts will not be intruded upon; that the therapist will not become a 'smothering' or any other kind of mother; and that their need for space in which to think, talk, act, or switch off will be respected. They learn too that they cannot impinge upon the therapists' space. At times the space becomes almost tangible; a symbol of change.

Transference and counter-transference

We know from our own experience how our behaviour in a given situation can be very different from the way we feel inside. Sometimes inner frustrations become momentarily beyond our outer control. (A passenger spoke very rudely to a ticket collector. His response was apposite: 'Just because you had a fight with your husband this morning, missus, don't take it out on me.') This displacement of feelings on to another person can be an everyday experience or something that happens on a deeper level, as in psychoanalysis. The significance of this phenomena was first put into words by Freud (1926), who recognised that transference, that is feelings from childhood especially relating to a particular person, most commonly mother, are usually trans-ferred on to others when we are interacting with them. These feelings can inhibit or facilitate our capacity to function, whether it be in play or learning. If the person we are with reminds us of a parent, sibling or other figure of significance with whom we have formed a good relationship (an attachment), our state of mind is likely to be calm and we can approach a task with equanimity. We feel good about ourselves, are ready to explore and expect to achieve our goals. Conversely, if our state of mind is anxious, our behaviour may become agitated and we are unable to function in the manner just described. The person we are interacting with for the purpose of completing a task may remind us of an upsetting, punitive or unpredictable attachment figure from the past. The feelings inhibit our capacity to learn; we are unable to think clearly and cannot contemplate exploring, or achieving a goal.

In what is known as counter-transference, the person with whom we are interacting brings his or her own feelings to a situation. He or she may be transferring hostile, negative or loving feelings towards us, because something in our behaviour brings back a memory from his or her own past. The manifestations of our feelings, conscious or unconscious, either from the past or in the here and now, will elicit a response in the other person, that is a counter-transference. If our behaviour towards them reminds them of a 'good-enough' experience from their past, they are likely to counter-transfer their own good feelings on to us. When our behaviour reminds them of a punitive or painful experience from a figure in the past, their reaction may in part contribute to our own anxiety, and thus prevent our functioning. Uncon-sciously transferred feelings of hostility can, when reciprocated, lead to confrontation, thus preventing any learning from taking place. This type of interaction may result in withdrawal into silence, or even self-cosseting, or in taking inappropriate action, like verbal abuse, aggressive behaviour or taking flight. Equally, one member of a dyad (pair) could feel impinged on by the other. Even at an ordinary social level one can experience the behaviour of a fellow guest or conference acquaintance as intrusive, either in manner or in speech. One can feel overwhelmed by their behaviour, and need to escape. Their behaviour is similar to that of a 'smothering' mother, a mother who cannot allow her infant/toddler/school-age child to behave in an independent manner. The term 'hard work' is often applied to one's interaction with a different sort of person who gives the impression of being unwilling or unable to enter into social exchange. We can rarely know, when working with a withdrawn child, whether this behaviour can be linked to an early experience of being ignored or rebuffed by care-givers. Children or adults whose behaviour is sometimes described in terms like 'I never know where I am with him/her', or someone who has 'mood swings', may have experienced unpredictable interactions from care-givers.

Analogies between food and learning have become part of common usage: 'an appetite for learning', 'food for thought', 'inwardly digest' are just a few of them. Caspari's description of the practice of educational therapy influenced our thinking, but, by focusing more on the interaction between adult and child, we began to place greater emphasis on the attachment behaviour that the child showed towards the educational therapist, and how her reception of this behaviour could affect his emotional and cognitive learning. When we looked at the patterns of interaction with the children with whom we work, we realised just how much their feelings seem to dominate their capacity for learning: not only feelings about their inner self-perception but also, of equal importance, their outer perception of self interacting with others, especially adults. So any attempt at achieving a task was often abandoned almost immediately, regardless of the way in which it was presented to them. The majority lacked the usual patterns of curiosity, or goal-seeking behaviour (Bowlby 1969) integral to the learning of the majority at any age. Our continuing ability to update and recognise a lifetime's need for attachments does appear to influence our adult 'appetite for learning' and creative thinking. Our observations of infants and pre-school children led to our own curiosity about cognitive learning and the conditions that facilitate or inhibit the continuation of that learning. If it is accepted that patterns of cognitive learning and patterns of attachment behaviour are interdependent, then it becomes possible to understand how both these patterns may be repeated again and again, either positively or negatively.

Inevitably, our interactions with others over time will encompass any of the above generalisations; if our internal working models of self interacting with others derive from a secure base, we are able to adapt to different encounters. For a person, child or adult, who sees himself as 'bad', it would seem that he must behave in a manner towards others that elicits a response (counter-transference) that in turn offers proof that he is right in his assumption. If, however, to use a term from Systems Theory, this self-perpetuating interactive cycle can be 'punctuated' (Bateson 1973) by a series of more positive interactions, the pattern can be changed. We agree with the findings of Sroufe (1983) in his research with pre-schoolers that children with 'disturbed patterns of behaviour' are (with rare exceptions) 'not beyond intervention'. For many adults, too, this view must hold.

We have tried in this chapter with our brief look at different concepts to emphasise the importance we place on the need to understand the concept of attachment. When this behaviour is looked at in the simplest terms, it just means that an infant or schoolchild who feels secure can take in a new experience without feeling unduly anxious. If he knows that he feels secure inside, a new environment such as school can be trusted. Then he can learn more about self, the behaviour of others or problem solving. A sense of 'going-on-being', even when momentarily challenged, is integrated into the process of play and learning, i.e. physical, emotional and intellectual development.

3

AN OBSERVATION OF SECURE ATTACHMENT BEHAVIOUR AND EARLY LEARNING AT HOME

The theoretical framework outlined in Chapter 2 helps us to understand the learning patterns of children referred to us for educational therapy who have formed anxious attachments to the adults responsible for their well-being. Observing the early interaction between infants and their mothers has enabled us to speculate about the developmental stage at which the learning pattern of anxious children appears to change. We have chosen to give a detailed observation of one infant, John, and his mother to illustrate the importance of secure attachment in the establishment of constructive learning patterns. Before describing John, who was 11 weeks old when the observation started, we take a brief look at the early learning patterns of infants.

FIRST LEARNING

The first stage of learning is primarily tactile, and an infant's most important tactile experience is an oral one. While feeding, he will slowly explore his mother by touch, with mouth, fingers and by bodily contact. Two other senses, those of taste and smell, are an integral part of the feeding experience. Shaffer and Dunn (1980), referring to the capabilities of the new-born, maintain that 'the infant's perceptual abilities at birth are likely to help the mother to consider her infant as a real person' within the first hour of independent life. By responding to their cries with offers of food, comfort and 'holding', physically as well as 'in mind', attachment figures demonstrate to their infants that they are valued, cared for and loved. These actions offer the infant a 'secure base'. Activities such as smiling and babbling form part of the reciprocal interaction between a mother and her infant. Stern (1985) refers to the organisation at a primitive level of the infant's experience of a process. Very slowly the infant's mother becomes 'an inner certainty as well as an outer predictability' (Erikson 1965). From the beginning the mother will respond to her infant, not only by giving, but also by setting limits on his demands. She has to let her infant perceive and later understand that she has feelings too.

Gradually the infant begins to recognise, unconsciously, that his skin separates him from his mother. The function of the skin as a boundary (Bick 1968) which contains the parts of the self rests on the acknowledgement of the image and feel of another person. In psychoanalytic terms this other is the mother, an external object in Freud's sense, in which an object is defined as 'the thing in regard to which or through which the instinct is able to achieve its aim' (1915b). As we have already indicated, Bowlby (1969) prefers the terms 'attachment' and 'attachment figure' when describing what he calls 'the child's tie to his mother'. He considers that much of the infant's behaviour in this dependent state of mind is directed towards maintaining proximity to the mother. Stern (1985) refers to the infant's 'emergent sense of self', that is his experience of the process of integration and organisation, as 'no more than a form of learning'.

JOHN

The initial arrangements for the observation of John were made by the health visitor following his normal birth at full term. At the introductory meeting with the infant's mother, the observer clarified with her that the observation would be a non-participatory regular weekly observation of 45 minutes. The following account describes interaction within the nuclear family. The mother continued her usual household activities throughout the observation, occasionally sharing her own thoughts and feelings about her son and their interaction together with the observer.

Mother described John as a planned first child. Her untroubled pregnancy was followed by a short labour and rapid birth. The parents were together throughout and seemed to have received sensitive and caring treatment. John was fully breast fed from birth and his mother reported that this was a satisfactory experience for both of them. He slept soundly and well from the start and his mother accepted night feeds as a perfectly normal part of caring for her baby. She described feeling rather depressed during the second week after delivery, having a sense of anti-climax after all the excitement. This mother had the constant support of her husband, who came home every day for lunch, and her extended family, the grandparents, all lived nearby.

A facilitating environment: exploring attachment behaviour

John was already showing an intense interest in his mother when the observation started. He was watching her closely and gave the impression that he was trying to understand her.

'John lay happily on his back on the bed as his mother changed his nappy. His eyes never left her face. Making frequent eye-contact, she talked to him. She left spaces for him and he responded to her with a wide range of sounds, with the intonation of speech. They were engaged in conversation together, a two-way process of communication. Mother verbally encouraged John, imitating both his sounds and actions. Their responses to one another were an extension of the concept of mirroring as defined by Winnicott (1971). Sometimes mother appeared to take the lead while at others John took it. This interaction was playful, with mother making no excessive demands on her infant. She did not need to urge him into a response. Their shared pleasure was evident and they respected one another's space. As mother put John on to his tummy he raised himself right up on his hands, arms straight, and he turned his head around to see her. Already he seemed confident that she would be there. Then she knelt beside the bed for a moment, making eye contact and confirming her presence before moving away. For the first time John became silent. Mother quickly returned and whisked him up, holding him high. Immediately he puked down her cleavage and she screamed, putting him hastily back on the bed again. The only indication of his concern about these sudden changes of position was the placing of two fingers in his mouth and the stroking of his ear with the other hand. Then he laughed at his mother who responded and another "conversation" ensued; this time it seemed to be initiated by him. I was struck by John's ability to tolerate both mother's shriek and his sudden return to the bed; each had happened so unpredictably. Was putting his fingers in his mouth an example of self-cosseting at a time of stress? He had sucked his fingers and handled the muslin nappy, which had been used in place of a pillow in his cot, since the observations began. This muslin later became his "transitional object".'

'The cot itself appeared to become a symbolic container for John, part of his secure base. Initially John's mother held him until he slept before gently lowering him into the cot. Having received this experience it seemed he could accept the cot as a continuation of his mother's "holding". She continued to describe him as a good sleeper. How much this was due to an inherited disposition and how much to his mother's handling in the early days it was not possible to say. When he was in his cot mother periodically checked to see if he was asleep, talking to him wherever she was in the bungalow. Using her voice in this way seemed to be an unconscious preparation for helping her infant to hold her in mind during later separations.'

Play and cognitive learning

We see the next phase of John's observed behaviour as part of the process of continuation which Stern (1985) refers to as 'domains of relatedness' instead of the more common stages of development.

'Mother placed her son in a low reclining baby chair with plastic gingerbread figures strung across it on a wire. John instantly became silent. He looked intently at the figures and he hit them with his right hand until they spun around. He was clearly very happy and his whole body was involved in the effort and concentration. Over a period of fifteen minutes he continued the exploration quite deliberately without uttering a sound. Mother came in and out of the room, talking to him as she did so. He appeared oblivious of her presence until she moved his chair so that he could watch her ironing. He then stopped playing with the plastic figures and the pair resumed a "conversation". At about this time mother reported that both she and her husband had become fascinated by what they thought was their son's first recognisable task-orientated exploration. They changed the colour order of the figures and observed that he continued his struggles to specifically hit the blue ones. The concentration with which he tackled the task was reminiscent of the total absorption observed when he was feeding at the breast.'

Feeding and acknowledging feelings on the infant's behalf

'When John was 15 weeks old his mother reported that she had found the experience of breast feeding to be both an enjoyable and a gratifying one. That John shared these feelings was, I felt, clearly demonstrated. Mother did not hold him in her arms while feeding (in what for many might be regarded as the more conventional method); instead she made herself comfortable on the sofa, with her infant lying peacefully on his back across her lap, arms loosely by his sides, suckling her left breast. His left hand gripped her left index finger. He momentarily stopped sucking and mother stroked his hand. He resumed sucking until she decided it was time to change breasts. John was very angry and upset. Quite calmly mother held him close, talking soothingly and encouragingly, empathising with and assuaging his feelings by telling him that he would be all right. He relaxed again, hands by his sides once more and settled on the proffered right breast. Her behaviour exemplified an adult's capacity to anticipate, understand, and respond to the anxious and angry feelings that the infant expresses. I felt that John was beginning to explore the differing boundaries between self and mother during this interaction with her.'

Because all the observations took place during normal working hours, John was rarely seen interacting with his father. However, if father did return home early the observer noted the ease with which he settled into a comfortable and mutual way of communicating: holding his son's hand, offering him toys and, at the same time, talking quietly to him.

A period followed when John slept through the observations. When he woke he would lie very quietly, apparently unaware of the observer sitting on the bed opposite his cot. It was some months before he initiated any interaction with her. He appeared to accept her presence unquestioningly, and she commented 'it was almost as if I had no real existence for him unless he consciously conjured me up'. How does this relate to Winnicott's idea (1965) of an infant being able to conjure up a picture of mother as an

43

introduction to symbol formation? The presence of an observer over a period of two years cannot be addressed here but does raise many questions as to the effect on the infant, and the mother.

Weaning began during a month's break in the observation. At 4 months the frequency of breast feeding was slowly reduced until the process was complete at about 9 months. The observer felt that for this mother the process was regarded as a natural continuation of care for her infant, as no untoward difficulties were reported or observed. Bowlby (1969) talked about the maturation of a 'behavioural system' taking precedence over a previously active system. He said 'For example, the behavioural system responsible for sucking remains extant long after infancy but is less frequently activated' as we develop. He suggested that a 'new' system then becomes more active, weaning is one example when biting and chewing supersede sucking.

CHANGES OBSERVED IN A MOVE TOWARDS A MORE INDEPENDENT STATE

The following series of observations give some idea of what Winnicott (1971) called the 'not-me' stage of development already referred to, when an infant gradually becomes 'a being separate from' the mother and no longer 'merged' with her. An infant's behavioural system at this stage is most likely to be activated by what Bowlby (1969) calls 'proximity-maintaining behaviour', that is, the infant likes to be sure that he has easy access to mother's presence, especially when his own actions, or those of others, bring about feelings of anxiety.

'I watched John pull a toy dog towards him and rest it against his head; at the same time he was making a lot of sounds. He then became cross, and his sounds became increasingly irritable. His mother sat him up and gave him his old favourite, the rod of gingerbread men. As he settled happily to examine it she left to get lunch ready. When she returned she picked John up and took him into the kitchen, putting him in his high chair. He screamed and arched his back. Mother strapped him in with difficulty as he slipped down in the chair, screaming again, and he seemed extremely angry. Mother started feeding him, but he went on crying between mouthfuls of chopped liver. He turned his face away from her until she said, encouragingly, "come on then", and he responded, looking back at her. The sounds that followed were different and enthusiastic as he ate his dinner. He picked up his drinking mug with two hands and drank. Mother helped him to put it down. He picked it up again and drank, preventing his mother from placing more food in his mouth. His exploration then extended beyond his high chair tray. He tried to reach things on the table. Father came in and greeted his son, who made his mouth into a funny shape as he responded. He returned to his drinking, but continued his efforts to reach things from the table.'

This behaviour we think belongs to the phase that marks Bowlby's concept of a 'partnership' within which the infant/young child makes use of 'simply organised goal-corrected systems utilising a more or less primitive cognitive map' inside his head. Gradually the infant learns to recognise that mother is part of this map, or internal working model, and that she has her own set goals, which may conflict with his own. However, Bowlby (1969) states that real understanding of their separate behavioural systems is at this stage 'likely to be still far beyond his competence to grasp'.

Exploratory behaviour and cognitive learning

Here we see John taking what we regard as quantum leaps. The following examples of his exploratory play were observed when he was 6 months old.

'He was lying on his stomach and appeared to be working out a way of reaching the toys that were in front of him. Mother encouraged this goal-seeking behaviour but waited before offering help. At about this time, in my opinion, John was continuing to demonstrate what I saw as his "advanced planning" with increasing efficiency. He explored the number of possibilities and attributes of nesting beakers, rolling and stacking them, before he tried to place different sized things inside them. He knocked them together, blew on them and scratched them with his fingers. This type of experimentation involved all his senses and was characterised by sustained and silent absorption in the task, again reminiscent of his suckling at the breast. He was continually extending his store of knowledge and extending his body awareness. These skills I saw as a sophisticated part of his problem-solving armoury that (with hindsight) I recognised was a preparatory stage for later learning.'

Mother's concern

'On one occasion when I observed John, at 7½ months, his mother was very tense and anxious. The health visitor had apparently arrived late to test John's hearing, so he had had to be woken from his sleep. (Concern had been expressed by the health visitor and her assistant about John's earlier lack of response to sounds, which obviously contributed to mother's anxiety.) John, in a "baby-bouncer" suspended from the door-frame, appeared to be in a cheerful mood. He was playing with a toy which he dropped from time to time while he bounced. Freud observed the activity of throwing toys, recognising this as significant as early as 1920. This kind of activity is now more commonly recognised as an infant's exploratory attempt to understand his feelings about separation from and reunion with mother.

'Mother made coffee and played peek-a-boo with John through the hatch. He was still in his bouncer, and he responded by bouncing very hard like real jumping, bobbing his head. He stopped, thought for a moment and then scratched the harness with the nails on his left hand. Then he began to fret. Mother appeared and returned the dropped toy, which he immediately put in his mouth. He bounced again, stopped and then "talked". Dropping the toy again he listened to it rolling away, turning to follow its passage. He stretched out his left hand, but then turned back, rocking himself on his toes. Becoming quite still for a while, he examined the pictures on the mat under him. He touched his mug with his toe and watched it roll away. He then noticed the observer drinking and became very excited, making many sounds with his mouth closed as well as open. The activity that John embarked on next enabled mother to move outside her own anxious feelings and place herself in a mood to address his needs. She gave him a cheap plastic food tub which he bit and broke. He immediately dropped it and rolled it away saying "ubble ubble". He turned around and back again, screwing up his eyes and reacting in a startled fashion to the broken tub. He was given another one which he also broke. His mother then presented him with a larger plastic pot, which he immediately tried to bite. When this proved impossible he attempted to break it with his hands, becoming very angry when it wouldn't break. Mother interceded, "Don't get so upset." She tried to engage him in play but he threw the pot away. Interestingly, he was able to accept a rattle in place of the plastic pot, and a quiet period of play followed during which he bounced gently.

'I became very conscious of mother's anxiety during this visit, and she expressed her concern. In addition to her worries about John's hearing, she talked about the difficulties she felt he might experience in school. She expressed the fear that he would be uncooperative with teachers, as he was so "strong-willed", and would focus only on activities of his own choosing. In the event her predictions proved correct to some extent, and she and John's teachers had to work hard together to help him to adjust, since her ability to allow him to struggle gave him the space he needed to maximise each learning situation so that he could achieve his goals. I saw these as vital components for learning in a school setting.'

Towards independence

'As John's mobility increased (sitting steadily alone at 7 months, crawling and pulling himself into a standing position at 9 months) he was given plenty of freedom to choose where he wished to explore. He began to test his mother with direct challenges. He gained her attention by choosing to get into their pets' food or by interfering with the record player and television controls. These pursuits seemed short-lived as the "ground rules", established by mother and supported by father, provided an unobtrusive structure.'

Mood

We have already had some examples of the effect that John's changing moods had on his task performance.

'During one of my visits, mother gave him some "Play-doh". He was not in the mood for it and kept throwing it on the floor. After a moment's irritation, mother was able to resign herself to this with a minimum of fuss. She again worried aloud about how her son would manage in school when he was expected to carry out tasks and he was not in "the right mood".'

JOHN AS TODDLER

'As John became more accustomed to his greater freedom of movement he returned to a very careful study of specific objects and their attributes. At 15 months he was exploring a hammering toy. This had three balls that could be tapped through holes into a box from which they would roll out again. He appeared to be trying to understand what was happening at every stage, checking with care that the box was really empty and so on. He also mastered the use of the hammer as a croquet mallet. He repeatedly struggled until he managed to pick up three balls at once, and to predict their paths as they rolled to one side of the sofa. This "experiment" was still being enjoyed, with variations, weeks later, with ever-increasing skill. John used Lego pieces in a similar manner, fixing the bricks together and playing with Lego people. He put them in and out of the doors and windows of "houses". Sometimes mother would be in the same room, at other times she would be within earshot, chatting to John from the kitchen or bedroom as she worked. (This was another example of a child "playing in the presence of an adult" as described by Winnicott (1971).) I could not decide whether John was able to play without becoming too excited or his play becoming too threatening because he was used to being "held" by an adult, or if his manner of playing with such concentration precluded any element of threat or excitement.'

'When he was 22 months old John gave me the impression that his play now incorporated "work" (as defined in Chambers dictionary, "effort directed to an end"). He managed intricate, fine motor co-ordination when playing with a winding mechanism which operated a lift and turntable on a garage toy. Although his mother remained available to him, John chose not to interact with her; he remained apparently oblivious of his surroundings. His self-motivation allowed him to find his own solutions to problems.'

More mutual play towards intellectual development

'When John was problem-solving, as described above, his mother very occasionally offered suggestions, though her support was always available. At other times she was an important participant in his learning. She would discuss new toys and their potential with him. They were observed, over many weeks, taking pleasure together in a book which had pictures with opening doors, an activity that had a ritual and rhythmical quality to it.

'Many of John's actions were based on his observations of his parents at work. He could use a screwdriver efficiently to turn the plastic screws in his toy tool kit and a spanner to turn bolts. He could also use his father's screwdriver. John enjoyed washing up with his mother, passing items to her for drying in the order that she asked for them.'

Imaginative play/creative thinking

'On one occasion when John was in an irritable mood, he was unwilling to play with an animal puzzle his mother had offered him. He took a cow-shape from it and started pushing it around the floor making a car noise. This clearly gave him an idea and he jumped up and ran to his toy corner. He sat in front of a vegetable rack where his cars were stored, taking each one out and examining it in detail before waving it about in the air. This play activity lasted for fifteen minutes, and his humour was apparently completely restored. I thought this activity demonstrated his creative thinking; he enjoyed it enormously.'

Language

In spite of the early babbling conversations with his mother, John was not heard attempting to use words at any time during the observation period (which lasted almost two years). He appeared to be able to understand everything that was said to him, and in spite of the health visitor's concern he proved to have no hearing problem. Subsequent follow-up visits demonstrated that John's speech was developing normally.

Mutual learning

'I was struck by the quality of the interaction I had observed. The partnership helped me to become more aware of how this new mother gained in confidence as a person. Her self-esteem increased as she discovered in herself skills and talents that she had not known she possessed. She described herself as having had a rather unspectacular and unrewarding school career. In my opinion, both mother and child benefited from their intuitive understanding of the attachment process.'

FOLLOW-UP VISITS: AN EXAMPLE OF UPDATING AND MORE EXPLORATORY PLAY

'My first subsequent visit was made when John was 2 years and 6 months. My original role as observer changed when the regular period of observation was completed. I became involved in the family interaction on my visits, although interest continued to be focused on John. He was now a sturdy toddler, chatting in a very sociable way; his speech was perfectly intelligible. John was no longer an only child, due to the arrival of his baby sister Victoria, who was 5 weeks old.

'Mother had clearly prepared John carefully for my visit after an interval of six months. She told me that he had been keen to meet me and his greeting was calm and friendly. He accepted my small gift while his mother took the one for his baby sister, who was being breast fed at the time. Carefully unwrapping the parcel, John remarked on the identical wrapping paper on the two presents. Before opening the box he carefully scrutinised the picture on it, then he removed the pieces from inside. These needed assembling to produce a go-cart with a passenger. Without prompting or hesitation he approached the visitor for assistance. Presumably he was aware of his mother's preoccupation with the baby and felt secure and confident enough to approach another adult. (Mother expressed surprise at the relaxed way that John accepted me, since he was going through a very "shy phase". I found it interesting to speculate about his memory of my presence as the silent observer of the first two years of his life.) John proceeded to experiment with the new toy, trying to run it down a narrow-gauge track from the roof of his garage to the floor. He seemed to sense that the wheel span was too wide. Nevertheless he carefully ran it the full length of the track, with the wheels overhanging the edge, first on one side and then the other. He commented, "It's too big!" His mother suggested he get his car box and find a car that would run freely down the track. John found the box and proceeded to seek out all the vehicles that were too wide. He was serious and purposeful with no sign of frustration. It was clear that he was exploring the concept of 'too big'. John was by now chatting with ease, giving a running commentary as he played.'

This type of exploration also occurred during a later visit when John, now 3 years old, was tackling a well-loved floor jigsaw puzzle. This time the emphasis was a little different, as John brought a shared fun element into the activity. His eye would instantly go to the correct piece of puzzle before he rejected it in favour of one that wouldn't fit. Methodically he worked through all the pieces which were 'not right' until finally he made the 'right' fit. All these actions were accompanied by a twinkle in his eye, deliberately teasing his mother, in what was clearly a game for both.

'I found these constructive examples of "negative exploration" (Trevitt) thought-provoking. I was able to recognise the similarities between this behaviour and that often encountered when working with learning-disabled children, who so frequently need extra time to explore the impossible before being able to discover and accept the possible. I was conscious, too, of the frustration that can result for teachers who are unaware of the importance of this process in developmental terms.

'Between the two activities outlined above, mother suggested that John might like to help his little sister, who was still feeding, by opening her present. Mother had already removed the wrapping paper so John opened the box which contained a rattle in the shape of a windmill. When the sail turned it revealed a man's face with a smile in one position and a grimace in the other. He was fascinated by this and experimented for a minute or two before offering it to his sister, who was still totally engrossed in feeding (lying in exactly the same laid-back position which John had adopted in the past). Mother encouraged his gesture by suggesting he might get Victoria to hold the rattle. Very gently he uncurled her fingers and wrapped them around the handle with just a little help from his mother, who merely supported the infant's arm at a suitable angle. John fetched tissues when asked and mother got him to mop the baby's milky chin. This he did gently and quite effectively. I was unable during this visit to observe any signs of distress or jealousy in the way John related to the baby, his mother or to me. Mother remained sensitive to her son's needs, showing respect for him as a person in his own right, allowing him to function in his own space....

'I saw this major life transition for John and his family as enriching and without trauma. Father returned briefly and immediately, in his unobtrusive manner, became absorbed into the scene I was observing and yet in a sense I felt a part of it.'

Dunn (1988) in her discussion of 'normative life events as risk factors' looks at several factors that contribute to this event of the birth of a sibling. She considers the individual differences in response to the event in the child whose position in family is changed by it, the 'quality of the mother-child relationship' before the sibling birth, the change in 'family structure', and the implication that extended family and outside support systems may also have an effect on this normal part of many family lives.

An example of tolerating a brief separation

'During this visit a stranger came to the door. Mother handed the baby to me and, telling John where she was going, went to answer the door. He continued to play without showing undue concern. When mother returned he asked about the caller and she explained that it had been a man delivering parts for the greenhouse.'

FURTHER FOLLOW-UP VISITS: THE FAMILY DYNAMIC
AND PRE-SCHOOL LEARNING CONTINUUM

A further visit took place when John was almost 3 years 10 months. He had been attending a local playgroup for three sessions a week for a year.

'On arrival I was greeted by mother holding Victoria (now a shy toddler) in the kitchen; John was lying back on the sofa in the sitting room, watching television. He greeted me in a very grown-up fashion, saying "hello" rather solemnly. I replied equally formally and offered him a small parcel, as well as giving one to Victoria. John examined the box which contained a construction toy. He politely thanked me and looked for a way to open his gift, expressing his delight at the same time. The concentrated effort seen in a visit six months earlier, and the request for help from mother, were noted again. John looked like a 5-year-old. He was tall and his hair had grown darker. His speech was clear, his vocabulary was sophisticated, his sentences were complex, and his syntax correct. He showed an ability to use language to organise and control events and actions. He was able to make links between past and present as well as predicting a future. John was now able to acknowledge things on his own behalf.

'Mother had clearly been anxious about the major separation that playgroup presented for John and her. I recalled her earlier fears that John's total preoccupation with the things that interested him would prevent his managing to do what he was asked in the playgroup. These fears had apparently proved groundless, though mother still did not seem really reassured. She again expressed her concern about the effects that John's apparent maturity might have on adult expectations of him in school. The playgroup that he was attending was on the school campus. Mother reported that John was looking forward to his entry into "proper" school, due in the new year. Mother had already helped John to negotiate two major transitions – the birth of Victoria and his start at playgroup.

'In spite of all the obvious indications that things were going well, John's mother spoke of what she felt was her difficulty in managing his behaviour. She described his "tantrums" and aggression towards his sister and said that he still frequently wet his pants. During this conversation John was observed assembling his new gift of Lego. He extended the play, testing how much weight the new friction toy could pull by using an electric motor of his father's. This involved connecting two very small leads on to terminals and needed very fine motor skills and endless patience. He decided to add a propeller and bricks to the four-wheeled vehicle. He began to pout and silently stiffened up in frustration, looking very angry. He took a deep breath. "I'm feeling very cross," he said, almost as if surprised. Mother empathised with the feeling and offered her help, which he accepted. Similar incidents occurred on several occasions allowing John to calm down and continue. He was able to tolerate an interruption of his work by his sister, deliberately engaging her in the play by propelling the helicopter blades gently against her legs, much to her delight.

'Shortly after this the children's father came home. Victoria climbed on his knee. John greeted his father then engaged him in his play, accepting a suggestion that facilitated the construction of a different model helicopter. Father looked tired and glanced at a book related to his job. Mother encouraged John to tell me a riddle. He said, "Why does a bee hum?" I responded appropriately. Then he said, very fast, "because he didn't know words" (omitting "the" in his excitement). He was tremendously pleased with himself and the laughter that he caused. Father said they had found a joke book in the library.

'I was taken by surprise when I noticed that father was using John's transitional object (a muslin nappy from his infant cot) to mop up his daughter's wet and messy face! John caught sight of his "cloth" and, climbing on to the sofa, snuggled up beside his father, sucking his thumb and watching a cartoon on television. Mother then went to fetch her daughter's transitional object, a small teddy bear. Victoria tucked the bear under her arm, and also snuggled up to her father. At this point mother confided that her friends thought she demanded too much of her children, with her high expectations of politeness and obedience.

'There had been several considerable changes in John's life-style by this time. Mother now worked full-time with her husband in their business, her part in which was largely home-based. John went to his paternal grandmother on Saturday mornings, while Victoria went to another member of the extended family or stayed at home with her mother while she worked. I felt that in spite of these changes John's family provided the same continuity of security and understanding as they always had. There was no evidence of conflict between the parents in their attitude to each other or to their children. Mother was seen as the person taking on the role of disciplinarian, while father supplied them all with quiet contact and support.'

The observer commented that she felt this augured well for John's entry into school.

ENTRY INTO 'PROPER' SCHOOL

It seemed that the transition into school had been a gradual process for John and his mother. His part-time attendance at the playgroup in the school grounds had provided him with an opportunity for relating to adults outside his family and of mixing with a peer group. Mother reported that he had been very tired at first but she felt he would be ready to become a full-time pupil the next term, when he was 4½. He would be joining a vertically grouped reception class.

It was another year before the observer visited the family, again during the summer holidays. John was approaching his fifth birthday. He had started what many children call 'big' school half-way through the previous autumn term. He went for mornings only until the Christmas break; when school resumed in the January he attended full-time.

'John's teachers had reported that he had settled well into the routine of school life. He was already beginning to read and write and his mathematical skills were well advanced (and a special favourite with him).

'When I arrived on this occasion, John, Victoria and mother were all in the kitchen together where they had been "junk modelling". As on each of my previous post-observation visits, John greeted me without a trace of shyness, although it was a year since we had met. He was very tall for rising 5 and could easily have been taken for a 6-year-old. I gave both children a small gift as I had done before. As usual, after removing the wrapping paper, John steadily studied the box, which contained another construction toy. He already had one that was similar but he still expressed his pleasure at getting another. He settled down on the floor to make the model, which had very tiny complicated pieces, and followed the complex instructions meticulously. He appeared to gain great pleasure from the step-by-step process. It was a long slow endeavour, but he neither needed nor sought any help, although I noticed that his mother manoeuvred a little break for him as she sensed he was getting tired. He reluctantly left the task but accepted a drink and an apple before resuming his work with enthusiasm.

'While John was busy, his mother talked about the happenings of the previous year. She seemed very relaxed about John's progress, and compared him to Victoria, John being the easier of the two. She said Victoria was essentially a "people person" who needed company and lots of interactions to be happy, while John was much more self-contained and independent. She went on to comment that, although he got on with his peers well enough at school, he did not have any special friends, concentrating much more on his own personal interests.

'I watched John working painstakingly on his model-making, and was amazed at his persistence and the patience with which he struggled to make sense of the instructions and to correct his mistakes. He was not, however, totally oblivious of those around him, as he kept looking up at me, beaming with obvious pleasure, revealing his sense of well-being. Once the model was complete we moved into the sitting room, while Victoria went off for her morning sleep, settling, it seemed, in the same relaxed way as her brother had before her. John went straight to his toy shelf and brought out a box containing similar intricate models to the one he had just made. He proceeded to play a complicated game on the carpet, which lasted until the visit was over. He chatted freely with the adults about his game and contributed to the general conversation. Several times he ran off to get things to show me, such as examples of printing that he had done at a workshop exhibition. In spite of the long gaps between visits John appeared to accept them, and I think he experienced me as a familiar family friend.'

John's emotional development and cognitive learning was monitored from infancy through to his entry into school. We consider that the interaction between him and his mother exemplifies secure attachment behaviour. We also acknowledge the contribution of the extended facilitating environment. There was no opportunity to observe John interacting socially with anyone other than members of his immediate family.

SUMMARY

In her examination of the predictive validity of attachment patterns Ainsworth states: 'With the more secure infant confidence in the accessibility of that [attachment] figure enables the child to venture forth to learn about his surroundings and what effect he can have on them and them on him' (Ainsworth 1985). She continues to discuss the fact that 'consistent maternal responses' allow the infant to perceive that his behaviour has an effect on his mother. He builds up a picture of himself as able 'to exert some control over what happens to him'. We have referred to the work of Sroufe (1983) with pre-schoolers, who found that securely-based children are more able to manage new situations like playgroups and school. Their internal working models of self interacting with mother enabled them to have an expectation that other adults could be approached and would be responsive to their requests. Main *et al.* (1985), studying individual differences of attachment behaviour in 6-year-olds, also found that the more secure children who had been seen at 1 year old in the Ainsworth Strange Situation study (Ainsworth and Wittig 1969) were better able to tolerate the idea of separation from their parents. This was shown by their responses to photographs of parents preparing to leave for a vacation. Similar predictions for John's propensity to cope with change were made at the end of the educational therapist's observation, and later confirmed by her follow-up visits. (It is hoped that further follow-up studies will reveal how John manages additional major separations and transitions.)

Part II

WHAT IS EDUCATIONAL THERAPY?

4

INTRODUCING 'SECOND-CHANCE' LEARNING WITH A 10-YEAR-OLD: ANXIOUS ATTACHMENT BEHAVIOUR

We have chosen to introduce the practice of educational therapy (the process is outlined in Chapter 6) by describing some sessions with a 10-year-old boy, Luke. His behaviour appeared to be more like that of the anxiously-attached children described by Ainsworth and Wittig (1969), 'The less secure child may have so much uncertainty about the availability of the attachment figure that he is preoccupied with keeping proximity to the detriment of exploratory activity.' The experience of John's interacting with his mother described in Chapter 3 provided an example of reciprocal attachment behaviour in a mother/infant dyad – first learning. In this chapter we examine the interaction which takes place in the educational therapist/schoolchild dyad – 'second-chance learning'. The relationship between the first and second-chance learning is shown in Figures 4.1 to 14.3 which are similar to Figures 1.1 to 1.3 (see pp. 8–10) but are here used to illustrate a different point.

PREPARATION AND ARRIVAL: INITIAL INTERACTION AND DEPENDENCE

The mother thinks about her unborn infant, preparing for his arrival (birth). Both lives change at the birth: both experience the loss of their former state. The educational therapist also thinks about the referred child and prepares for his arrival (the first session). Although the educational therapist is likely to have met the schoolchild at least once in a preliminary interview, they will be alone together for the first time in the initial session.

The mother and infant have to adjust to one another in their new, unknown relationship. They depend upon the support and encouragement of those around them. The mother has to respond to the dependent state of her infant, providing for his physical and emotional needs and be aware of his active participation in the dyadic relationship.

The educational therapist will take responsibility for the child within each session, helping him to manage the transition from the known to the

Figure 4.1 Preparation and arrival: initial interaction and dependence

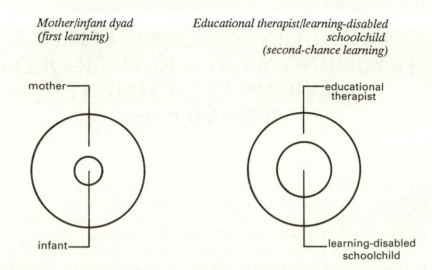

unknown, in a strange room in a strange building with a strange person. The child's anxiety levels are likely to be high and he will not know what to expect in spite of the therapist's advance explanations. The therapist is also likely to be apprehensive. Whether the child is withdrawn or acting out, the therapist will accept his dependence on her to meet his needs while maintaining her professional boundaries as a teacher. She has to provide educational 'food' and support, recognising and responding to his interactional behaviour.

ATTACHMENT BEHAVIOUR: ESTABLISHMENT OF A SECURE BASE AND EMERGING INDEPENDENCE

The mother who is consistently emotionally available for her infant will recognise and respond to his need to be close to her (especially when he is anxious) and encourage his exploratory behaviour. The establishment of a secure base allows for movement.

The educational therapist has to establish a predictably secure base within the 'here-and-now' of the session, building up a memory of a shared experience and a predictable future for their work together.

Both adults in these dyads initially acknowledge feelings on behalf of the infant and the schoolchild until they are ready to accept and own them for themselves. They accept negative and ambivalent feelings and manage behaviour relating to these feelings, keeping the children safe and giving a message of belief in their potential for growth.

Figure 4.2 Attachment behaviour: establishment of a secure base and emerging independence

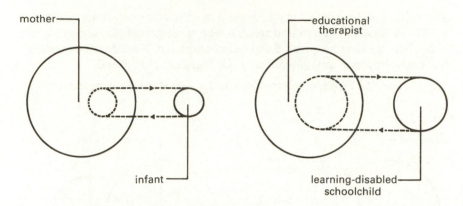

Differentiation – 'me/not me'

Reciprocal mother/infant interactions (secure attachment behaviour) allow the process of individuation to begin. The mother keeps her infant safe, manages his frustrations and sets limits for him. His confidence in her emotional availability allows him to explore his environment and to begin experiencing himself as separate from her – a two-way learning process.

In the therapy sessions, the therapist interacting with the child offers herself as an educational attachment figure. She responds to the child's active, independent contribution within the dyad. She keeps him safe, sets limits and helps him to manage his frustration and distress. His emerging confidence allows him tentatively to discover or rediscover a sense of self.

Playing in the presence of an adult

The securely-attached infant will play happily in the presence of his mother while she is busy (ironing, for example). He will be able to pursue his own explorations confident that she is near at hand if he needs her.

The therapist helps the child to find ways of managing his play and work within the session, encouraging him to use his own initiative.

Internal working models

The infant builds up internal working models of his interactions with his mother. As these interactions and his exploratory experiences extend and become increasingly complex, involving other people, the models are updated. The educational therapist offers the schoolchild a similar opportunity within the sessions. Like the mother, she also validates the self-worth of the child.

EXPLORATORY BEHAVIOUR: CREATION OF A
PLAYING/WORKING SPACE

The mother and her infant create a space in which they can make discoveries about one another. This shared space is where reciprocal play and work take place, feelings can be expressed and tasks completed. The infant's exploratory behaviour becomes goal-orientated as he learns to plan ahead.

Figure 4.3 Exploratory behaviour: creation of a playing/working space

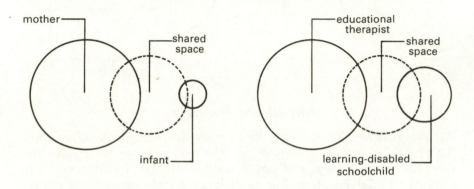

The exploratory behaviour of the learning-disabled child is often inhibited and his capacity for playing and learning lost. The therapist creates a playing and working space for the schoolchild in which the lost skills can be recovered.

Separation

The securely-attached infant will be able to hold his mother in mind during her absence and learn to tolerate separation from her, confident that she will return. These positive experiences prepare the child for the separations that lie ahead as his world extends beyond that of his immediate family and friends.

The learning-disabled schoolchild will need a lot of support and encouragement from the therapist to manage the separations that arise from the breaks in therapy due to holiday periods. Memories of earlier painful and often traumatic separations are reawakened. The therapist offers the child a new experience, carefully preparing him for the breaks and confirming her reliable predictability by resuming sessions at the time agreed.

Anxiously-attached children have few positive experiences to draw on, and the advent of school can be daunting. The separations, both expected and unexpected, that form a normal part of school life can prove overwhelming, preventing a child from acquiring basic skills, or provoking a later loss of those skills or an active resistance to the process of learning. The educational therapist works towards the renewal of a child's confidence in his own ability to survive and move towards age-appropriate autonomy.

SCHOOL EXPERIENCE

Children with secure attachment behaviour (like John in Chapter 3) will be able to continue to play and learn, using goal-seeking behaviour in school. These children can extend their interactional experiences with their mothers, transferring them to their teachers in the new setting. They can also learn to share the working space with a classroom full of other children of similar age, interacting creatively and with enjoyment in the new social setting.

The anxiously-attached child who has not been able to adjust well enough to his experiences in school cannot concentrate on learning. All his energy is taken up with his struggle to either avoid or attract the attention of his teacher. Sharing a teacher is often impossible for these children. The educational therapist offers a second-chance learning opportunity for the child in which he may form another, more positive attachment. As a result of an increasing sense of self-worth, the child can experience a renewal of hope and a belief in the future, exemplified in the following account of our work with a 10-year-old boy of at least average ability.

LUKE

Luke had no specific learning disability, so was not typical of the majority of the children referred to us. He had simply lost his capacity to learn, and we show his recovery of himself as a schoolboy through his interaction with an educational therapist and the use of stories. Luke's stories graphically demonstrate a child's use of the metaphor to express what he is feeling and illustrate the recovery of his capacity for learning. (The creation of the stories, in fact, formed only a part of the therapeutic process.) Another reason for using the example of a boy without a specific learning disability to introduce the intervention is to allow us to focus on his emotional development. We think the account illustrates the premise that unless due attention is paid to the state of mind and feelings of children their cognitive learning is unlikely to move forward.

Luke came from an intact middle-class family, the elder of two boys. Both parents were in full-time employment, though mother was able to be at home during her children's school holidays. Mother described his transition from home to school as 'difficult', although the reasons for this were never clear. Going to school continued to be 'stressful' for him, and he was still struggling to manage at the time of his referral. In his penultimate year at primary school he had become very attached to, and dependent upon, his 'motherly' class teacher. After the long summer break he returned to school to face a new teacher and in the knowledge that this year would be his last within the primary school before transfer to a large, more distant secondary school. As the autumn term progressed he became increasingly anxious. His ability to cope, already precarious, decreased. He was under-functioning in all areas and his behaviour resembled that of a helpless infant. This was emphasised by his small stature at the time. He was very withdrawn, out of contact with his peers and 'full of helpless-seeming misery'. The prospect of his transfer to secondary school in nine months' time dismayed everyone. He was referred to the clinic by the family doctor who, together with Luke's parents and teachers, had become increasingly concerned about the boy's inability to make any moves towards 'growing up'.

Luke's mother was naturally apprehensive as they prepared for his transition into what she described as the 'Big School'. She acknowledged that her son had formed a close attachment to his former class teacher, but she had difficulty in understanding what had 'gone wrong' with his present class teacher. Luke's own comparison of this teacher to the previous one gave an indication of his difficulties in school. The first, he said, 'did everything for me', while he described the second as being 'unavailable' to him. He had evidently expected the first teacher to be ready at all times to meet his needs, in a way that was reminiscent of his mother's description of her earlier interaction with him at home: 'I did everything for him.' No major traumas in Luke's early years were reported by the family, and we know of no event that might have accounted for their possible unavailability at a crucial time in his development, for example when he was beginning to explore becoming an individual separate from his mother – the 'not-me' of Winnicott. The birth of Luke's brother inevitably changed the lives of all the family members, but the parents' preparation for the event seems to have been sensitive. It was difficult to reach any conclusions as to how the family dynamic may have contributed to Luke's present state. The following short account of the family interview with the educational therapist who worked with Luke gives a picture of interested and concerned parents, and also an indication of Luke's behaviour as a family member.

'Luke and his parents came to the educational unit situated in an annexe of the clinic, but did not bring Jack, their younger son, because he was described as having a "low boredom threshold". Overtly both parents were at pains to minimise the difficulties that Luke was experiencing, while covertly emphasising them. I noted the difficulty that they seemed to be having in speaking openly in front of him. Directly addressing the problem in this way appeared to free him and he said that he did not seem to be able to manage anything for himself and that he needed help. He sat on the edge of his chair, looking desperately at me. (Although his legs were long enough for his feet to touch the floor he sat in a way that made this impossible.) I described the type of work that I was offering, namely a working space in which he and I, together, would struggle to understand at what stage his learning had become "stuck". We would find ways of unravelling the problems. I defined the confidentiality and privacy of the sessions and the use of time as a boundary, one hour a week, and explained that we would probably use stories, among other things, in our work together. I stressed that the sessions would provide him with a space on neutral territory, away from the pressures of school and the worries at home. I suggested that if we were to work together we would be thinking about transitions and the possibility of providing a bridge for him into his senior school. The family left to consider the proposal and the next day mother telephoned to confirm Luke's wish to proceed and the family's support for his decision.'

In this chapter we shall focus on Luke's interaction with the educational therapist, showing how she responded to his feelings of helplessness. By sharing her understanding of what was happening, he very slowly recovered enough to accomplish an educational task.

Preparation

At a practical level the therapist arranged for a specific room to be available for one hour each week at the same time, where she and Luke could work together undisturbed. A box was provided for his exclusive use, containing play and educational materials: paper, card, tags, elastic bands, paper clips, round-ended scissors, felt pens, pencils, eraser, pencil-sharpener, glue (non-toxic), Sellotape, animal families and fences, and modelling clay. A small collection of books was also available. (The significance of this box for different children is described in Chapter 6.)

Part of an educational therapist's preparation is creating a space in one's mind to think about each child (group or family) before beginning the work. The therapist working with Luke reported 'that it seemed important, prior to our first session, to hold in mind the part of Luke that could not learn, and to think in terms of a concrete task that was chronologically, rather than emotionally, age-appropriate. Perhaps focusing on this helped me not to feel overwhelmed by his "hopeless-seeming misery".'

The first session

'Luke duly arrived for his first session looking both apprehensive and expectant. He was a neatly dressed and well-coordinated "little" boy. He sat quietly beside me at the table, facing the box. After greeting him I referred again to the working space that we would be creating for ourselves, trying to establish a link with the family meeting of the previous week. Luke's apparent total lack of interest in what the box might contain was very striking. I wondered whether the sight of the box, a symbolic container, might be emphasising for him, on an unconscious level, that he felt very uncontained, with no expectation that anyone could be available to hold his helpless feelings. I felt that the need for me to provide some containment for him was paramount.'

The therapist became aware of being in danger of responding to Luke's helplessness in the same way as his mother and previous class teacher by doing everything for him, instead of maintaining her professional boundary. She recognised what was happening and took action.

'I acknowledged both our feelings at the time of this interaction: his sadness at being unable to do anything, and my temptation to do all the thinking for him. We sat quietly for two or three minutes. He didn't look at me directly but raised his head slightly. I mused aloud, "We might make a story together." There was no response so I continued, "I think we could look at ways of struggling to understand just how and where your learning seemed to have stopped." Luke remained very still but made eye contact with me and said, in a melancholy voice, "I can't get started. I'm having a real problem getting started." Indeed, this was an exact description of what I was observing. His tone of voice and drooping body, sunk into his chair, expressed a feeling of total helplessness.'

It is at this point that the therapist allowed herself a momentary space in which to think about what was happening.

'I was reminded of my thoughts a few minutes earlier about Luke's lack of containment and state of apparent total dependence, and I resolved to provide him with some symbolic (educational) "food" (Caspari 1974a). His statement, however, made me realise that this was an important beginning, because for the first time Luke had taken the initiative. He had helped me to understand, with words and body language, the depth of his hopeless and helpless feelings. I acknowledged the helpfulness of his statement and there was a lightening of his mood. I chose to proceed from there and suggested that it might be helpful to us if we made a list of things he felt we should think about first.

'At this he was able to move, open his box, and look inside for the felt pens and paper that he needed (sparing only a cursory glance at the other contents). In flowing italic writing he wrote "starting and choosing". I asked him if he could give me examples. "Starting school work, getting up and making choices of any kind," he volunteered. Choosing was very much associated with starting, every choice meant a beginning. He said he couldn't make up his mind and never knew what he wanted. He mournfully contrasted his state of indecision with that of his younger brother who knew what he wanted and how to get it. Although Luke managed to give me this information without too much difficulty, he suddenly became limp, almost feeble, with the effort required to speak about this difference. I reflected back his statement. "Jack always knows what he wants and how to get it?" He nodded. "But I don't," he added. He sounded almost resigned to his problems and I wondered what motivation, if any, he had to alter this state of affairs. I found myself questioning whether he really wanted to stay "the little one" in his family and to have everything done for him. How much did he care if his younger brother surpassed him, like a resigned baby bird being ousted by a cuckoo? Luke then went on to say that teachers don't make anything clear and that they don't generally like being asked for help. His self-esteem appeared to be so low that his whole life seemed a burden.'

(As already indicated in the introductory family meeting, Luke had become very closely attached to a maternal class teacher in his penultimate year in primary school. The degree of his total dependence upon her to meet his every need emerged gradually. The trauma of separation from her to start his final year was further aggravated by her retirement from teaching, which had made her totally unavailable.)

'I accepted all Luke's anxieties and feelings of inadequacy, restating that we would work together to understand his problems and start unravelling them so that he could really begin to grow. He looked at me very directly and the possibility of a future was silently acknowledged.'

'I can't'

'I suggested that we make a start on beginnings and think about making a choice at a practical level by creating a story.'

To engage so directly is unusual but it seemed appropriate for Luke. Inevitably, each therapist chooses to begin work with every child in the way that seems most likely to engage the individual. Certain patterns may emerge over time, but each child is unique and the response must be equally so. Returning to Luke, the therapist continued:

'The thought of creating a story paralysed him and in a very small voice he said "I can't" and looked helpless again. This phrase "I can't" was to characterise phase one of our work together. I reminded him that we would share the struggle to find ways that he could manage, and that we would go one step at a time. I accepted his feelings, saying that I would help him. The contrast between the confident, flowing handwriting that he had used on the label he made for his box and his appearance at this moment was very striking.
    'The first decision that had to be taken was a practical one – who was to

65

do the actual writing? His handwriting was excellent, as I had seen, and I wondered if he might like to write the story himself. Or, alternatively, he could just be the author and I would be his scribe. Having to contemplate these questions, not surprisingly, initially proved impossible for Luke; after a miserable minute or two he said, "Will you do it?" I praised him for managing to choose and he glanced at me with a flicker of hope. Taking a book from the shelf I asked him to give me a random page number, then a line and finally a word. He wrote down that word on a piece of paper. We repeated this process until he had a collection of five words, which included "path". I remarked, "Mm, a path, that's likely to lead somewhere ...." He glanced at me and I smiled. He solemnly acknowledged my smile with a slight change of expression. His apparent recognition of the symbolic implications was an encouraging sign for the work we would be doing within the metaphor. I felt we were beginning to find a way, but it seemed necessary to continue to provide him with enough support to keep the momentum going. I spoke out loud, "Once upon a time there was ....", a familiar starting point. He completed the sentence with, "a path leading to the river". He looked anxiously at me again, the words had been halting. A silence followed.

'I recognised the pressure that Luke was under and also the pressure that he was placing on me to do the thinking for him. I expressed my understanding of what was happening between us: that this was our first session together and that already we were stuck, with Luke looking to me to help him out. He nodded and I said that together we would find a solution by helping him to discover how to help himself and that I must discover how to resist doing this for him. He smiled at this. I said that I would simplify the task by doing the writing for him and that together we could sort out a few more techniques that he might find useful for story writing. Next we had to find a way to continue the story. I asked Luke if he could close his eyes and visualise a path (very difficult for many children, but he managed). He sat very still and then began, "It was a very old path, which was hardly visible, it was all overgrown." He described the path with tremendous feeling, then stopped again. I responded to his silence by repeating, "It was overgrown," and added, "It was unused but it was there, and would there be a way through?" (My choice of words was deliberate.) This allowed Luke to dictate, in a very halting way, the rest of his paragraph:

The old path

Once upon a time there was a path leading to a river. It was a very old path which was hardly visible, it was all overgrown. On the bank of the river the water rats were swimming about. Suddenly one darted into a hole as a fox appeared along the path. The fox sniffed at the river bank where the rat had once been and tried to reach the hole.

'As Luke finished dictating this I told him that I would type his story ready for him to read in next week's session. I asked if the story was complete or whether he would continue it next time; he chose the latter.'

The therapist had already begun to establish a 'here and now' in this first session; the beginning of a secure base. She made reference to their shared 'past' by recalling the family meeting. A 'future' was predicted by the promise of the typed story, which also gave the boy a message of her belief in his ability to recover the skills that had become suspended.

'The remainder of the session was spent with Luke, now less tense, telling me more about himself. He said that he liked drawing cartoon figures but couldn't draw otherwise. He told me that he didn't go outside at play-time in school, and that he always went home at lunch-time, albeit to an empty house, getting his own lunch of soup or baked beans. He didn't like playing football, finding it "too cold". He reckoned that bed-times were "about the same as for all children" but getting up was "really bad". After indicating to him that the session would have to end in five minutes' time, I talked again about what he had told me of his difficulties which seemed to be associated with transitions. I commented on the problem he experienced with the beginning of a new day. He looked at me with surprise and nodded. He was thoughtful as he put his things away and left quietly and calmly.'

Reflections on the first session

'In retrospect this session seemed to have been a full one, and yet I felt it to have been very desolate. I was very aware that Luke was showing by his behaviour how he would have liked to take on an infantile role, so inappropriate for a 10-year-old. By his attempts to become totally dependent upon me, he was showing me his wish to relinquish the schoolboy role. I felt somehow that he could not summon up enough energy to show any defensive behaviour in the new, unfamiliar setting, away from a known environment. The only way in which I could respond to these needs was by empathising with his wish to behave in this way. But I was, almost simultaneously, trying to respond to his other needs by helping him to take on a task which might reasonably be expected from a normally intelligent boy of his age. Reflecting his own statements about himself back to him often took him by surprise. His affirmation of his statements by his non-verbal communications made me feel that we had made a start on establishing a secure base.

'The subsequent sessions, which included a continuation of the story, clearly mirrored the struggles that were being experienced, although the resultant story set out below cannot reflect the full impact of its traumatic creation. The story continued from where the fox was trying to reach a rat in a hole.

He missed and walked away. Suddenly he stood still. A little mouse ran across his path. He jumped out and caught it and put it in his mouth and began to walk home to his den. His den was further up the river, under a big oak tree, almost hidden by dead leaves. He crawled in and dropped a mouse in front of his three cubs. Eagerly the three young fox cubs began to attack the mouse and play around with it. Then he came back out of his hole to look for food for them.

He sniffed the air around him – someone had been there – quite recently. He was worried that they might find his den if they came back, especially as the cubs were probably too young to look for another home.

He went to the side of the river to look for fish. After a while of seeing nothing he walked away. It was now night. He crawled back into his den and went to sleep.

'The second chapter started with the long wandering search for a new and safer den for his family.

He turned and walked a different way, but he had no luck there either .... He turned back and looked again. He was searching all day. By the end of the day he had found three possible spots, but none of them was quite what he wanted. He turned and walked back home. He was still quite a long way from home when he came to a small glade. He sniffed – he could not smell anything. This place, he thought, was perfect. Now his worry was would his cubs survive the journey? They were still too far from his den to be there by nightfall, so he settled down in the leaves and fell asleep.

'In the third chapter the fox returned to the den to collect his cubs, but disaster had struck.

He looked where the den used to be under the tree. The tree had been pulled up and destroyed, and he saw tyre marks leading into the forest. He was not sure what to do .... He didn't know whether his family were alive or had been caught. He searched everywhere he could think of.

'Luke described how it was getting dark by the time the fox had tracked down the van which was parked by a big house.'

Slowly and quietly he circled the house. Round the back he found some rabbit hutches. He ran up to them and was delighted to see his wife and three cubs.

'Luke vividly described the valiant efforts of the fox to rescue his family who were captive in the hutches. Overcoming apparently insurmountable odds, he led them off towards the new den. The journey was a hazardous one, with one small cub getting caught in a rabbit snare. After a great struggle the fox saved the baby and the family reached the new den safely.

'Together we considered the problems experienced by the fox and recognised the animal's growing ability to manage better. The fox story made good reading and Luke was clearly very satisfied when he heard it read aloud each week. We talked together about the pains of achievement and the satisfaction to be felt when overcoming things that are really hard to manage. The actual physical process of looking at the growing book also seemed important, providing a tangible reinforcement to Luke's efforts.

'As Luke gained some confidence in his sessions he began to draw parallels in his own life with those of the fox. He described a school project which he had found impossible to manage, becoming completely stuck. To his surprise he managed to "free himself", as he put it. He had recognised the possibility that he could move on, like the character in his story. He struggled with a drawing for the cover of the fox book for the three sessions leading up to the Easter break, but became more and more frustrated, and eventually abandoned his efforts. I commented on how hard he seemed to find it to make up his mind what to do. Finally he said "I could manage if I were on my own!" I reflected back, "If you were on your own?" He nodded and looked at me. I wondered aloud about what seemed to be his frustration with me for not helping him enough; not just with his drawing, but also with how he should end his story. I added that this probably had something to do with having to think about the ending of our sessions for the Easter break. I also recognised that the next end of term would signify his transition from primary to secondary school, and I reminded him that we would continue to work together after the change. I wondered if he thought I should be helping him to manage his feelings about these issues. In spite of the enormous impact my thoughts appeared to have on Luke, verbalising them seemed to have a positive result and he relaxed momentarily and nodded before fussing around again. Then suddenly he made the decision to stick his circular drawing of the fox on the cover. I watched as he did this, and he seemed to experience great relief. Then he said quite firmly that he was going to outline the circle. With this completed he had no difficulty in dictating the end of his story:

> The fox had a brilliant idea. He lifted the baby foxes up on his back; this way they got to their new den a lot faster. He told them to hold on tight and they ran off to their new den.

'Then Luke punched the holes and assembled his book with a great sense of purpose. He sat back upright in his chair, expressing pleasure in his achievement, clutching the book to his body. The tremendous struggle required to produce this book, culminating in drawing something alive (the fox) that was not a cartoon, symbolised for me the renewal of an interest in life for Luke, who seemed to be acknowledging the existence of a future for himself.

'Our relief was short-lived because, however well the ending had been managed, it inevitably meant another beginning. Luke was clearly very dismayed and we turned again to the fox story, together reflecting on the difficulty we, and the fox, had experienced throughout its creation. Again

Luke appeared to take real comfort and strength from the presence of the book which so readily allowed us to review his progress. There was a real possibility that new beginnings could be managed and lead on to other things.'

'I'm not sure'

'The next stage of our work together was characterised by this phrase. Was this a useful step forward from the former "I can't" position? It seemed to represent a shift from the totally dependent wished-for state. At the start of the summer term prior to the proposed transition into secondary school, Luke began dictating new stories with more confidence. The characters were interestingly different from those in the fox story. In the first instance Luke appeared to have been exploring the two parts of himself that were represented by the anxious parent (the fox) and the helpless babies (the cubs). The fox was constantly struggling to feed and protect his helpless babies from ever-present dangers, searching for a place where they could be kept safe, which he achieved in the final passage. The characters in the new story were Thomas (a small boy) and a large, sad, helpless dragon. In this series of stories (which continued throughout the remaining weeks of therapy) Luke explored the possibility of these two characters becoming friends and helping one another to become independent. Thomas and the dragon seemed to be a less extreme pair, perhaps reflecting Luke's own movement away from the earlier position of infant and parental distress, towards a measure of autonomy.
'The new stories began:

Once upon a time there was a peaceful village in the middle of the country. Everybody lived in harmony and everybody was happy apart from one thing. There was a dragon living in one of the hills just outside the village. He often came into the village but everybody ran into their houses and shut the windows and doors because they were scared of him. Sometimes they organised dragon hunts to catch the dragon, but no one was brave enough to go near him. There was one boy, the farmer's son, who was inquisitive about the dragon. He asked his father whether he could go to the dragon's hill and see what he did during the day. But the farmer was scared for his son and would not let him go.

The boy, who was called Thomas, thought this was very unfair, because he thought the dragon looked too small to hurt anybody. When Thomas got close to the dragon he discovered that the odd sound that he could hear was the dragon crying: 'He was sitting in a corner sobbing in a pool of tears.' In spite of the dragon's pleading for Thomas to come back the boy was petrified and fled away home.

All the rest of that night and the next day Thomas thought about the dragon. 'Why was he crying?' he asked himself, and 'why did he want me to come back?'

Thomas found the dragon crying again alone in his cave. He (Thomas) crept in further until he was right next to the dragon. Just then the dragon wiped his eyes and saw Thomas next to him. 'Hello', the dragon said. Thomas raced out and the dragon chased him. They ran round and round the field until finally the dragon caught Thomas and went back to the hill.

'What is this we've got?' said the dragon.

Thomas was not really listening and was wondering whether he would be fried or roasted and wondering how much tomato sauce he would have. Thomas was too scared to run away and looked at the dragon. He was very small for a dragon, Thomas thought, and why was he crying? Thomas didn't dare ask the dragon why.

'Who are you?' said the dragon.

'Er ...Thomas,' said Thomas.

'Oh!' said the dragon.

Thomas said, 'Dragon, when are you going to eat me?'

'Eat you?' said the dragon, 'I wasn't going to eat you,' and started crying again. 'They're all scared of me,' he wailed. 'I'm only a baby dragon, only a thousand and three.' Thomas, who was now sorry for the dragon asked, 'Why were you crying?'

'Because I want to be friends, boo hoo hoo!' said the dragon. Thomas was now up to his knees in salty water from the dragon's tears. He said, 'But don't you want to eat us all up?'

'I would but I'm a vegetarian dragon. Anyway, the clothes get stuck in my teeth.'

Thomas was feeling very sorry for the dragon and decided that he would tell the villagers that the dragon wasn't so bad after all. It was now almost morning so Thomas said goodbye and told the dragon he'd be back next morning. Then he crept back to his house.

'Luke's growing confidence was reflected in the ability of Thomas in the story to make decisions even though he was frightened. He was able to explore the fearfulness and sadness of both the characters within the metaphor. (The majority of children make use of characters and settings that are reminiscent of many other well known books and stories where the problems of relative size are explored. Jack the Giant Killer or David and Goliath being just two examples.)

However it took a long time for Thomas and the dragon to evolve a plan of action that would allow the dragon to be accepted in the village. He (Thomas) and the dragon thought and thought until a month had gone by. Still neither of them could think of anything.

'Luke resolved the characters' dilemma. The dragon had an encounter with a burglar, who attempted to rob the mayor's house. The dragon unexpectedly dropped from the sky and overpowered the burglar. In true fairy tale fashion

71

the dragon became the hero of the village people and was accepted by everyone.

'This happy state of affairs was not sustained and a series of separate adventures found Thomas and the dragon floundering again.

'As the sessions continued the story gradually became more humorous and Thomas and the dragon were joined by friends. Luke began to talk more directly about the coming transition into secondary school. He extended his consideration to include the minor transitions that he would have to make from activity to activity in different rooms in a secondary school to encompass major changes in life. At this time Luke's very real apprehension about his eleventh birthday surfaced. He started talking about feelings of frustration and fury which he had experienced "since he was 6". It was then, he said, that he was told to do things. "To do things?" I repeated. He nodded. "For yourself?" I added. He nodded again. This simple exchange again seemed to free him and for the first time in our work together he took some modelling clay out of his box. He modelled a dragon and while he did so we went over the original list of problems, focusing particularly, as always, on beginnings. He then began to explore the relationship between loss and gain, and the implications of movement. We considered together yet again the question of endings leading to new beginnings and the relevance of making choices, and the movement away from the familiar into the unknown.

'At this time I was becoming increasingly aware of the importance to Luke of the actual story books he was creating. They seemed to be providing him with more than just tangible evidence of the growth that was taking place within the sessions. I began to feel that the books held a deeper significance for him. Luke could be observed thinking about his book, particularly as he assembled it. He appeared to be preoccupied with his own thoughts as he handled it. I wondered if he was unconsciously reminded of an earlier experience, possibly with a transitional object. He now appeared to be looking towards the books themselves, not only the stories, as a tangible reminder of his competence, a validation of his self-worth, and a reminder of the frustrations which he had overcome by himself and for himself. I wondered to myself about his early experience with books and the part that they may have played in his interactional relationship with his mother? Did he continue to have stories read to him once he could read for himself? If not, had this been a painful loss? His appetite for the stories that I read to him within the therapy sessions seemed to be voracious, almost greedy, and was difficult to satisfy.

'Luke still continued to reflect on the fox stories, making his own direct links between the similarities he observed about himself and the fox. He appeared to have used the character of the fox to explore feelings of himself as an inadequate adult as well as a helpless infant. The characters in the dragon story were both young and less extreme. The boy was small but curious and brave, the dragon was large but lonely and helpless. In these stories Luke continued to explore the possibility of small people and animals solving the problems that beset them by using their brains to find solutions. Increasingly he moved from the metaphor to his own situation.

'In spite of these new insights, the shared preparation for the long summer break was another painful struggle, acting as it did as a reminder of the major impending change. Ending his sessions for the vacation heralded yet another beginning for Luke, that of entry into a new school. This trans- ition, too, stood for the physical change of growing up that he had so dreaded.'

The senior school

'When we resumed our work together after the holiday Luke was often very tired, physically as well as emotionally, and he expressed very negative feelings about school. As time went on this state of mind gave way to a more positive one. Luke seemed to find the clear expectations in his secondary school reassuring. He managed the transitions from task to task, room to room, and teacher to teacher, with comparative ease. The very different structure seemed to provide him with the containment he needed and could use. In one of our sessions he was able to be openly angry at the thought of writing yet more stories. This seemed to be real progress and I verbalised my thoughts, noting his growing confidence. He gave me a very direct look and started dictating, at high speed, about a burglar. The story was long and involved with everyone in the family and the dragon being rescued by a very tiny mouse. I made no comment. None was needed. He had utilised the session in a manner that gave it a feeling of being complete. He left the room looking tall and strong. He was still a small boy, but this was no longer significant. I felt he would not need the sessions much longer.'

Towards a more independent state

'From this time we began preparing for the ending of our work together. Luke was telling me more frequently about what he experienced as positive things at school, and he was describing anticipated events. The future was no longer a taboo subject. He appeared to have made a number of friends and was able to go out alone as well as with them. He was enjoying playing football and looking forward to playing hockey after half-term. We continued, period-ically, to talk about loss and gain. He still looked tired when he arrived for each session after a day at school, but the fatigue seemed to drop away from him as he worked. By this time he was cycling alone to each session.

'Just before the half-term break, earlier patterns of behaviour recurred briefly: Luke could not work again and his behaviour was anxious, but we were able to think about this reaction to a break. Together we reviewed his past feelings about gains and loss and how, in order to move forward, certain changes had to be tolerated. During this final period of our work together the dragon in the stories had grown bigger and stronger, changing out of all recognition from the sad little creature at the beginning of the series. Interestingly, he became "Dragon" not "the dragon" as he had been before, a person in his own right, perhaps. The progress continued until at last the dragon was ready to leave home. The sadness of separation was acknowledged and feelings relating to this were explored through an exchange of letters between characters.

'The final chapter was dictated as our work together was drawing to a close. It is only possible to speculate just how important the creation of these stories was for Luke in helping him to come to terms with himself and his life. Sometimes he appeared to move from the story to his own life experiences as if they were interchangeable. I no longer had to struggle to maintain my professional role with Luke. His helpless infant behaviour had given way to more appropriate feelings of independence and with them he had gained a measure of autonomy. The final words of the story were completed in the last session and I typed as he dictated them.

'I was acutely aware of the crucial part which the stories, within the two books, had played in the therapy. They had provided a vivid, symbolic picture of the journey that took Luke from a helpless, miserable, infantile state towards the development of a more age-appropriate sense of autonomy. Although the creation of the stories dominated the sessions, they took up only a portion of the time. Luke seemed to have been creating for himself a metaphorical vehicle which allowed his internal fears and fantasies to be tested against his external realities. He appeared to experience holding the books and working on them as reassuring proof that he could manage for himself. His worth was revalidated within the working space that we had created together. I came to believe that the books put him in touch with a "lost" experience. The memory of the books and whatever they symbolised for him could be carried forward through each stage of his development.'

Comment

We began our introduction to the intervention of educational therapy, second-chance learning, with the work of a boy who had no specific learning disabilities. In spite of this, according to both his parents and teachers, his learning had become impaired. In addition, he seemed to have given up growing, too, although full medical investigations showed no physical problems.

It is clear from these sessions with Luke that there were wide discrepancies between his intellectual and emotional development. We can also see how the therapist tried to maintain a balance for him, by attempting to respond to his feelings, while at the same time catering for a currently realistic expectation of scholastic achievement. Although we always use specific teaching methods for reading, writing, spelling or mathematical topics, the questions we are constantly endeavouring to answer are, how can we begin to understand the child's state of mind? What are the feelings affecting his or her approach to a task? And how can we discover at what earlier stage of learning the child's capacity for scholastic and often social learning became lost?

Luke's earlier patterns of attachment behaviour

To begin the process of assessing this boy's perception of himself interacting with others, we focus our attention on some emotional aspects of his development. In the account given by the educational therapist it quickly became apparent that, although Luke was potentially an able and articulate 10-year-old, he was behaving like a dependent infant. Mother reported that he had always had difficulty in separating from her, and starting school had been a particularly painful experience for him. He had just managed to cope both at home and at school until the beginning of his final year in junior school, which entailed the loss of his previous class teacher upon whom he had become very dependent. He could not adjust to his new class teacher, whom he described as being 'unavailable'. (We think he must have been reading Ainsworth!) It became clear that she appeared, for him, to be an inextricable and negative part of the process that would lead to the inevitable transition from his small, familiar local school into a large, unknown and distant senior school. He appeared to have been overwhelmed by the prospect of this major change and could no longer function intellectually; an unconscious unwillingness to relinquish the infantile part of himself, perhaps.

We have only limited information about Luke's early life experiences and we can only speculate about his attachment behaviour. He seemed to have been left with the impression that he had to manage by himself. Mother said, 'I tried to encourage him to stand on his own feet.' We are not told what his (or her) experience of weaning was like. Did it end suddenly? Was he separated from his mother in the pre-school years? Did losses or family circumstances mean that Luke was expected, or expected himself, to become independent before he had experienced a predictable dependence on an attachment figure?

Inevitably there are many possible interpretations that can be placed upon Luke's stories. We have used them to chart his progress from being unable to function towards a recovery of exploratory and goal-seeking behaviour. We can see the steps he took (often two forward and one back when there were breaks in the therapy). Gradually it became possible for the therapist to help Luke to prepare for these transitions, having established a predictable continuum in their sessions together. The establishment of a secure base allowed for the existence of a shared past and present, and for the emerging possibility of a previously inconceivable future. The fox story illustrated the first faltering steps towards a satisfactory outcome between parent and infant, while Luke explored the natural progression towards maturity as he developed the Thomas and dragon story. The work took a comparatively short time, nine months in all. This was no doubt due to the absence of specific learning disabilities and to the fact that Luke was able to respond to the therapist's expectations. His small stature became increasingly irrelevant as his confidence grew and he finally looked and behaved like the 11-year-old boy that he was.

Observations of other learning-disabled children

Luke's behaviour and that of other learning-disabled children interacting with an educational therapist confirm the observations made of them, whether with their families, in small groups, or in mainstream classes. It is difficult to equate their behaviour with their chronological age. What were their inappropriate behaviours (active or withdrawn) expressing? Why were they unable to understand signals given to them by others and unaware of the effect of the signals they themselves were giving?

Educational therapists recognise the wisdom of differentiating the child from his problem, and viewing his behaviour as an expression of his feelings about both. Barrett suggested in 1985 that we do well to remind ourselves that each child is a member of a 'myriad of systems', the most significant of which are, of course, the family and school. We try to gain a picture of children as members of clubs, street gangs, choirs, sports centres, where they interact with adults as well as peers, in addition to recognising self-as-system as suggested by Duhl (1983). Ours is an intervention that has put many children in touch with patterns of earlier learning about their attachment behaviour and the losses they have suffered, losses both of people and of skills.

Skills are more readily acquired (at any age) when our level of anxiety is under our control: we are aware that we can learn when we feel secure, both inside ourselves and with the knowledge that we are not in a dangerous environment. If for any reason we have not had an experience of forming attachments to people on whom we can rely, we may be less able to take in knowledge, or trust new situations.

5

THE ROLE OF THE EDUCATIONAL THERAPIST

The idea that children, or indeed adults, find it more difficult to take in new information if their state of mind is preoccupied with other matters has already been introduced in the earlier chapters. We have given an overview of the likely experience of learning-disabled children at home. How can the minority of children, who are unable to 'make use of' a teacher and the range of educational provision, be helped to take advantage of the intervention of educational therapy?

Bowlby (1969) refers to our 'internal structures' from which we select what we perceive and reject what we choose to ignore; and 'how a new situation is construed and what plan of action is likely to be constructed to deal with it'. He suggests that these 'structures' influence our choice of people to whom we can relate. A small number of children when they enter school are unable to relate to their teachers. Even when a specific attachment person is available some children reject them. Their capacity for updating seems to be impaired, and many adopt a 'plan of action' that is frequently inappropriate. If their behaviour arises from their earlier experiences is it possible, for some of them at least, to shift their previous patterns of behaviour or learning? Those referred to us have often chosen to see themselves as so 'bad' that they feel no one wants to relate to them; others 'switch off', thus making themselves unavailable. An 'I don't care' stance may be taken to mirror their own feeling of being uncared for; or they are so hurt that their behaviour becomes aggressive. Any one of these plans of action is an attempt to manage in a new situation such as school.

We feel the acceptance of the concept of attachment to be crucial to our role as educational therapists if we are to help a learning-disabled child to recover his 'loss' of the memory and meaning of his earlier attachment experience. As educational therapists we assume the role of *educational attachment figures* who are available to learning-disabled children for one hour a week. The use of this term delineates our professional boundary, although we note that Mattinson and Sinclair (1979), in their description of working with marital couples, boldly state 'We were in effect offering ourselves as attachment figures. We came to believe that such a role was a prerequisite for change.'

Luke (Chapter 4) showed very clearly that his choice would be to remain an infant, relating to his mother in a dependent state of mind. He attempted to continue on this 'pathway of development' (Ainsworth 1985) in his first encounter with his educational therapist. He tried to transfer his infantile feelings for his mother to his therapist and to perceive her as mother. She accepted his wish to behave in this way, but responded to him as the 10-year-old that he was, and he was then able to express an age-appropriate wish to 'get started again'. If an educational therapist has no true understanding of the meaning of transference and counter-transference (Freud 1926), her own learning and teaching skills are likely to be ignored, or at least inhibited. Luke was slowly and painfully put in touch with 'lost' scholastic skills; but, more importantly, with himself. For whatever reason, his 'internal structures' had not incorporated the capacity to update his earlier experience of first learning. His 'internal working model' of himself interacting with his mother had remained stuck in his infancy. He had not been able to change his internal structure, so that unconsciously he was trying to ignore how a new situation is construed. Nor was he able to make a plan of action to deal with it.

We try to intervene, or interrupt a child's previous 'pathway to development', and to put him in touch with earlier perceptions and feelings that will lead to a re-evaluation of self-esteem and self interacting with others. Like the mother with her infant and toddler in Chapter 2, each child with whom we work needs to discover his confidence in our ability to be 'consistent and accessible' and to know that we will listen attentively. He learns to recognise our willingness to respond to anxious attachment behaviour by assuaging it appropriately. One of the more obvious differences between maternal and professional assuagement of anxious behaviour is that of physical comfort. The question of how much (if any) physical comfort is offered to children in individual sessions by an educational therapist remains problematic. Physical restraint is occasionally necessary; young children may sit very close to a therapist, or on her lap when a story is being read; one of us had the unusual experience of a 6-year-old girl spending all but the first 5 minutes of her first session asleep on her lap. She had been suspended from school for her violent behaviour towards peers and staff. When children show great distress, resting a hand on their shoulder or holding their hands can be more effective than words alone. In their description of the aims of a teacher/therapist, working with severely reading-retarded children, Heard and Barrett include 'modes of communication' to fulfil some of their aims for 'assuaging care-giving' behaviour. These are: '(1) bodily posture, gesture, and facial expression; (2) tone of voice; (3) the way syntax is used in utterances; and (4) the overt information in utterances; and a high level of congruence and consistency between the messages and signals conveyed in each of the four modes' (Heard and Barrett 1982). If we had to choose one ingredient from the recipe for becoming an educational therapist for individual learning-disabled children, it would be the keeping of professional boundaries, by *never* adopting the role of the child's primary attachment figure, however much we know from our own value system that he has been starved of affection and care-giving.

The dual roles, educational attachment figure and teacher, are in practice integrated throughout the process.

We have chosen two young children, Leslie aged 6 and Mark aged 7, to illustrate the dual clinical role of the therapist. The work with Leslie ended abruptly, so it is possible to see that more work was needed to help him to resolve some of his conflicting feelings relating to the attachment behaviour he showed towards his therapist. The intervention with Mark too was only marginally successful. He did well in school and managed transitions until the final one into the world of work, when the patterns of delinquency of his stepfather proved a temptation that was difficult to resist. The therapist reported. 'I felt that events had come full circle for Mark. The pressures placed upon him as a 2-year-old appeared to be repeated now that he was 16.'

Leslie

Leslie was referred by his head teacher because of aggressive behaviour towards his peers coupled with a 'refusal to learn'. His manner was said to be 'aloof'. Leslie's class teacher spoke of his 'superior' attitude towards her, especially towards the end of the day when she read a story in class. He said repeatedly that this activity was too babyish for him and he stood away from the other children, who were sitting on the floor ready for the story.

Leslie and his parents attended family interviews during which they revealed their resistance to learning. Neither parent could discuss their son's aggressive behaviour, or his adoption of the role of a third family adult. (The power this gave him appeared to amuse rather than worry them, but they were concerned about his lack of scholastic progress.)

The therapist described her first impressions of Leslie in his individual sessions.

'I was immediately struck by the repetition of his behaviour with me that I had to some extent observed in family interviews, but even more so by its similarity to that reported by his class teacher. This was illustrated by the things he chose to have recorded in a book about himself. He liked a well-known brand of baby food and roast potatoes – part infant and part adult, which seemed to indicate his uncertainty about whether he was little or grown-up. He was unable to tell me his dislikes or anything about himself as a person. For the next 7 or 8 weeks Leslie's behaviour remained aloof. He asked numerous meaningless questions that were repeated time and again. No answers seemed to be required. There was little indication from his eye contact that he perceived me as a person who existed at all. I felt I held little reality or meaning for him, even when the questioning moved forward to the "why" stage of a toddler. In his distracted efforts at play his choice of puppets seemed to hold little significance, although I noticed that the baby puppet was held most often. His second choice of activity was typing, again a rather adult activity possibly indicating some of his confusion?

'One day Leslie was trying to type his "spelling" (gobbledegook) with the baby puppet on his knee, when it slipped to the floor. He picked it up and placed it in my hands. As he did so, the previous blank (Tinbergen and Tinbergen 1973) or "switched-off" expression in his eyes appeared to alter, leaving me with the impression that for the first time I was perceived as someone to whom the care of the baby might be entrusted. I felt that Leslie was giving the baby part of himself into my care.'

This action was the first of many that showed Leslie's seeking for an explanation of his role. Could he explore himself as a little boy of 6, was he a baby, or was he really an adult asking questions that he knew caused his parents amusement and were never answered? His therapist felt he would need to understand who he was as a 6-year-old, before he could even begin to think about feelings related to basic skill learning. Subsequent sessions confirmed this. The therapist held in mind what she considered to be some of the more fundamental of Leslie's needs, but knew that psychotherapeutic techniques were outside her terms of reference. She chose, therefore, to stay within the bounds of the educational material, suggesting that the baby could be placed in a box while the 'typist' typed his name, Leslie.

'Leslie seemed to understand and carefully placed the puppet back in its box. It was as if he unconsciously recognised that the puppet was symbolically representing the baby part of himself that could be "held", in the Winnicott-ian sense, while he got on with some basic skill learning appropriate to his chronological age. He returned to the typewriter and immediately asked how to spell some "four-letter" words. The request was taken seriously and we approached the task together. Leslie showed pleasure in this activity, and listened to my comment that perhaps the baby puppet was not sure if it wanted to be very little or grown up enough to write very rude words.'

Work with Leslie continued for another term until he was suddenly withdrawn from the clinic. He did not return after the summer break, his parents no longer wished to maintain contact with the team, and they were quite unable to consider any other form of help for their son. The educational therapist by now felt that Leslie's worries had little to do with scholastic skills, which to a small degree is illustrated in her account of his final session with her. Reluctantly the parents agreed to allow Leslie to return once more to give him and his therapist the opportunity to say goodbye to one another. The therapist continued:

'Leslie moved very swiftly towards me in the waiting room as usual, but instead of challenging me to a race, as he had done each week of the previous term, he walked very slowly beside me on the way to the room. He looked carefully around it before asking if we could play hangman. The progress he had made in his reading was very much in evidence at the beginning of this game. It seemed that unconsciously the choice of this aggressive game mirrored some of his angry feelings about the unplanned ending to his sessions, and was probably chosen to express anger towards me for apparently "allowing" this to happen. When I warned him that we had only a short time left, Leslie, who was winning the game, made his final choice: the word he chose was "home". I said that I thought he was telling me that he would rather be at home than here in this room having to face the painful feelings associated with having to say good-bye. Leslie sat very quietly, looked directly at me and said, "Home is here".'

The account ended with the therapist's description of her own conflicting feelings.

'I felt sad and said so to Leslie. I was aware too of my own sense of helplessness, because I would have preferred to know that Leslie was being transferred to a psychotherapist. In the waiting room, I had unexpectedly to deal with more conflicting feelings. Leslie's mother jumped from her seat to greet me and began to recount her amusement about a social event from the previous evening, ignoring the return of her son. Leslie was sitting with tearful countenance in a far corner of the room. I acknowledged what his mother was telling me, but said I thought Leslie was feeling rather sad at having to say good-bye, and that I hoped he would continue to do well at school. He was jollied along by his mother and I realised how angry I felt as I witnessed this insensitivity. Later, reflecting on the events in the waiting room, I was reminded of the process of mourning described by Bowlby (1980).'

Mark

By the time Mark was 7 years old family life had been interspersed by periods of time, both long and short term, spent in the care of local authorities. The following brief account of a first educational therapy session with him seems almost to resemble his life experience.

We do not know what prompted Leonardo da Vinci (who in one sense could have been labelled learning-disabled because he wrote in reverse form) to think 'that every part is disposed to unite with the whole that it may escape from its own incompleteness' (translated *Notebooks* 1938).

Mark gave the impression that he felt 'incomplete', unsure of who he was in time and space. Like many other children, his past experience of numerous transitions from home to being placed in care and then back to his family again, must surely have contributed to his bewildered state of mind. He was referred for 'severe learning difficulties'. The referral was made by a consultant psychiatrist, who also stated that 'there was a danger that Mark was becoming too cynical in his relationships'. The family was well known at his place of care and it was recognised that he had received 'good-enough mothering' for the first two years of his life. However, his environment then became cruelly rejecting. His mother became pregnant and lost all interest in him, and at the same time he was being mistreated by his new stepfather. When he was taken into care his internalised picture of his attachment to his mother made it possible for him to form an attachment to a 'specific attachment person', a member of staff in the home where he had been placed. When this person left the home Mark's behaviour began to change. The second loss of a significant attachment figure proved intolerable for a 7-year-old to manage. This initial impression of Mark was given by the therapist who worked with him for three years.

'I observed Mark, a pale robot-like little boy, sitting silently beside his escort in the waiting room. His demeanour remained the same until he entered the room where we were to work, which had an "educational bias" (Duve 1965).

'Mark immediately began examining everything on the shelves and all the play materials, touching most of them. At the same time he kept up an apparently meaningless commentary, often asking questions that required no answers. He seemed to be trying to fill the space with words and actions.

'I tried to assuage what I assumed were Mark's anxious feelings by introducing an educational task. I showed him a notebook and felt pens and suggested that we used the task as a way of getting to know one another. I asked him if he would like to write his name and tell me something about himself. Mark was unable to say anything or look in my direction. I further acknowledged feelings on his behalf and empathised with the difficulties of wondering who you were and why you were here, in a strange place with a strange person. Mark immediately stopped what he was doing, although still avoiding eye contact, and said "She sent me", indicating with his thumb in a general direction towards the door.

'I explained briefly why I thought we were here, and said I was sorry he was finding school work difficult at the moment. I asked Mark if he would like to sit down and write his name on his book. He did this, but when he was invited to write something about himself he immediately started walking around the room again. I mused to myself, "Shall we say Mark has brown hair? Yes, I can see that he has. I wonder if we should write it in his book?" Mark's response, still from the other side of the room was "Mark has brown eyes. Write that down. He is 7." His behaviour became more and more excited as he began to dictate in a very controlling manner. At this point he came to look at what had been written in his book, and then returned to a box of bricks that he been looking at. On being told that he could tip them out and play with them, he began to build a house.

'I felt that this house in some way represented a tentative acceptance of his present environment, as well as possibly symbolising an attachment figure. I made use of the building to establish a "secure base" for our first session by using terms like "firm foundations", well understood by this intelligent little boy. When the building reached a precarious stage I introduced the idea of a builder's mate (myself) who could be useful to the builder (Mark) when he was in difficulty. Again there was a sudden change of mood when he demanded that I wrote the word "house" on the board. When I had done this I said out loud, "h for house". Mark then asked me to write the word "witch". I repeated the initial sound of the word "witch" as I wrote it down. In a very excited manner Mark picked up a book, selected at random from a shelf. Rather frantically he began searching for words beginning with a "w", but abandoned the task and asked me to look for him. He quickly lost interest and asked for the lavatory. On our return to the room I had my first indication of a more integrated boy with a sense of humour. "W for wee-wee," he said, looking directly at me with a smile, "Go on, write it down, that's something about Mark, isn't it?"

'When I warned him that his session must end in 10 minutes his behaviour became very agitated and he ordered me to roll out some modelling clay. He placed some plastic animals on the clay, imprinting their foot marks as quickly as he could. This behaviour did not change until I acknowledged his anxiety about the end of the session and commented that the animals had made their "mark", too, and would still be there next week, like his book. I suggested that perhaps we could write down something else about him next week.'

Because of the limitation of space we have not included a full account of Mark's work, but we think it is possible to see how much happened in this first session. The witch featured throughout the first two years of work with him. He made use of the metaphor to work through many of his feelings about past rejections. With the help of his educational attachment figure he was able to begin uniting the fragmented parts of his life in an attempt to make it whole.

One way in which memories of painful feelings associated with specific school learning are sometimes expressed is in miscues or word substitution. A boy of 8, at the time of his mother's fifth pregnancy, could not read the word 'mum', at least not aloud. He chose a book, the cover and title of which made the content clear. The words of the title were 'My mum', so it seemed that the boy was quite able to read 'mum'; but each time it appeared in the text he replaced mum with random names or 'gobbledegook'.

When we suspect that children are secret readers, we usually take it up with them, though they may continue to deny it over long periods of time. Pretending, or even almost believing, that you cannot read is a convincing way of 'punishing' adults with whom the child is feeling angry or disappointed.

The boy just mentioned allowed himself to discover and momentarily to share his 'secret' reading with his therapist, but this was quickly followed by a denial. In several subsequent sessions he settled for a compromise, and sang all his reading books.

Miscues like these can reveal the child's state of mind and give the therapist some clues about his inner world or indeed his reality. A boy of 12 always read the word 'sad' as 'tired'. He experienced his sadness as fatigue. His class teacher had reported how he often yawned in school. She had assumed that her subject held no interest for him or that he watched too many late-night films. Later, in his therapy, he was able to share his sad feelings about the absence of his father. Bettelheim and Zelan (1982) state 'The meaning of what he [a child] is reading is distorted both by the feelings he brings to it and the material he is reading arouses in him.' Another boy who had no knowledge of his father compiled a list of words which he cut up. In each session he read the word and then posted it into in a 'gobble box', his own invention. The words 'dad' and 'dead' were always left until last, but it was not until his fears were expressed by the use of several stories that he could bring himself to read them.

The deliberate choice of a word or words by the therapist when working with these children frequently intrigues them when their appetite for learning has been rediscovered. The interest in words expressed by Gordon in Chapter 10 began with his wish to identify with his father, who was a journalist. His search for the meaning of words seemed to be unconsciously reflecting his search for his father, whom he had not seen since he was a small boy.

Some years ago the term 'reading readiness' was used in schools (Chazan 1970). It seems to us that when an educational therapist has developed a sensitivity to a child's communication she is able to gauge the 'right' moment to introduce direct teaching. Unless the child is behaving in a very compliant, passive or 'switched off' way he will indicate somehow when the moment is not right.

THE CONSULTATIVE ROLE

The majority of clinically trained educational therapists are invited to consult with head and individual teachers, a particular school department, or occasionally a staff group. When the educational therapist is well known to a school, she is likely to be invited to a consultation about children who are not necessarily attending a clinic or other setting where she is a member of staff. The title 'work discussion group' is frequently used by teacher's groups, and we function as active participant members rather than group leaders. This aspect of our role is a valuable resource, and we work within whatever limitations others place on our use of the term 'consultant'.

Michael

Michael, aged 9, was a member of a family of seven children, two of whom had been referred for educational therapy some years previously. The parents had been supported by several members of the community network whenever a crisis situation arose over a period of years. The deputy head-teacher of Michael's school invited an educational therapist to discuss Michael's behaviour with the staff, several of whom were concerned about his safety. For some weeks he had been climbing to a dangerously high level on the roof of the school. He usually did this at the end of the school day, and neither his parents nor the school staff seemed able to control the situation.

At the first meeting with the staff, feelings appeared tense and angry. Michael was described as being quite out of control in school. In response to a request for examples of this behaviour, a few members of the staff group described Michael running out of his classroom, hiding in the toilets, shouting in the corridors and disturbing other classes, tipping over fire buckets or rushing up and down the stairs. The educational therapist took as her starting point the separation of Michael, the boy, from his behaviour. She noticed that his interaction with staff and peers was not mentioned. It became apparent that all the staff liked Michael, that he was intelligent, and that he worked well when he did manage to stay in the classroom. The educational therapist posed the question, 'What must it be like for Michael when he is disappearing, or shouting, or endangering his life climbing up the drain pipe? Does he enjoy behaving like this?' It was then suggested that it might be very frightening for a 9-year-old to find himself in apparent control of the adults he liked and in whose care he was placed. The realisation that Michael's behaviour thus placed him in a very powerful position led to a reappraisal of the adults' behaviour. The deputy head-teacher recognised that his own uncertainty and lack of action had contributed to Michael's behaviour, and must have made it even more terrifying for the boy. All the staff members, except one, nodded or murmured agreement with this. The discussion, which took place during a lunch hour, enabled this caring staff to respond to the deputy head's lead. He used his authority to take full responsibility for Michael, and suggested that he would talk to the parents in the presence of their social worker. He invited the staff to monitor Michael's behaviour, including any positive aspects of it.

When the educational therapist met the staff a month later, it became clear that they had worked together in such a way that all their previous positive feelings about Michael as a person had been reinforced by the actions taken to monitor his behaviour. Each member of staff had found ways of letting the deputy head know how Michael had managed each day, and he in turn had seen Michael for a few minutes every afternoon to discuss his day with him. The class teacher gave the boy some classroom responsibility, whenever possible at times to coincide with previous 'danger' points such as the interval between a school assembly in the hall and the return to the classroom. The social worker was able, to a limited extent, to help the family to show less admiration for their son's daring exploits.

Regular consultations

When a special needs department, a school counsellor or other teacher with specific responsibilities asks to work with an educational therapist on a regular basis, one hour a week for instance, many children can be discussed. If the teacher can find time to write up any interactions that have taken place between him or her and a group of children, and then share these notes with their colleagues and/or the therapist, this can lead to a greater understanding of the group or one-to-one dynamic. The adult learning that takes place (including that of the therapist) can be evaluated, and may lead to an examination of how the peer-group behaviour of the children is being reflected in the interactions of the adult group discussing them.

An inherent difficulty for a therapist when working with a sub-system, perhaps a special needs department, is that the group may shift the emphasis away from the children they have chosen to review into a session of complaints about the position of 'their' department in the whole school system. One then has to decide if this issue is felt to be affecting the functioning of the group of teachers with whom one is working, and of course indirectly the children. We usually manage to address this question with the group, for example, by inviting other staff members, or heads of other departments, year tutors or the head teacher, to join a discussion on which to base decisions. However, we find that if we allow ourselves to drift into tasks other than the ones agreed at the beginning of the consultation, the children and the concerns about them can be lost sight of, leaving all members of the group with a feeling of dissatisfaction.

Another difficulty that can arise when one is invited to discuss one child, perhaps with a head teacher, is the sudden presentation of a dozen more children as problems. This may well be the true situation for that particular head, but again we usually find that more can be achieved by arranging an agreed discussion time, during which one or more children can be talked about on a regular basis. This allows the therapist to make a realistic commitment to the school, and the head to invite classroom teachers to express their perception of each child, before deciding to invite school psychologists, members of other disciplines, or a child's family to become involved.

A head teacher who was already working with a particular educational therapist asked if she would observe twin girls, whose behaviour was causing problems for their class teacher. The hidden agenda was the head teacher's concern about the newly-qualified class teacher's management of her class. She was described as extremely anxious, and the presence of other teachers or the head made her even more so. In spite of the fact that the school layout was open-plan and the presence of colleagues therefore commonplace, the head had felt that this teacher had needed time to find her own solutions, but she did not now feel that this decision was helping either the teacher or the class.

The educational therapist had already met all staff members over a period of several weeks, but nevertheless re-introduced herself to the class teacher concerned and spoke to her briefly about the twins. She then asked if she could sit and listen to the story that was to be read to the class. When the teacher nervously agreed, the educational therapist recalled her own feelings about having another adult sit in on her lessons in the past. She continues:

'There was a lot of interaction between the teacher and children during the story, and when it was over the children went out to play. The teacher became even more anxious and said, "Well, what do you think?" I felt this comment indicated that she had been all too aware of her head teacher's hidden agenda. I replied that I found that the two children I had been asked to observe elicited the opposite response in me from that described by her. I said that I found myself becoming increasingly angry with Lottie, "who sought your attention so often, but you were so patient with her. My thoughts about Elin were that I just wanted to pick her up and put her on my knee, she looked so sad, but ...." At this point the class teacher interrupted. "Oh, I get so fed up with Elin, she never seems to pay attention and she's always trying to distract the other children." The ensuing discussion about other children in the class seemed to lead the class teacher into a new-found belief in herself in role. The realisation that there could be no wrong or right way to deal with children about whom one was worried was a shared one. I reminded her that although we had reacted differently to the twins, I also felt concerned about the effect their behaviour was having on the rest of the class. We agreed to meet again two weeks later.'

The follow-up visit showed quite clearly that the class teacher was working in a more confident manner with the whole class. She was observed to be more encouraging to the twin who was withdrawn and very firm with the one who tried constantly to gain her attention. The whole tenor of the classroom was more relaxed.

When acting in a consultative role we try to help teachers to make sense of the de-skilling effect that troubled children can elicit in them, and counteract the resultant feelings of inadequacy. When they understand the complex interactive processes involved, they become free to exercise their professional competence. Teachers at all levels frequently become very defensive about not having 'noticed' the distress of withdrawn children. They find it difficult to share anxieties about aggressive behaviour of others or find ways to seek help and specialist advice early enough. Whether we are teachers or psychologists, we share a common professional background with those with whom we consult. Because we are not members of the school system we can offer an objective view. Given time and space teachers can discover the effect of their behaviour on children and vice versa (Hanko 1985).

The first roles we talked about contribute to the process of the intervention which we examine in Chapter 6. Equally important are the tools used in the practice: in a sense, the therapist herself is a tool. Unlike the psychotherapist who 'becomes' a witch in the transference, most educational therapists begin by thinking about the behaviour of the witch together with the child. By this use of the metaphor she shares, not only the child's feelings about the witch, but also the effect the character's behaviour might have on the child. The educational therapist enables a child to manage his feelings about what the witch might do to him in fantasy, until he is ready to deal with his feelings about a person he perceives as witchlike in reality.

6

THE PROCESS OF EDUCATIONAL THERAPY

The process of educational therapy has a structure similar to that of a good story. The beginning has to engage the reader by introducing the characters, setting the scene, establishing the plot and hinting at what may be coming. The middle is concerned with the unfolding of a tale about the vicissitudes of the lives of the characters: explorations, discoveries, excitements and pain. The author provides continuity by referring to the present, the past and the future. The ending can leave the reader with feelings of satisfaction or of frustration and dismay.

The educational therapist, like the author, has to engage a child by introducing the characters, of which she is one. The child represents the reader in our analogy. In the case of a story, of course, the author is usually invisible, whereas in therapy the adult is part of the interactive process with the child. The therapist sets the scene by talking about the features of the room and the 'rules' of the setting. The plot is established by describing the nature of their work together, followed by an intimation of future activities; each session is like a chapter from a book.

During the middle or 'on-going' phase of the therapy the child, like the reader, is offered time in which to think about the developing story and to reflect on any feelings evoked by the material.

There are other similarities which continue the analogy. Author and therapist need to maintain the reader's/child's interest in the here-and-now of each chapter or session, to make it possible to build a memory of past events that can then be retained, and at the same time to inspire feelings of anticipation that make the reader and the child eager to find out what happens next. Reader and child identify with the behaviour of the characters at conscious and unconscious levels, and their feelings are likely to be affected by the situations in which the characters are placed. It is reasonable to assume that, to some extent at least, readers are aware of the effect that a book or story is having on them. The educational therapist uses the characters and their situations to help the child to begin exploring his feelings within the metaphor, until he is able to equate them with his own reality. As his understanding increases he becomes able to accept or reject what he has learned.

Naturally each phase of the work of author and therapist can be of equal importance in relation to the whole book, or the whole intervention, but the therapist is likely to place even greater emphasis than the author on the preparation and management of endings. This is because, as we have already indicated in our earlier chapters, referred children's experiences of endings appear to be closely associated with unpredicted loss, most frequently the loss of people with whom they have formed an attachment. For the child in therapy, like Leslie in the previous chapter, an unexpected ending can be very painful, leaving him with feelings of sadness and bewilderment – which could have been very different if the ending had been planned.

PREPARATION

Reference has already been made to the arrangements that we make to ensure that a room (or part of a room) will be available on a regular basis. This is particularly important for those children who have lived for many years with uncertainty. It is not always easy for a school to manage this, though the benefits can be clearly seen in the work reported in Chapter 9. Interruptions cause problems for the child and the therapist when they remain unacknowledged, though when it can be managed children quickly recognise the advantage of open discussion about the way in which disruptions can affect our feelings. We cannot emphasise enough the importance of maintaining the boundaries of time, place and privacy of the sessions. The following account demonstrates how this can be done constructively but also highlights the distress that interruptions can cause. One therapist's acknowledgement of the shared problem posed by the interruption of an unexpected visitor provoked a surprising response from an adolescent.

Rick, aged 15, had returned to a clinic at the suggestion of his social worker to discuss the possibility of resuming work with his educational therapist, following his 'failure' at yet another school. When he was at the point of acknowledging the ambivalence of his feelings, the session was interrupted by an uninvited visitor, who had by-passed the clinic 'rules' that normally ensured privacy. The visitor, an education inspector stated her wish to watch the educational therapist working. The visitor refused the invitation to wait until the boy's session was over in less than 15 minutes. Aware of her anger at this intrusion at such a difficult moment, the therapist introduced the visitor and the boy to one another, but then, feeling nonplussed, she sat down again at the table where they had been working. Both remained silent for a few moments. She then posed a rhetorical question to the boy: 'Rick, I'm not sure what we should do. I'm sorry that our time together has been interrupted, but Mrs Lamb has the right to watch me working...' Rick interrupted, 'I don't think anyone has the right to interrupt my time, whoever she is, she must know that this time is private.' This difficulty was resolved by the therapist inviting Rick to either stay and continue working or to end the session now.

90

She said, 'I'm free until 12 o'clock today, and if you feel able to wait we could resume our discussion then.' Rick said 'OK', packed up his books, picked up his gloves, nodded to the visitor, and left the room in dignified silence. The therapist was very surprised to find him still in the waiting room after the departure of her visitor, knowing how painful this adolescent's return to the clinic had been.

Before we begin working with the child we think about him as an individual person by observing his behaviour within his family and school systems. Consideration is given to his 'problem' as it is presented by the referrer. It is helpful to learn about the child's experience if he is in the care of the local authority.

Thought is also given to the provision of materials and activities including books appropriate to a child's interests whenever feasible. (The rationale for the choice of materials and activities is given in Chapter 7 and in clinical examples throughout the book.)

The educational materials supplied for each child's exclusive use are contained in his own box, which is kept safely by the therapist between sessions. In addition, there is always an unlimited supply of paper and drawing equipment in the room. We also like to provide water, sand and paints for those children who need to regress educationally to the activities which they seem to have either missed or 'forgotten'. (The term educational regression was first used by Barrett in a workshop presentation.) Educational therapy with an 11-year-old girl, Maxine, provides an example of the use of material associated with early educational learning. She had attended a nursery school from the age of 3. While she was there her father was killed in a car accident. She continued to enjoy all the activities in the nursery school, but subsequently denied all knowledge of this experience. Learning in school had little meaning for her until she was helped by her educational therapist to re-learn at a nursery school level, employing the 'forgotten' activities.

We like the room or corner in which we work with children to give a message of educational bias (Duve 1965). This Norwegian professor developed a psychological assessment procedure for children referred for learning disabilities in Norway, which stresses the importance of this type of setting. She felt that it contributed to the adult's understanding of the child's reaction to a classroom situation in which he was said to have 'failed'.

THE BOX

The box (referred to briefly in the work with Luke) always has a lid, which may be labelled or decorated as each child wishes. It contains some basic materials for the exclusive use of every child, regardless of his age or level of ability. It contains the following: scissors (blunt-ended but with a good cutting edge), glue (non-toxic), modelling clay, Sellotape, a pack of playing cards, elastic bands, paper clips, families of wild and domestic animals and several fences. Not all educational therapists include doll families with this basic equipment in each box; some prefer to have them visibly displayed and easily accessible, as part of the more general provision of play and educational material in the room where the sessions are held. One reason for not including a doll family is a reservation, sometimes expressed, about the educational therapist becoming a quasi-psychotherapist. A more mundane reason for the restricted choice is one of expense; toys placed on a shelf can be shared with the other children who may use the room at other times, either with the same therapist or a different one. Having to share material can help a child to deal with his resentment at not having everything in the room – but only the things in his box – reserved for his exclusive use, and may also help him to come to recognise and manage rivalrous feelings towards siblings and peers. If we are working in medical rooms or other such spaces in schools, we have to improvise, borrow or bring material that is easily transportable. The therapist rarely adds to the original contents of the box; any child who makes excessive demands for more and more material will be helped to understand why he is making these demands.

Whether the real or ostensible reason for a referral is a reading problem or not, we always have a selection of books within easy reach. Most of the children need help in choosing a book. Some cannot choose because making a choice is impossible; others are too frightened of books even to contemplate opening one. Frequently young children ask for books that are beyond their reading ability, while others claim that they have read all the books in school. When the choice poses a problem, which it frequently does, we may decide to postpone any decision and say, 'Shall we choose this one for today?' This leaves the option open for a later date and relieves the child of the responsibility for deciding. When a child is able to choose a book it may remain in his box throughout the span of the intervention. Occasionally a child wants too many books kept in his box, and it is not easy to convince him that they will be available for him in subsequent sessions even if they won't all fit in. Helping him to choose one 'for today' and then, when it can be managed, to place the others on the shelf, may help him to overcome his reluctance to part with them.

Even opening a book can be a dreaded action and present a real threat to a few children. A 7-year-old boy could not even touch a book, and if one was opened for him he would close or avert his eyes. It was several weeks before he could let himself look at picture books and even longer before he could face the simplest of texts.

The child needs to know that, like the box, any material, models or paintings that he makes will be stored in a safe place until the next session. We show our acceptance of their efforts, however torn or misshapen they become. As a break in the therapy approaches children often take their work out of the box and look at it again. This activity sometimes takes place in silence, but more frequently the task becomes a mini-review of past sessions with the therapist. The feelings recalled and associated with even apparently insignificant, subtle drawings or models vividly demonstrate most children's capacity for understanding symbolism. Their memory of past pain and sadness seems to be an important aspect of their capacity for 'going-on-being' (Winnicott 1971).

Sometimes children cannot give themselves 'permission' to open the box, and we accept this unless the child indicates by non-verbal communication that he is afraid to do so. The therapist may then ask the child's permission to open the box and talk about the contents. Selecting something like a pack of playing cards, likely to be familiar to most children, can help a child to understand that sessions will be a learning experience that is not quite the same as lessons.

At the end of the session the child may want to take something from the box away with him. It is unlikely that we would comment other than to say that all the contents of the room belong to the particular institution and can only be used there, and to remind him again that his box and everything in it are kept safe for him alone to use each week in his sessions. If children persist in this over a period of several sessions we attempt to help them to understand why they are feeling the need for some concrete evidence of their session. Once the concept of internalising their experience with a therapist and how they can make use of this is explained, even young children can understand and accept it, which obviates the need to take away a tangible reminder of the session.

The box becomes, for most children, a symbolic container of feelings as well as a physical confirmation of educational tasks achieved. The feelings may remain private until the child is ready to express them to his therapist in the form of games, drawings, stories or in other ways (see Chapter 7). When the children begin to discover how much can be expressed within the safe boundary of the material, which in turn is contained symbolically by the therapist and by the temporal limits of each session, they find that these feelings need no longer be sealed inside the box and can be explored more openly.

In addition to the practical arrangements we make for the work, if we ignore our own preparation we do so at the expense of the child. In discussing the figures comparing the dyad of mother/infant to that of educational therapist/schoolchild (see p. 57–8), we talked about creating a space in which to think about a child prior to our interaction with him. A continuation of this thinking is the concept of 'holding in mind', which from our experience we know to be essential to the quality of the process. (Initially it can be quite difficult to hold in mind a child whose behaviour is withdrawn, very compliant or passive.) When a session is cancelled or a child just does not attend, it is tempting to become so involved in other activities that the child in question is forgotten. We are not suggesting that the child is thought about in silence for an hour (this would be unrealistic because of other pressures), but work that relates to him can be done in that time: a letter to him, or a telephone call to his school or social services, are just two examples. In the session following an absence, if the child has not been held in mind it is surprising how often he unconsciously picks this up, unless he is very depressed or confused both within and outside his therapy time.

SESSIONS

It is not difficult to imagine some of the feelings of children or young people sitting in the waiting room with their parents or other attachment figures, knowing that at any moment they will have to leave with an adult who is almost a complete stranger. Even if they have previously visited the building for a family interview, or have met the stranger in another setting (for example school), what are their fantasies? They do not know where the stranger will be taking them, let alone what she will be doing to them. If they already have an image of themselves as 'bad' they may fear further punishment. Most of the children we see have low self-esteem because of academic or social failure in school, so they may well conjure up pictures of a scolding teacher. Because so many of them have suffered loss or unpredictable parental behaviour, do their fantasies include doubts about whether they will ever see their parents again? (These anxieties are frequently expressed during sessions, particularly towards the end. Unfortunately there have been occasions when parents have not returned to the waiting room at the time agreed, thus confirming their child's fears.)

Individual children's reactions on entering the room with their therapist can vary widely. Their behaviour may range from withdrawn or compliant to aggressive, and can be an indicator of the type of preparation they have received, if any. They may feel troubled or guilty initially if they are not immediately working at recognisably school-orientated tasks, although most have already understood in family meetings that they will be working on understanding how their feelings may be inhibiting their capacity to learn.

We referred briefly to the term 'educational regression' with Maxine. In addition to our attempts to link past events to loss of social or academic skills, we take children back to earlier 'educational' activities. When presenting these to adolescents, we include a face-saving introduction of them (for example Gordon, see pp. 177–84). This is very helpful, too, for those children who are having difficulty in coming to terms with the loss of their infancy as they are forced to face the inevitability of becoming older (a common phenomenon.) Not everyone working with children finds it acceptable to allow them access to water, sand, paints or materials such as building blocks if they are well past nursery age, but we think it beneficial because opportunities for enriching play experience at home are often limited and limiting. Other activities like drawing around hands, talking about the senses, or playing in the manner described in Chapter 13 take a child back to an earlier stage of play and learning that he has forgotten. Children are often moved on to another stage of cognitive learning before they have really understood the previous one. If a child's behaviour is such that he is endangering himself or his therapist, then it will be made clear that limits will be set. Should he attempt to destroy the room or its contents, these actions have to be curtailed.

In the first few minutes of the session the therapist is actively involved in observing, thinking and speaking. Our observation of a child's behaviour helps us to gauge his mood; observation of our own behaviour helps us to understand the response that the child's response is eliciting in us.

While thinking about the interactional behaviour, the therapist tries to be aware of the possible effect that events which occurred immediately before the session might be having on either the child or herself. This is particularly important where the child's experience of being alone in the presence of an adult has been one in which he has been shouted or screamed at, simply ignored, or had excessive demands made of him.

Colluding with children, for example 'allowing' them to cheat in a game, or telling them not to bother if they can't read a passage, can, like reassurance, gloss over the reason why they need to cheat or not face words on a page. We may empathise with their feelings about their need to cheat or give up but spend time discussing the underlying reasons for this wish to do either. We saw in the therapist's work with Leslie and Mark how the simple use of 'we' can be supportive when things start going wrong. There is a difference between saying 'You don't seem to be able to read today' and 'Shall we look at the book together?' Standing back and looking objectively may help with upset feelings about a task or activity and can give both child and therapist space in which to reconsider.

On returning to the waiting room or classroom, a child may suddenly proffer a very personal piece of information. A family may have been given several openings to express their thoughts about a particular member or event, but have been unable to take this up during an interview, until at the very last moment they slip it in when it cannot be adequately addressed. This can create a dilemma, especially if it is something that one has felt the child has been waiting to hear openly expressed or wanting to say for some time. We try to acknowledge the importance of the information or statement and suggest that he wait to discuss it in the following week, although some family therapists are able to have flexible family interview times. Most children quickly value the privacy of their sessions and readily accept their therapist's changed mode of speech and content of exchanges (social only) which make it clear that the session is at an end. Other children try to extend the session outside the therapy room. When a child attempts to begin a session on the way to the room, the therapist helps him wait by just saying 'hmm', or if he persists 'That sounds rather private/important/difficult, shall we talk about it inside our room in a minute/next time?' Time is used as a boundary: if the child is late the session is not prolonged.

95

First session

The educational therapist re-introduces herself to the child, recalling the reason for their meeting, for example: 'I expect you remember, Oliver, when I met you with your parents/social worker/teacher we talked about the work we might do together.' The therapist then describes the practical arrangements, stresses the privacy of the sessions and the boundaries of time, gives a careful explanation of the box for the child's personal use, and introduces any other materials or activities in the room.

The first session provides the therapist with an opportunity to begin establishing a second 'secure base' for the child. Children need to have evidence that the therapist believes in their ability and can help them, and most of all that she is trying to understand them. How she handles different situations in the early stages sets the scene for their working relationship together. It is important to respond to the child's feelings while endeavouring, at the same time, to avoid collusion or confrontation. A child can accept a statement, 'that makes me feel sad', or 'I'm beginning to feel angry', if the adult remains calm and does not cry or express anger with harsh words or punitive actions. Children can feel very threatened if they fear, unconsciously, that some of the angry feelings they have projected on to their therapist might be reciprocated and acted upon.

Activities which allow for 'aggressive' actions, like playing with plasticine or tearing up paper, will help some children. Others may need an 'opponent' to channel some of their angry feelings more appropriately, and games like draughts or snap are useful. Reading to a child can be paradoxically reparative. It is essential that the therapist takes up what she guesses to be the child's feelings about any upsetting behaviour or incident that occurs in a story. We have referred to a shared space, both playing and working, and we try to ensure that respect for individual space is retained, both for the child and for ourselves. Initially, the therapist does not allow herself to withdraw into inaccessibility like the rejecting mother, but remains available even when the child himself chooses to withdraw from the interaction. She takes care not to impinge on the child's space like a smothering mother. She must also try not to allow the child to impinge on her space by colluding with manipulative behaviour; most children come to understand the concept of intrusive behaviour. It may be difficult not to behave like the spinning mother, mirroring the behaviour of the child who is restless and difficult to engage. It is important to remain still and help him to recognise and understand what is happening.

If a child makes a comment that is not understood, reflecting it back to him in question form can both give the therapist time to work out what the child means, and allow the child an opportunity to develop the thought or retreat from it. He may indicate his need for space by ignoring the therapist's intrusive comment or answering monosyllabically. He may enter into a displacement activity as a distraction if the therapist has interpreted his feelings too accurately and he is not yet ready to own them. Non-verbal communication is normally just accepted in a first session, though held in mind by the therapist. Later, the child will be helped to understand and recognise that actions can express or disguise inner feelings.

At least five minutes before the end of each session the therapist warns the child that it is nearly over. If he attempts to curtail or prolong the session his feelings relating to this are taken up. Warnings may need to be given earlier or more frequently in the future. Forward-looking statements about the next session are made and the child is reminded that the time and room will be the same.

Second session

We like to begin the second session by giving a brief recapitulation of the first and reminding the child of the reasons for being there and why we are meeting again. He may need time to re-examine the room and its contents. Some children are quite unable to show any interest in the therapist, their box or the room, but sit silently avoiding eye contact. Again the use of the word 'we' demonstrates that the responsibility for the silence can be shared. 'We seem to be finding it difficult to know how to begin again today, don't we, Dianne?' The onus is not then placed on the child; the adult acknowledges the fact that neither of them knows how to proceed. For a child who is not used to having his feelings taken into account, let alone having them put into words, the therapist's statement may be experienced as a relief or as a threat.

Should the therapist make a promise to a child, for example to produce a typed version of story or poem that he may have dictated the previous week, she should make every effort to keep it, but if this proves impossible she hopes that her apology will be accepted. It is extremely important to try and establish trust for these children, who often have little reason to expect it. Even quite small examples of openness like this contribute to the creation of a second-chance secure base.

The recall of activities or statements from the first session will help the child to know that he has been 'held in mind'. As we have previously stated, this helps to establish the idea of building a memory, initially on the child's behalf, of the interactive process. At this stage it is probably useful to make a statement acknowledging and empathising with his loss of the relevant 'scholastic skill' and, if appropriate, to begin exploring with him his feelings about this loss. The therapist needs to state her belief in the child's ability and capacity to recover the lost skills. Any educational tasks offered should be at a level which he can achieve.

If the child is unable to make a choice of any of the available material, the therapist will take up his feelings relating to the difficulty of making choices before helping him to do so. An example of just how painful decision making can be was illustrated in Chapter 4 in the work with Luke.

Open discussion about the here and now contributes to the child's 'new' understanding of work in an abstract form, with the therapist constantly aiming to make links between tasks and feelings. It is important, too, to have fun as well as taking the child's efforts to communicate seriously, in whatever way he chooses – though this can be difficult if he switches off, cries, screams or attacks physically or verbally. His behaviour sometimes may be provocative: one example is talking in 'gobbledegook'.

Subsequent sessions

These are likely to move forward slowly, with the therapist making constant reference to the shared memory of earlier sessions, re-affirming the security of the here and now of the current session, anticipating the potential of future ones and the activities within them. Reviewing progress helps the child to 'up-date' his internal working models and eventually to share the therapist's belief in him and his skills. What she does not reveal is her expectation of his capacity to tolerate change; later this may be explicitly stated to confirm and validate his self-worth and capabilities. Part of this change may be a painful relinquishing of an earlier state of 'not knowing', linked to an unconscious wish to remain dependent.

Another aspect of the process is the growing number of comments or indirect interpretations made by the therapist as the child becomes increasingly able to make use of them. Much of the work is conducted by the use of the metaphor: characters in a story, drawing or model are used to encourage children to express their perception of what the character's feelings might be (anthropomorphic ones are particularly useful). A child may use the same story to express different feelings, and may identify with any character. In the story of Jack the Giant Killer, Jack may be allotted some feelings of guilt by children when he steals from the giant; they may become upset by the demise of the giant; they may enjoy the delinquent aspect of Jack's behaviour or any other behaviour of the characters. One child thought Jack's mother was cruel to provide her son with an axe to kill the giant. When a child is ready to 'own' these feelings for himself, they can be examined in the light of the experience of the characters in the story.

The recovery of a child's lost capacity for play can take a long time. The activity of peek-a-boo or a variation of it is sometimes entered into in the first few sessions; for other children it does not seem appropriate for several months, depending largely on the length of time it takes to bring the child into a 'state of play'. The game frequently takes the form of hide-and-seek with the therapist, just as any little child plays with a familiar figure at an early stage of development, the 'me' and 'not-me' of Winnicott (1965). It can take place on the way to a session or, if the setting makes this unsuitable, the child may run ahead of the therapist to find a hiding place in the therapy room. Even adolescents seem to need to re-enact this playful memory from childhood: this may take the form of hiding pencils, or playing guessing games that seem to symbolise the discovery of a lost or forgotten skill. Some of them just stand momentarily behind a pillar or doorway and say 'Boo' to the therapist, who they know will have to pass that way to collect them for their session.

With the approach of breaks in the therapy the behaviour of children often changes. They may ask for repetitive tasks or express a wish to return to very easy ones. Often they ask for activities requiring the use of glue or Sellotape, which symbolically seem to express a wish to stay. Questions about the therapist's personal life are asked, long stories are requested, or a game of chess or Monopoly may be suggested a few minutes before the end of the last session before a break. For many children Christmas is the most painful time of separation from the therapist to tolerate, as it frequently evokes both past and current crises for many of their families. When any breaks occur questions arise as to whether the therapist sees other children, and if so whether they use the same room as themselves? (Surprisingly, it often takes children some time before they become aware that others use the same room.) The implication is 'does the therapist care for him enough, has she enough care to share or is it possible that she cares for the other children more?' A fear, usually only covertly expressed, is 'will she survive the break?' This curiosity about a therapist is an important part of the process. The child is moving on from knowing the me and not-me developmental step, and beginning to reveal that it is safe to admit to curiosity.

The need to prepare children for all breaks, whenever possible, cannot be overstated. If they have formed an anxious attachment to significant care-givers in the past, it must be very difficult for them to hold on to a belief that a transient (educational) attachment figure can be relied upon to re-appear. Unconsciously they may feel that their destructive feelings towards adults are so powerful that they will be reciprocated by the therapist, or destroy her so that she cannot return after a break. The account of the work with Jason in Chapter 9 illustrates these fears.

Even after a year or more of therapy, some children's painful memories of earlier separations from significant attachment figures make it extremely difficult for them not to feel abandoned by their therapist on the advent of a break. An unexpected break, occurring as a result of a therapist's illness, can of course give rise to many fantasies for children. Their feelings need to be taken up on the therapist's return, and letters will have been written to them in the interim – by the therapist if possible.

It is important that children can show their distress or anger when long breaks are approaching. Some will have experienced their mothers 'slipping out' when they were younger thinking they would not notice, or as schoolchildren not being told that a teacher would be leaving. Although preparation cannot reduce the feelings associated with separations, it can allow the children to mourn their loss and hold the person in mind, freeing

99

them to believe in the safe return of mother or update their feelings for the new teacher.

We look at the enormous significance of the question of loss and mourning here in a very simple way. We know from our own lives the feelings of regret and sadness we have when we cannot say goodbye to a friend we know we shall probably never meet again. When someone close to us dies, the complexity of feelings of anger and guilt, in addition to great sorrow, remain with us if the process of mourning cannot be managed (Bowlby 1980). The advisability of preparing children for changes in school has been touched upon, and the fantasies about what happened to a teacher who disappeared, especially for children who have hated or hurt him or her, can be far more difficult to manage than talking about the loss of that person. They may think of this as a confirmation of their untoward behaviour, especially if the effect of an earlier experience of loss within their family has not been acknowledged. The attitude of the adult influences the way that separations can be managed. The mother who can show tolerance and understanding of her child's response when she returns after being absent can help to prepare him for the next separation. Teachers who are changing schools need to prepare children for their permanent departure, providing opportunities for and acceptance of any small gestures of reparation that children may offer, particularly the troubled and troublesome. They also need to say goodbye to colleagues and own to their feelings about loss.

Final sessions

At different times, children of all ages will spontaneously recall past experiences about the sessions. At late stages in the therapy they tentatively begin to make links for themselves between the loss of skills and the acquisition of new ones on the one hand and events in their lives outside their sessions on the other. They frequently reflect back to the therapist statements which she has made to them in the past, about either their feelings or approaches to tasks.

It is impossible to do justice to the multifarious aspects of each experience of the interactive process when working with a child or adolescent. There are certain broad patterns, like those outlined above, but each experience has a pattern unique to that child. (Work with peer or family groups, to a degree, follows similar patterns, but again each group is inevitably different.)

Preparing the child for the end of the therapy is as important as the beginning. Endings mean change and change encompasses loss, like so many experiences from the past, for the therapist as well as for the child. Sometimes children, especially adolescents, may choose not to attend sessions leading up to the final one, particularly the penultimate session. Excuses are given, sometimes by telephone or hastily uttered on arrival five minutes before the end of a session time, if work towards the separation is being resisted. The

100

therapist too has to tolerate any feelings of sadness or frustration when goodbyes cannot be completed. The use of a story to help children to understand that 'their' time and experience cannot be taken from them is described in Chapter 7. Most children are able to appreciate the concept of 'internalising' in this way when an interaction has been good-enough. A child may have to deny his experience with the therapist if his subsequent experiences are too dreadful for him to retain it.

The educational therapist has to risk taking an imaginative leap into each child's inner world. The variation of the therapist's response in her attempts to meet the needs of the individual schoolchild echoes that of the mother responding to her first born and each subsequent unique infant.

In her attempts to find solutions and resolutions the therapist must be prepared for a rejection of her ideas or suggestions, or indeed a rejection of herself, from time to time. The overall aim is to help children to learn how their feelings contribute to their acquisition and attainment of academic skills; to reawaken their capacity for play and learning; to help them to enjoy and understand the process of interacting with others and to reach age-appropriate autonomy.

7

THE USE OF STORIES, CREATIVE MATERIAL AND EDUCATIONAL ACTIVITIES

STORIES

Stories in one form or another can assume great significance for children of all ages and abilities, and they can be used in a variety of ways. We have chosen to evaluate their contribution to the practice of educational therapy before discussing additional educational materials and activities.

A few extremely restless children find it impossible to listen to a story, whether it is being read or told. Many are likely to have heard stories for the first time in playgroup or nursery school rather than as part of their early learning experience at home.

Assessing the amount of time required for story reading is very important and on occasion it seems advisable to ensure that the beginning, middle and end can be encompassed within one session. Some children have had to tolerate too much 'not knowing', and leaving the story characters in an uncertain state may be too close to reality to be bearable. It is essential that children can predict events that will actually take place within the sessions. This is especially true for those for whom adult behaviour and expectations of future events have proved unreliable in the past. If the content of a story proves too stressful for a child, or he is already engaged in a task that he wishes to complete, he may choose to have a change from the regular story-reading pattern. The therapist takes responsibility for suspending whatever activity is taking place if time is running out, so that the child can decide whether to continue what he is doing or have the story read as usual.

The completion of a tale is important too, especially for children who have no confidence in their ability to finish any task. These are the children who tend to rubbish their writing, throw their work across the room or simply say 'I can't.' Story characters who achieve their goals can help children, even adolescents, to overcome their feelings of helplessness at what they see as their failure in acquiring scholastic or social skills, even over a period as long as seven or eight years. Other children, like Luke in Chapter 4, may prefer to overcome hurdles and beat opponents, metaphorically, in their own stories, drawings and models until they are able to equate the achievements of their characters with those of their own. It is very rarely that children cannot accept and value working in the metaphor.

In Bettelheim's introduction to his book *The Uses of Enchantment: The Meaning and Importance of Fairy Tales* (1976), he talks of the need 'to find meaning in our lives', and suggests that one way of achieving this is to develop 'one's inner resources, so that one's emotions, imagination and intellect mutually support and enrich one another'. There have been many examples of story-telling furnishing the human race with a belief in their group's or tribe's survival. Bettelheim's interpretation of fairy tales (1976) is invaluable to educational therapists working with learning-disabled children.

Many stories epitomise the feelings of a small creature or person who is able to overcome a much larger and stronger opponent. A boy's fears and fantasies of what will happen to him if he 'beats' or surpasses a punitive father are unlikely to be resolved by reading a story, which cannot alter the real situation. But stories can contribute to an examination of alternatives, or enable the child to come to terms with feelings about his reality. The word 'ego' is rarely used in this book and yet it is a child's ego strength, a better sense of himself, that leads to a resolve to stand as an individual in spite of circumstances. Stories in which the youngest or weakest character carries out impossible tasks set by father figures, very often kings, and overcomes or outwits them, give a message that it is permissible for a boy to surpass his father, leave his family and become a man. Many of these characters gain the hands of princesses, another symbol of adulthood.

Tracy

Cinderella, Snow White and Sleeping Beauty are just three of the tales that have a hidden agenda about a girl's development. Tracy, a very small, thin girl of 13, had a mother who could not allow her daughter to grow up. In her special school Tracy looked, behaved and functioned like a pretty, delicate 7-year-old. In a family interview about the slow progress their daughter was making in school, it became clear that her parents felt very protective towards her, because they thought they had been told that she had been born with a very small brain. They expressed particular worries about her sexuality. Mother said she would not tell her about menstruation until she was 18. At the next parental interview mother was unable to attend, due to 'female troubles'. Father came and asked the educational therapist if she could tell his daughter the facts of life, 'everything, otherwise she will end up pregnant'. He then implied that the whole subject of menstruation and 'sexual matters' was taboo at home, although his wife's greatest fears lay in this area: she had reluctantly agreed to this request being made in her absence.

The therapist working with Tracy chose to read the tale of Sleeping Beauty. Bettelheim discusses the various merits of the different versions of this story, but as he says:

'However great the variations in detail, the central theme of all versions of The Sleeping Beauty is that, despite all attempts on the part of parents to prevent their children's sexual awakening, it will take place nonetheless. Furthermore, parents' ill-advised efforts may postpone the reaching of maturity at the proper time, as symbolised by Sleeping Beauty's hundred years of sleep, which separate her sexual awakening from her being united with her lover.'

(Bettelheim 1976)

The long sleep followed Sleeping Beauty's discovery, as a result of her curiosity, of an old woman with a spindle on which Sleeping Beauty pricks her finger. This drop of blood symbolises menstruation. The reading of this story to Tracy and the accompanying discussions, initially within the metaphor, gradually leading to a presentation of the real 'facts of life', had a dramatic effect. It was clear that at 13 Tracy already had some information about bodily functions, but she had not allowed herself to hear the meanings, perhaps out of respect for her mother's views. Prior to a long summer break, Tracy picked up a family of dolls that had been lying on a nearby shelf for several weeks. A large proportion of the session was taken up with Tracy's silent play, which demonstrated human interaction culminating in sexual intercourse. When the play ended Tracy pushed the dolls to one side with a loud sigh.

On her return after the break the therapist described her thus: 'I was very surprised to see Tracy standing at my door' (she was normally collected from the waiting room). 'She smiled and, looking what I can only describe as radiant, she said, "I've started!"' As in the tale itself, the happy ending was the acceptance by the parents of their adolescent daughter. Both were able to face the reality of Tracy's leaving school and growing up.

Beryl

In contrast to the fragility of Tracy's appearance at the beginning of her therapy, Beryl, who also attended a special school and was the same age as her at the time of referral (13), was large, very plain and smelt of stale urine. Her manner was aggressive and truculent. The very thought of helping Beryl to make use of a fairy tale in the way described by Bettelheim (1976) seemed unlikely. His reference to unconscious fears of separation and starvation suggests that a fairy tale can 'speak to his [the child's] unconscious, give body to his unconscious anxieties, and relieve them, without this ever coming into conscious awareness'. Beryl chose The Seven Little Kids to express some of her feelings. Not only did this story 'speak to her unconscious' but it was eventually used to speak to her conscious awareness of her here-and-now.

Beryl had stated that she had no need to learn anything in her sessions. The therapist concerned summarises her work:

104

'For about a year, Beryl often behaved like a toddler in her sessions and whenever attempts were made to engage her in a task she became very angry; however, over a period of time, and in close co-operation with her class teacher, Beryl learned to read some simple books. She often became extremely dictatorial and ordered me to read or tell the story of The Seven Little Kids to her over a period of several weeks. Beryl then told me the tale until she decided it had to be dramatised. If I made any mistakes in word or movement I was castigated. It was not until I was told that I must play the part of a judge that I became fully aware of the significance of the story for Beryl. (There is no judge in the fairy tale. It is about a mother goat who leaves her seven kids, warning them not to open the door to the wolf in her absence. The wolf character enters the house by subterfuge and devours all but one of the kids who hides. On the mother's return she cuts open the wolf and the six escape.) Borrowing from Walt Disney, Beryl then commanded me to sing "Ha, ha, ha, the wolf is dead." It was at the end of this jubilation when the drama faced Beryl's reality by the introduction of the judge, a jury, the police, and social workers.

'Beryl gave a graphic commentary on events unfolding in a court scene. It became clear that the wolf represented the power of authority, from which the kids, Beryl and her siblings had to hide. I felt Beryl adopted the role of the clever and cunning seventh kid, and her grandmother, with whom she lived, was represented by the mother in the story. Together they outwit and destroy the wolf/judge. There is a minor character in the story who aids the wolf; in Beryl's drama this character became a social worker, many of whom featured in her life. The policeman was there but played no active role. I wondered if her introduction of this character served a dual purpose: to keep Beryl's enacted rage under control but also to represent me who kept the play from becoming too threatening. I felt anxious too about helping Beryl to regain her equilibrium in the here and now of the session before it was time for her to leave each week. Whenever the drama was repeated the warning time became earlier and earlier, so intense were the feelings engendered. I used to say to Beryl, "I must stop being a judge for a moment to tell you that we have x amount of time left." I knew this worked when Beryl, still in role, announced in sonorous tones, "I have to tell you that the court will adjourn until next Wednesday" (her next session). At no time did I enter into any discussion about Beryl's reality: court proceedings were taking place at the actual time of this girl's use of the drama that stemmed from a fairy tale.'

Probably one of the stories most used by educational therapists is *Amos and Boris*, by William Steig (1972). The language is quite sophisticated but it has been read to countless children of all ages (frequent reference is made to the story in this book), very often as part of the preparation for endings. The story of Amos and Boris is about the friendship of a whale and a mouse, who after several adventures (somewhat similar to those of Androcles and the Lion) have to part. It is a sad and moving end to a friendship, but Steig conveys the concept of internalising a memory beautifully. Many children can accept the separation of the two characters, which in turn enables them to feel secure in the knowledge that the memories of their own encounters with 'their' therapist can be retained.

Stories written or dictated by children are also valued. Several common themes from the world of traditional tales are incorporated, although adapted to express certain elements from the children's current concerns, as we demonstrate later in this chapter.

A number of educational therapists make use of the dictated story method. The child dictates a story or part of a story each week. This is typed between sessions and read at the beginning of the following week. The rationale for this method is at least twofold: the child is offered a means of expressing himself in words, often for the first time, but is not made to feel inadequate because he cannot write; and he is granted 'permission' to be in 'control' of an adult. This role-reversal where the adult becomes the scribe is reminiscent of an earlier phase of learning, like the games of 'mothers and fathers' or 'teachers and pupils' that many children play. Linda, described in Chapter 13, shows this kind of behaviour in action. The presentation of the child's story in the session following the dictation, with title and author's name boldly typed at the top, normally provides a sense of achievement (though not all children find this easy to acknowledge).

A child is encouraged to read his story with the adult, and often chooses to illustrate it. Having it typed each week is concrete evidence of his effort, validates his creativity, and acknowledges his achievement in assembling his thoughts. The activity provides, too, a tangible link from one session to another, part of the building of a memory referred to in other chapters. A different kind of process is in evidence when the child decides to collate his material and make a book. We saw earlier, in the work with Luke, that this in itself can require an inordinate amount of decision-taking. To assemble the book means too that order is required; the pages must be placed in sequence; holes have to be punched and aligned; all must be cut and fitted together. For a child who is functioning well this could be an enjoyable activity, involving many skills of dexterity as well as creativity; none of it is easy for a child whose behaviour is chaotic and confused. It is interesting to observe that, in spite of the difficulties involved, most children's motivation is very high, and the concentrated effort with which they tackle the task is reminiscent of that observed in toddlers.

Keith

The following story, written by a boy of very limited intelligence, illustrates a remarkable achievement. Keith had a verbal IQ of 59 and a performance IQ of 68 on the WISC-R (1976), and he had experienced many traumas during his 11 years of life. He had been taken into long-term care and was admitted into a children's psychiatric unit to help to prepare him for fostering. At weekends he returned to the children's home where he had been placed.

He spent each day in a children's psychiatric unit classroom; here his teacher (an educational therapist) recounts her work with him. 'Each child started their educational day with a writing task and Keith was not excepted. Initially Keith found this difficult, resorting frequently to furious tantrums.' We think the following stories illustrate the way Keith used them to make some sense of his experiences, allowing him to look back and come to terms with his past. His capacity to express his thoughts also enabled him to reveal a glimpse of the hope of a different future for himself in the content of his stories.

Punctuation has been added to Keith's stories to match his reading them aloud. In the first story the animals were killed:

> One day there lived a cat and dog. The cat and dog got killed on the road and the cat got killed.

In the second Keith introduced a farmer who was pleased when his cow was good. He appeared to be exploring the possibility of a move from the permanent 'bad' position with the help of the 'farmer':

> One day there lived a cow and then the cow wasn't a good boy, and then he was a good boy and then the farmer was pleased for the cow and then the cow was a good boy and then the farmer was pleased.

The next story was more complex:

> One day there lived a dog in the town and the dog got killed in the road because he was (not) looking where he was going. And then a man came along and then the man picked up the little dog and then took him to hospital because he got killed and he got better and he went home.

It seemed that death was no longer an irretrievable condition. It could be reversed provided help was at hand; reparation became a possibility:

> One day there lived two baby kittens and the big cat was the mother because the two baby kittens were a nuisance. The mother cat had two baby kittens, their names was Tommy and the other kitten's name was Lisa because they were born like that.

We can speculate as to whether this is a reference to his own family – it seems likely as Keith and his sister had been taken into care together. The next story, written the following week, seems to make a clear link to what happened to him in the past:

> One day there was a dog in the town, and the dog was a bad dog and then his mum and dad put the dog outside because he knocked something over

107

and it was a flower pot. So they put the flower pot in the bin because he knock the flower pot.

The following story was written at a time when Keith was making token attempts to run away from the unit:

One day there lived a donkey in the town. The donkey lived in a field because that's where he lived. So he doesn't run away from the field. So if he ran away again he will not have him. If he doesn't run away they will not kill him at all and they will never kill him again.

The dog again became the central character in the stories:

One day there lived a dog in the town, and the dog should not be in the house because he might bring footprints in. If he brings footprints in he will be booted out the house and he will not come into the house after he brings footprints in the house.

The following day he wrote:

One day there lived a dog and the dog didn't wipe his feet so his mum was very cross because he brought mud into the house and mum said to dad that we should put him outside because he was a naughty boy, [he hastily corrected himself] "dog" – and said that he will sell him or keep him inside. If he keeps bringing mud into the house or they won't have dog again, so they said to each other they will not put the dog outside because he keeps bringing mud inside from the puddle. And they said to the little girl who looks after the dog so they said they will put him outside every night before they go to bed at eleven o'clock.

This was the longest story Keith ever wrote. The themes were continuous but it seems possible that when he made reference to puddles and being put outside he was addressing his problem with bed-wetting; this problem was being tackled with some success at the time.

Following a meeting between Keith and his natural parents, at which they gave their approval for his long-term placement in a foster home, the boy wrote:

One day there lived a dog in the town. So his mum said he had to go out the house because he kept on bringing mud into the house. So mum and dad said right they will sell him to another person because they might like the dog instead because they think he would be a nice dog in the house.

Keith visited his new home that day. The next story, written the following day, introduced a completely different character:

One day there lived a pixie, and the pixie said to another pixie that she should live in another house because she is a naughty girl so all her other friends came back to see her when she settled in her new house.

The final story of the series was written a week later:

> One day there lived a horse and the horse said that he should go in another
> field because they think he should go in another field.

It is impossible to convey just how much emotional and scholastic effort Keith put into his stories. He appeared to use them as a means of coming to terms with all that was taking place in his reality.

We have included this example to demonstrate the importance of providing children of limited intelligence with the opportunity to use stories to express their fears and fantasies within the metaphor as we believe Keith was able to do. It was possible to make simple verbal comments and reflect upon the content of the stories to help Keith to feel that he was being heard. For example, 'The dog must have been very sad when he kept getting into trouble.' Keith responded by making excellent eye contact (not something he found at all easy) and replied 'He just couldn't be good.' The therapist wondered aloud about how the horse that had to go to another field must feel. Keith replied very strongly and positively that 'he liked the new field because he was safe there'.

Supporting a child by 'staying with' a weekly task is an experience that is often a new one for him. It is particularly important for the chaotic children. Once they begin to see that their 'book' is becoming thicker it provides convincing evidence of progress. It is often used to review a term's sessions when a holiday break is due, and some children will make grand plans for their future stories at this time, as if to ensure that they and the book will survive the break. The fact that the therapist shares the reviewing and the looking forward in some way confirms that she, too, will be there after a break.

CREATIVE MATERIAL

We cannot devote as much attention as we would wish to children's drawings, paintings and modelling. We offer one or two examples which, like the metaphors in stories, might be described as 'archetypal'. (In a classroom a large percentage of the children may choose to draw the horror figure that was shown on television the night before. This can be interpreted as a lack of individual imagination, but the likelihood is that most of the children will be using that figure to represent any number of different and individual fantasies.) For a number of children, especially those who have been abused, drawing is often the only way in which they are able to show a trusted adult what is happening (or has happened) to them. These drawings are often frightening in their intensity, and can be all too explicit when sexual abuse is part of their experience. These drawings, sometimes quite colourful and artistic, may contain 'mistakes', which to the expert eye indicate a covert expression of what is taking place (Wohl and Kauffman 1985).

A series can relate directly to what a child feels about the sessions. One

109

boy, aged 10, prior to a holiday break, dashed into his sessions and drew a boy leaping over a chasm: as the break drew nearer each week, the chasm widened and the hazards at the bottom became more and more dangerous. Others may convey their feelings in only one drawing or painting.

Clive

This boy was referred for his 'apathetic attitude to all subjects' by his year head. He was 13, and gave the impression of being grey and downcast at all times. After two terms of working with his therapist (who was also feeling downcast, as scholastic and interactional progress seemed exceedingly slow). Clive admitted that he liked art at school. The first painting he produced was very large, and executed entirely in shades of grey. It was of a skater, with his hands behind his back, head down, skating towards a patch of broken ice. The landscape was one of desolation, the only life being the sad central figure. The therapist, although she felt that the skating figure so acutely resembled the boy in front of her, chose the indirect method of discussing the painting.

'I talked about the stance of the skater and mused to myself about his thoughts. Clive responded by talking about the skater's feelings of hopelessness, especially about his future. We remained silent until Clive looked at me. At this point he allowed himself to show some pleasure when I mentioned the artistic merit of the painting. Following a long discussion within the metaphor, Clive's voice became more animated, and he switched to talking about himself and his family.'

(At the end of the term in which this activity took place, an interview with Clive's mother revealed the fact that this boy had, as a small child, been locked in a room with his father who had uncontrollable rages. Clive was the only member of the family 'who seemed to be able to quieten his father ... sometimes he was in there for hours', mother reported.)

Clive in subsequent sessions revealed how much he missed his father and 'saw no future' for himself as his working mother and siblings were 'too busy to notice' him.

If a child is unable to communicate feelings that the therapist thinks are hovering close to verbalisation or expression of some kind, she may decide to make her own 'artistic' contribution. One simple example is to draw a smiling, sad or angry expression depicted on two sides of a face, which is then cut out and stuck on a stick, like a lollipop. These figures are particularly useful when a child cannot accept or understand feelings of ambivalence. We have seen children who show compliant or passive behaviour and who can only indicate their wish to play with modelling clay or paint non-verbally. Others may resist or deny their non-verbally expressed wish. Richard, aged 15, looked longingly at paints and brushes for weeks. Occasionally he touched the brushes, but denied his wish to use them by stating that he was no good at art. The therapist invited him to play a game with paint, and straightforwardly told him to pick up a brush, dip it into a colour and guess what she was saying to him with her brush. The boy's initial reaction was of amused embarrassment; he took some time to choose a colour. Gradually the fun of the game took over. ('Paired painting' involves two people trying to communicate with one another by using brush strokes but without speech for five minutes; this is followed by a discussion about what they had each been trying to convey.) Richard enjoyed the game and although he did not use paint again the activity opened up the possibility of discussions about shyness, during which he was able to raise numerous questions about his problem of communicating with others.

Painting in pairs or small groups is similar to the game of 'Squiggles', a marvellous means of communication devised by Winnicott (1971) while he was working with children in a London hospital. It is the serious attention that Winnicott gave to a child's use of 'art' that we would like to emphasise. For a few this medium becomes the main channel of communication and creativity.

Although the majority of the learning-disabled children with whom we have worked are quick to seize on a way of expressing their feelings symbolically, our use of the metaphor, or indirect comment, does not always work. A child may persist in moving away from the metaphor into a more personal and intimate communication about his concerns. We then have to make a decision, usually based on consultation with colleagues and discussion with the family, about the advisability of referring the child for psychotherapy if this intervention would be more appropriate and could be supported by the family. Occasionally a psychotherapist may suggest educational therapy for a child, reversing the situation. The whole question of why certain children are considered to be able to make use of educational therapy rather than psychotherapy is an interesting one but is outside the scope of this book.

Sometimes modelling material such as plasticine is used to teach letters, words or numbers, particularly when children cannot form them correctly. The problem of reversals of 'b' and 'd' can be helped in this way. Banging a newly formed 'b' while saying 'b' for 'bang' helped one boy of 7; another delighted in 'writing' the word 'bum' in plasticine. Tim, a boy of 8, gave the impression of being obsessed with anal material. He was forever using brown and yellow plasticine to make faecal shapes, or drawing planes that bombed people with what he called 'plop-plops'. When he began to bombard different objects in the room with his plasticine faeces the therapist felt she was not helping the child at all. In the next session, when he began to mould his missiles she suggested that they were targeted. She placed a small container on the table and invited him to throw the missiles into it, each 'success' scoring a point. If he missed she would score a point. Tim played this game with increasing excitement until all the plasticine was placed in the container, at which point he calmed down. The idea of targeting letters and then words written on a chalkboard with pieces of plasticine was a development of the container 'game'.

In modelling, we often note the infinite care that learning-disabled children take when using a different medium. Their plasticine models are sometimes minutely detailed, even when the child in question is unable to write either coherently or legibly. One boy, Reid, made a multi-coloured monster of clay that he named 'Hontipoozle'. It was the only thing he made, but it was used week after week to take part in exciting and dangerous adventures that he was verbalising from his inner world. The significance of a simple and constantly collapsing model of a swing is given in the account of the work with Anthony in Chapter 10.

The use of craft materials, drama or music in group work is valued and recognised as a way of helping a group to understand the individual and group behaviour. We also use a range of craft materials with individual children. A girl of 11 chose to learn Chinese calligraphy and a boy of 9 constructed a one-man-band from old boxes and tins which he 'played' each week. Music has occasionally been used, but incidentally rather than systematically. Singing nursery rhymes for fun was used successfully with an adolescent, as a way of taking him back to an earlier 'educational' experience in his playgroup or nursery school. This is another example of 'educational regression'.

It is important to take his efforts seriously whatever the media a child chooses to use, even when we are not sure what it is that he is struggling to communicate. The therapist usually chooses to share her puzzlement with the child, making a statement such as 'I'm sorry, I don't understand', or 'I'm wondering if ....' Verbalising and accepting 'not knowing' can help a child to try again and to recognise the adult's fallibility. If he can say 'What a dumbo!' So much the better: a very clear communication.

The range of other activities is enormous: only a few have been selected to give a flavour – if we stay with the food analogy – of the practice.

EDUCATIONAL ACTIVITIES

Phillip used Lego in a family interview to express the taboo subject of his separated parents. He made half a house, which at the end of the interview was entrusted to the care of the therapists. At the next family interview his first words were, 'I bet you haven't still got my house.' The fact that it had been kept safely enabled the subject of his feelings about living in half a family to be more openly broached. This boy's relief in discovering that we had taken care of his symbolic model enabled him to feel that we would in some way be taking care of his 'half' of the family.

Criticism has been levelled at therapists who have made use of very structured material like Lego, on the grounds that it leaves little scope for creative thinking and is not 'educational'. This has been far from our experience, and it has proved to be very useful in the early stages of interaction with children who have difficulty in communicating verbally. The therapist can readily place herself in the position of learner, at the same time encouraging a withdrawn child to ask for help when pieces prove too difficult to assemble. The fact that the material has different shapes and colours can be incorporated into the language used by the therapist. The combination of the tactile, visual and auditory senses can be built up, like the material, for a child who has had a very limited play or exploratory experience.

If a child is given a cognitive task and chooses to misunderstand or misinterpret our instructions, we need to ask ourselves why. What is the child saying? Is there a simple answer: is the task too easy, too difficult, too familiar, boring? Is the child ill, not in the mood, unhappy, angry or just perplexed? The children themselves are very inventive once they feel secure enough in their sessions. Kunsa, aged 9, invented a character for herself, an American she called Mrs Porkway. Like other children in care, Kunsa spent part of each session for several months playing in the play house in this role, while the therapist was expected to sit quietly in the corner. Kunsa refused to read or write, but once she decided to give the therapist a role as a neighbour, Mrs Brown, the play entered a new phase. The therapist suggested that they wrote each other invitations to tea in the play house. Mrs Porkway (the child) of course could not read, so Mrs Brown (the therapist) had to pretend to think aloud when composing her invitations, so that when the letter arrived in Mrs Porkway's letter-box, Kunsa, in role, could 'read' it.

Whatever the activity selected for or by the children, the predictability of the pattern of each session confirms his trust in the continuity of the therapy being offered him, until he feels secure enough to initiate change.

Games enable children to express their feelings indirectly. They can be expressed without too much anxiety when given the boundary of certain rules. Keeping the rules is important for the therapist as well as the child, particularly with a child who has acquired the label 'delinquent'. We try to gauge at what point he is ready to engage in competitive games with us, especially those where aggression is expressed. For example, in the game of 'Hangman', a child who is winning by his reading or spelling skill may begin to prolong the game by attempting to abandon or change the rules if he becomes too anxious about 'hanging' the therapist (Caspari 1974a). (The child wins a point with a correct answer by drawing a gallows followed by the parts of a person, until the figure is complete or 'hanged'; the therapist scores only when the child gives a wrong answer.) Some children cannot continue if they are still at a stage of unconsciously fearing retribution from their adult opponents if they beat them, even though they know consciously that the 'beating' is not actually a physical one. The fact that the word 'beat' has two meanings makes it impossible for a few children, who are in reality being physically beaten, to contemplate playing this game at all; or alternatively they become too excited to contain their anxiety leading to an abandonment of the activity.

The creation of a game with or for a child, for his exclusive use, can give him a message that he is valued and offers him an opportunity for co-operative behaviour. Commercially produced activities such as draughts are of course also necessary for our work.

Jake

A 9-year-old, Jake, was behaving aggressively towards peers and teachers. This was particularly noticeable when he was asked to read. Generally a popular boy, he would hit out at peers if he thought they were taunting him for having a black father (whom he did not know) and a white mother. Jake was a skilful draughts player and enjoyed beating his therapist, although it took him several months to admit to this. He was able to express some of his angry feelings by banging the draughts pieces on the board. This activity was used to help Jake to 'own' angry feelings for himself; and to help him to link his skill in planning and placing the pieces on the board in order to win, with placing letters in the correct order to make words. The winning here was beating his 'problem'. He hated not to be as good as his peers at reading, especially as he was envied by them for his mathematical and footballing skills. The third use of the game was to talk about the differences and similarities of the black and white draughts pieces, which on a symbolic level addressed some of the conflicts that Jake was experiencing about his mixed racial background.

While paying due attention to the teaching (in the didactic sense) we aim to follow the child's communications at all times. We try especially to understand non-verbal communication: farting is one example, communicating by remaining silent is another. By trying to develop and maintain a state of awareness of what is taking place in the here and now, we can usually follow a lead given by the child and make use of it. There are numerous examples throughout this book.

Probably the single most useful commercial game for a learning-disabled child is a pack of playing cards. Even simple card games require rules, interaction and enjoyment. However, before embarking on any games, just to discuss the cards themselves, and their colour, value and suit, entails sorting and matching activities that, for many children, have never really made sense in school, resulting in their having only a hazy idea of basic concepts. Muddled thinking can be compounded for children if they are being moved on to the next 'stage' of mathematical or reading activities before they are ready.

A game such as 'Snap' can be a good starting point to consolidate the activities mentioned above. Playing cards can also offer an introduction to the idea that it is all right to express feelings; sometimes the results are unexpected. Clifford, aged 11, was referred in his final year in his junior school for having no basic skills. He was described as a very well behaved boy who 'sat at the back of the class and never caused any trouble: he is very good at drawing'. The therapist working with Clifford found his behaviour to be a mixture of withdrawn and resistant. She discovered that he could read the names of all the football teams of the world. One day he asked to play a game of his own invention, a version of gin rummy, a card game making use of sequencing and grouping of numbers and suits. He said the name of the game was 'knuckle-duster' rummy; if either player acquired a set or sequence they must hit the knuckle of their opponent with the same number of blows. When the therapist lost, Clifford had to be restrained from hitting her knuckles – first because his excitement was getting beyond his control and second because she was actually getting hurt. She reported:

'I was amazed that this quiet withdrawn boy, who found it so difficult to communicate in any way, became so aggressive. He jumped up and down with excitement each time he beat me, both metaphorically and physically, shouting "take that and that" over and over again, as though increasing his re-enactment of violent fantasy.'

This boy continued working with his educational therapist until almost a year after his transition to his secondary school, where 4 years later he passed five public examinations.

The choice of any manufactured game warrants careful consideration at the outset. A card game called 'Concept Snap' consists of sets of different photographs of familiar objects. A common attribute has to be identified in a pair before either participant can say 'Snap'. This is then challenged by the other player – the common feature could be colour, shape, or type of material of the two objects shown. This game is very useful for a child who is inarticulate or withdrawn or whose uncertainty in language and general demeanour is inhibited. The therapist can discuss the child's choice of common attributes chosen for the two cards placed on the table; initially the answers may be confused or monosyllabic, but usually the pleasure of the game takes over and the child can use it to extend his language skills. The increase in eye contact that follows enables the child to assess the therapist's reaction to his attempts and thus to become more inventive.

Games like 'Snakes and Ladders' are less useful because they introduce an element of chance. They can be used to practise numerical skills to some extent, but it is not skill that determines the outcome. When we think a child is ready to examine and tolerate feelings about winning or losing to an adult figure, they can be explored through games like this. Generally speaking it is when the child recognises the dual triumph of symbolically beating the adult, due not only to his game-playing skill, but also to his own scholastic achievement, that he gets the greater reward.

When working with children who have given up listening, for whatever reason, we try to choose our words with care. For example, if a child has become stuck, rather than saying, 'Why don't you do this?' or 'I think it should be done this way', we try to remember to say, 'Shall *we* do it like this?' The problem then becomes a shared one. Once children are free enough to know that words can be played with in the abstract, they become less threatening in the concrete form of writing or reading. Mark, introduced briefly in Chapter 5, made humorous use of the words 'transparent' and 'opaque'. After a break he often behaved like a much younger boy. On one occasion nursery rhymes were recited or sung to help him with his dilemma about whether he wanted to be very small or a schoolboy. One that captured his imagination was:

> Big A, little a, Bouncing B,
> The cat's in the cupboard,
> And can't see me.

He then chose to write it down, and wrote the last line as 'the cat can see me'. With great satisfaction he showed it to his therapist who said, 'Oh, the cupboard's transparent, then?' Mark thought this was a huge joke, and looking around the room said 'Oh, dear, the blackboard is so transparent that I can see those people in the next room' or 'What a pity all the trees have disappeared – those windows are opaque'. The importance of language as a shared activity is illustrated in other examples throughout this book.

We need sufficient confidence to allow a child to make use of the space we have offered him in a way that matches his mood, imagination and need at the moment. Moving into a mode of 'learning with' children about feelings as well as a subject requires us to take an 'imaginative leap' into ourselves too.

As we have already suggested children who are feeling 'fragmented', whose lives are chaotic, are frequently drawn to the use of glue and Sellotape. Bruce, aged 7, spent a long time punching holes in coloured paper and card with a hole punch. The 'confetti' that resulted was used in many different ways. For example, he would spread glue randomly on a sheet of paper and sprinkle the confetti on it. He gained great satisfaction from the results and after high excitement would become quite calm, as if reassured that the fragments could be contained and could even make patterns. Bruce discovered that, even if he had thrown the tiny fragments into the air and they were spread far and wide, he could collect them up swiftly with strips of Sellotape. Symbolically, he appeared to find comfort from his ability to take some control. The behaviour of another fragmented child is described in more detail.

Duncan

The therapist working with this 7-year-old boy described him as a chaotic and confused child, from a chaotic and confused home. He was said to be uncontainable in school.

'He arrived for his first educational therapy session with his mother and sister. When I collected him from the waiting room he was virtually running up the walls. He greeted me without any apparent anxiety, racing ahead of me with no idea in what direction we were heading. (This continued for weeks before he finally learned the route.) When we arrived he burst into the prepared room, scattering all the things from his box with only a cursory glance at the contents. He remained in perpetual motion, exhausting to watch, until his eye lit upon a kaleidoscope on a shelf. He became immediately absorbed and apart from his twitching limbs he was at rest. He repeatedly shook the kaleidoscope and then looked at the patterns he had made. He would hold it out for me to look, always taking it away before I had done so! I felt exhausted just being in the same room with him. Suddenly it occurred to me that the scraps of coloured paper in the kaleidoscope were flying about in the same hectic movement that I was observing in Duncan, but when they became still together they formed a complete pattern. I mused aloud about the confusion of the tiny pieces that were "all over the place" and yet could come together to make a very satisfying pattern. Duncan stopped moving, then he solemnly turned round and for the first time made eye contact with me. "Yes," he breathed, pausing again. He continued to shake the kaleidoscope that session and during many more, but gradually the frenzied shaking gave way to more exploratory movement. He then discovered, like Bruce, that confetti can be made by using a hole punch and paper. Duncan made paper boxes and envelopes for his confetti; he ate them by the handful; he stuck them in patterns on to a folder; he made "pictures" from them. He developed ways of collecting them together when they sprayed over the floor, and he too discovered that using strips of Sellotape was the most efficient method. It seemed that Duncan had an urgent and desperate need to have a space in which he could explore ways of containing all the fragments of himself before he could move forward. Eventually he was able to write letters on scraps of paper and find ways of organising them into patterns that formed his name. On reflection I realised that I was able to provide Duncan with an experience of playing in the presence of an available adult (Winnicott 1971). His frenzied activity became increasingly playful. His struggles to contain the fragments of paper reflected his experience of feeling "contained" within the session and his anxiety was reduced.'

A child may choose an activity that utilises glue or sticking tape, if he thinks that the therapist is not 'sticking' to the task, or to express anxious feelings about a coming break. Some children even envelop the box in sticking tape or string prior to a long break, as though placing feelings inside that they fear might 'escape' during the separation. It can indicate too that they do not yet trust the therapist to take care of the box, which may also symbolise themselves, and that she will not be able to hold them in mind while they are separated.

We have mentioned scissors, which are used for numerous activities. The activity described by Caspari (1974a) has become well known to educational therapists: she wrote vividly about the excitement of a boy who cut up the picture of an animal with its name written underneath. Once he realised that the animal and, more importantly, the word could be reassembled, and that he had not in reality destroyed anything totally, his equilibrium was restored too, and he began to learn.

When children are beginning to recover a lost skill, they are achieving something that has hitherto eluded them; they recognise that they are regaining control. Previously uncontrolled letters and numbers can now be placed or recorded where the children choose, and they can see that order makes sense to them and to others. Eventually they recognise that their feelings, too, can be controlled. The anger, frustration and misery that previously accompanied learning can now be examined and recognised, and in due course acknowledged and owned. If the therapist has succeeded in acting as a 'model', for example by admitting to her own stupidity when she fails in a game, or by stating that she does not seem able to play well today, a shared analysis of feelings relating to the game can extend to feelings about other situations. Bullying is a topic that can be dealt with in this way, and adult injustice is another one commonly raised. Adult shouting remains more problematic: it is an experience we all dislike and there are very few learning-disabled children who are able to relate cause and effect where shouting is concerned.

An example of the use of a mathematical jigsaw with an adolescent is given in Chapter 8. Alphabetical, word and number puzzles when presented straightforwardly may please or perplex; but we and the children become adept at devising games. It can be fun to make jigsaw puzzles upside down, guess which piece is missing, make up stories about the picture, or use them to extend an inhibited child's talking. We have already referred to a three-dimensional 'puzzle' like Lego which has endless possibilities for discussions about feelings, mathematical estimates and imaginative play. Drawing around the puzzle pieces, muddling them and then placing them on the outline can help a child who cannot 'see' the shape of letters or numbers. Symbolically, parts are being assembled to make a whole; a muddle can be placed in a certain order to create meaning. Children whose parents are separated or have left home can be helped to understand that even when a piece is no longer there, the missing piece retains its shape. They can begin to accept that the piece is, metaphorically, representing the person missing from their family. The empty space represents a memory of that person even though he/she is no longer physically present as a part of the whole.

Doll or animal families can be used creatively and educationally. They were referred to when we were describing the contents of the box provided for each child in Chapter 6. In our experience adolescents rarely use doll families, but the animals offer an acceptable vehicle for discussion. Although children may not have pets of their own they become familiar with animals from pictures, films and television. From an early age they are taught to imitate animal sounds, and are likely, for example, to associate 'grrrrh' with an aggressive animal. Many nursery rhymes and stories feature animals; anthropomorphic characters are extremely useful for exploring feelings. So many children readily identify with animal characters. When presenting the box to adolescents they may handle the animals and show feigned amusement or disparagement, dismissing them as irrelevant to them. They do however often make use of them, directly or indirectly, usually the latter. Daniel, a 14-year-old, looked at each one in turn and then recalled his sadness at the recent loss of a pet, followed by his anger because his father reprimanded him for making so much fuss over the loss of 'only a pet'.

Frank

Another use of the animal families is illustrated by the work of Frank, a 10-year-old, within his therapy sessions. He was the only child of a single parent who felt very ambivalent towards him. Frank struggled to meet his mother's needs for an adult 'partner', never having had his own needs met when he was an infant. He was referred for individual educational therapy: he had no basic skills, he could not relate to his peers appropriately, and his school attendance was erratic. His mother felt unable to attend except on a termly basis to discuss her son's progress.

In his first session the therapist said,

'His eyes lit up when he opened his box and found a female kangaroo with a baby in her pouch. (The inclusion of this animal pair had been deliberate.) The baby kangaroo became the central figure in an ongoing story which he dictated week after week over a period of eighteen months. The mother kangaroo's name was "Willma" (Frank's spelling) and was pronounced like "Will ma?" She was never available to care for her baby, Alice, who was constantly sick or lost. Fortunately a kindly farmer always saved the baby from disaster. As the therapy proceeded the baby kangaroo became less helpless, though when breaks in the sessions were looming dangers abounded for her. Eventually Alice came to terms with the fact that her mother could not provide for her and she became increasingly able to look after herself. Finally Alice took charge of her own destiny and courageously escaped from a kidnap incident by her own ingenuity. This seemed to reflect Frank's own experience: in the last three months of his therapy he transferred to a secondary school, where his attendance was regular. The school reported that he had made good scholastic progress, and had made friends.'

The animal families prompted Carl, a boy of 14, to speak of his feelings about the extinction of certain animals and the short-sightedness of man. This led to covert references to the nuclear age, a topic that, once his fears were expressed, dominated his sessions for more than a year. In common with a number of families discussed by Perlmutter and Ringler (1986), in a paper entitled 'Nuclear anxiety: social symptomatology and educational therapy', Carl's parents, we felt, belonged to the group they described under the heading of 'Parents Denying, Children Not So Compliant'. The authors see this group in the following way: 'their children come to exemplify the very kind of obsessive concern which the parents are desperately trying to avoid'.

When younger children play we do not always feel we understand their re-enactment of various scenarios, however dramatically they express them. If this should be so we either have to tolerate the 'not knowing' or risk becoming intrusive. If the latter is the case, the child may stop playing or just not answer. To question too directly is not necessary or indeed desirable; the message he is giving is clear: he wishes to play in the presence of someone who can be trusted to accept and not interfere. This is close to the description by Winnicott (1971) of a young child's play. Perhaps it is better to ask why we need the answers. 'If I do discover whom the dog represents for this child as it attacks the lamb or the tiger, how will the answer help me to understand why the child cannot learn?' The play may have repetitive sequences when the young animals are in danger, being attacked or devoured even when placed inside the comparative 'safety' of the fences. Whether or not the play is accompanied by a commentary from the child, it may take a considerable length of time to allow reparative feelings to be demonstrated following such destruction. We decided not to include examples of younger children's play in this chapter because we have already talked about Phillip and his puppets in Chapter 2 and there is a full account of play with Linda in Chapter 13.

8

THE SIGNIFICANCE OF MATHEMATICAL CONCEPTS AND WRITING

We have chosen to focus on mathematical and writing skills in some detail to draw attention to the very important part that they can play in helping us to understand children's scholastic difficulties. The symbolic significance of letters and numbers is also taken into consideration when thinking about a child's emotional disturbance. There are extensive studies of reading disabilities in the literature but there are very few concerned with the writing or (particularly) mathematical disabilities of children.

It is often erroneously assumed, in spite of research to the contrary, that having a learning disability does not necessarily constitute a major problem for the child, his family or his school. Yule and Rutter (1985) express the view that severe reading difficulties are common, persistent and handicapping; they are also frequently associated with psychiatric disorder. 'This association is not confined to clinic attenders.' While noting that reading skills affect a child's approach to and subsequent attainment level in most other subjects, we have found that children who are unable to master mathematical concepts, writing or spelling skills find the effect to be equally handicapping.

Very few children are referred to us for a mathematical disability alone, though Gordon, described in Chapter 10, appeared to have unconsciously selected mathematics as a way of initiating his referral. It was the area in which his suspended learning became most apparent in school and yet, as the account shows, the subject hardly featured except in the early sessions. A child's difficulties in understanding basic numerical concepts and with handwriting warrant attention at an emotional as well as a cognitive level.

MATHEMATICAL SKILLS

Poincaré's description of the development of a mathematical formulation encapsulates our ideas about the necessity to order and value each new experience, and to place them into a whole, particularly when we are working with groups. He states

If a new result is to have any value it must unite elements long since known,

121

but till then scattered and seemingly foreign to each other, and suddenly introduce order where the appearance of disorder reigned. Then it enables us to see at a glance each of these elements in the place it occupies in the whole.

(Poincaré 1952)

Poincaré's statement reminds us that we are trying to think about separate and sometimes disparate elements in the behaviour of the individual members of a family or peer group system, before being able to bring about a 'new result' for the whole system. He continues, 'Not only is the new fact valuable on its own account, but it alone gives a value to the old facts it unites.' A family or peer group sometimes leaves us with the impression that they are expending their energies on undermining our attempts to bring about any unification of their past experiences so as to make sense of the present. For most of the children in the families we see there has been little order. This seems to us to suggest that some of the children cannot risk making two and two equal four, when they 'know' that what is happening belies this fact.

Bowlby's thoughts in his paper (1979), 'On knowing what you are not supposed to know and feeling what you are not supposed to feel' also appears to be relevant here. Bowlby looks at the question of what a child may 'allow' himself to 'know'. He says, 'Children frequently observe scenes that parents would prefer they did not observe; they form impressions that parents would prefer they did not form; and they have experiences that parents would like to believe they have not had.' Some of these children then attempt to comply with their parents' wishes to 'forget' what they have witnessed. An increasing number of children who have been abused are now referred to educational therapists. Their experience has certainly been one that they wish could be forgotten. If the experience can be remembered then there is a possibility of a new result. Most of the children about whom we are writing in this chapter have had experiences long since known, and from our clinical work with them we infer that many choose to believe that they have no connection with one another. Educational therapy has the potential to help a child to integrate these previously scattered and seemingly foreign to each other elements or experiences into a whole. When order is introduced the parts and the whole can begin to make sense to the child. This is true not only of mathematical concepts but also of the signs placed on paper that signify letters (the parts). These when added together or ordered in certain sequences can be built into a whole – that is a word, leading to a sentence, a paragraph, and a story with a beginning, a middle and an end.

If one's experiences have made little sense, they do not 'add up': a term in common usage, meaning that one cannot make sense of, or discover, a connection of thought. It is especially difficult to think, to make sense of, or to add up when one's world is changing. If a child is a member of a family comprising four members and one disappears, his previously held understanding of the number of parts that added up to a whole of four no longer makes sense. When one or both parents form new relationships, following divorce or separation, a child may find himself to be one of five at weekends and one of two during the week. Can the concepts of multiplication or division have a true meaning for children of reconstituted families? Can they cope with the value of numbers if they are unprepared and confused by sudden changes and frequent transitions which result in the number of people at home changing dramatically? The situation can be aggravated by a compulsory move to another house or flat with a different number of rooms, and/or the giving up of a single room to share with new members of the reconstituted family.

How can children manage to calculate the true value of a number if they experience the breakdown of several foster families, which can entail transitions backwards and forwards from their family home to an institutional home? Berridge states,

> It is very important not to underestimate the effects of fostering breakdown on a child. The effects of fostering breakdown are highly disruptive and emotionally distressing. They disintegrate peer and other social networks, wrench children from familiar neighbourhoods and lead to a change of school.

(Berridge 1985)

He feels that transfers can 'shatter the fragile trust the children have in the permanence of adult relationships, resurrect memories they have of earlier separations and encourage emotional disturbance and learned indifference'. He reports that teachers of these children find that they 'function well below their potential for several years following the disruption'.

The observation in Chapter 3 gave the impression that securely attached children, such as John, are able to encompass the arrival of a sibling without losing the sense of their own worth and identity. Children less well prepared for the arrival of a newborn sibling might stumble over adding two and two to equal four, when unconsciously they would prefer to stay as two and one.

It is with the concept of 'one' that most children understand the beginning of mathematical thinking. The symbols for the number '1' and the capital letter 'I' resemble one another very closely, particularly when written by hand: they are almost interchangeable. A collection of Winnicott's essays posthumously published in 1986 includes a paper given to a group of teachers of mathematics, 'Sum I Am'. He says, 'the idea that arithmetic starts with the concept of one, and that this derives and must derive, in every developing child from the unit self, a state that represents an achievement of growth, a state indeed that may never be achieved.' (The latter part of his statement applies to the children referred to on p. 147 in our classification of children with no basic skills.) If children have not had an image of themselves that they can believe in reflected back to them, how can they recognise themselves as being valued as unique human beings? Without this experience their understanding of 'I am' will be tenuous.

In his 'Sum I Am' paper, Winnicott (1986) later makes reference to the contribution that a teacher can make to re-establishing a child's sense of 'I am.' Without this certainty it becomes extremely difficult for a child to master additional mathematical concepts. This inhibition may be linked to the loss of a family member (as suggested above) or to a traumatic event that brings about change in a previously facilitating environment. When a family member dies (or leaves home), children often assume that they are responsible and are overwhelmed with feelings of guilt.

Rupert

The work undertaken with this boy illustrates the difficulties he had in allowing himself to acknowledge his right to know 'I am.' Children like Rupert seem to have lost the wish to move on to new experiences, as if they have an almost compulsive need to remain at the stage of development which they had reached when the loss occurred. Rupert was very small for his age and became an elective mute at 2 years old following the death of his younger brother at a few weeks. When he was 3½ another brother, Neil, was born who at the time of referral was described as a 'confident and rather boisterous pre-schooler'. Rupert was said to have acquired some speech, but he often expressed himself in a muddled way. His articulation was poor and he presented himself as a toddler; his behaviour remained very immature for a schoolboy of 7. He was of average intelligence with severe learning disabilities in all areas and he had acquired no basic skills. He had previously been designated 'dyslexic'. In the classroom Rupert seemed unable to tolerate any activities that could remotely be associated with growing up. His problem was exacerbated by his apparent inability to think.

We would like to digress for a moment because we have found that many children appear to be unable to think. One boy, also aged 7, became quite fearful if the word was even mentioned. It was not until he and his educational therapist had been working together for almost a year that he began to say, 'I can't think.' Several months after this he was able to demonstrate that he was indeed thinking in two senses. He was able to think about and manage an abstract task, but also he thought about his feelings. We found that a lecture by a psychotherapist, Ricky Emanuel (in press), helped us to understand more about a child's capacity to think. It is based on Bion's concept (1962) of the mother as a 'container' of her infant's feelings:

> The capacity to think, or be curious in any way, or to pay attention, depends upon the child's experience of being thought about, or of someone being curious about or being attentive to him. In the same way that a child does not learn to talk unless he has been talked to, the same premise applies to

thinking, curiosity and attention .... A baby may be distressed and crying because [he] is experiencing an unpleasant feeling, a state of mind, or physical discomfort. His crying evokes distress in the mother, who nevertheless has to try and understand what this crying may mean. She reflects on it, thinks about it and relates it to her own experience as well as that of her baby, before attending to his needs, by changing, feeding or comforting him. The baby then is not only made more comfortable, but is also able to take inside himself the experience of his mother having a space in her mind for him, he feels understood.

(Emanuel in press)

From the brief description of Rupert's early years it seemed that his capacity to think might have been very slow to develop. In addition thinking may have become too dangerous and 'uncontainable' when his sibling was destroyed by death.

In addition to seeing an educational therapist individually, Rupert was a member of a group of three in a psychiatric unit. The therapist reported,

'Understandably, he had great difficulty in acknowledging, let alone believing, that 2 + 1 could make 3. The fact that he was one of a group of three also appeared stressful for him. The staff took every opportunity to verbalise the reality of situations naturally arising in the classroom; for example, when two children were carrying a table and the third child was not involved, they were all still members of a group of three. During the first few weeks of his admission, his behaviour became infantile if a child was absent for any reason.'

His educational therapist tells us how this boy began to understand 'I sum' by using letters, long before he could begin to contemplate the value of numbers.

'Books with pictures of animals held a particular fascination for Rupert, especially those with dogs, although he could not bear to look at the accompanying texts. One day he cut out each letter in his name and we began to play with the letters, moving them around, with him asking me what the letters said. Much later we discovered that it was possible to make "pet power" from some of the letters from his name. He found this very exciting and asked me to write a simple sentence about a dog. We read this together, the first time he had allowed himself to look at any text. He went on to create a story, dictated to me, about a dog named Pet Power. As the story developed his capacity to add and subtract numbers to five also developed. He began to explore his relationships with his peers, and seemed able to begin internalising better feelings about himself. His trust in adults developed in parallel with his newly discovered "power".'

He moved steadily through the next stages of his development. At the end of his therapy the therapist remarked, 'All his skills had been curled up inside him, and as they emerged I was strongly reminded of an infant unfolding from its foetal position on entering the world.'

We pause here to speculate about the power of numbers. Are numbers feared because they cannot be controlled when the child himself fears being out of control? Is power attributed to numbers by certain children because they symbolise the power of people who have such control over their lives? The very word 'power' is part of mathematical language. Mathematical symbols can assume great power for children, even in their early years in school. Can 2 or 3 be perceived as having constancy for a child whose family constellation changes from time to time? $2 + 3 = 5$, but $2 \times 3 = 6$. The symbols for two and three remain the same; the other symbols are different. Many learning-disabled children confuse the symbols for addition and multiplication. Does this have anything to do with the fact that children struggling and failing to make sense of numerical symbols have so many answers marked with an 'X'? The word for this symbol is 'cross', which teachers and parents can be when answers are wrong. What meaning does the symbol and word 'equal' imply, if one is feeling very 'unequal' as a result of unresolved feelings of jealousy towards siblings or a 'new' parental figure?

When a 9-year-old girl said, 'You can't really do maths without a ruler, can you?' was she making an oblique reference to rules that she was trying to understand or was she wanting the ruler to help control her sums? Placing and spacing are essential rules when undertaking numerical tasks using Arabic numerals. Other civilisations such as Sumerian, Egyptian, Greek and Roman were limited by having to calculate without the advantage of a symbol for 'nothing' – '0'. This sophisticated concept that 'something' could represent 'nothing' came only comparatively recently (probably from India) in the history of mathematics. Most of us readily accept that 1 followed by 0 (one and zero) – 10 (ten) – is greater than 9 (nine).

When a child is unsure of his own place in a family or in a classroom, where does he begin to find his own space? The task of solving problems involving fractions again presents particular difficulties to those children for whom the idea of sharing, or dividing, a whole can be intolerable. Thinking about the complexities of the sequences of numbers that are possible must be akin to contemplating infinity, either a daunting or an exciting concept depending on your perception of 'I am.'

Although the advent of mechanical calculators makes long-division sums a matter of pressing the right buttons, for many children this level of calculation has assumed gigantic proportions. Intellectually-able children who have no problems with any of the individual processes required appear to be incapable of managing the sequence of steps involved. When faced with this task they become quite rebellious and it becomes impossible for them to allow themselves the satisfaction of completing the sums.

Martin

This 10-year-old had managed reasonably well in school until he became ill just after his tenth birthday. He then became unable or unwilling to return to school. There were no signs of physical malfunctioning, and no solutions were offered by the school; so Martin was referred to a small educational unit. When he arrived in the unit he was unable to walk up or down stairs and would speak only in a one-to-one situation. His manner was extremely patronising with adults and peers alike. Martin's inability to climb stairs, to speak and to attend normal school (he had transferred aged 9 to a middle school before the crisis) could be related to his wish to stay little, preferably at home with his mother or father. Although there had been no major problems in school Martin had never separated easily from his parents, and had been very protected throughout his time in first school.

In the unit classroom Martin was resistant and uncommunicative. When he was presented with long-division sums similar to those he had already managed in school, there was a dramatic change in his behaviour. He became openly angry and expressed his feelings forcefully, 'I can't do sums with so many steps in,' he raged. Did the method of long division represent symbolic problem areas for him? The educational therapist decided that Martin could be helped to tackle his problems with the stairs, which apparently represented the threat of progress (growing up), through the symbolic step-by-step process of long division. It is not possible to be certain that accomplishing this specific task of long division was a contributory factor to Martin's recovery. He undoubtedly experienced considerable job satisfaction from mastering the process, which marked a change in his relationship with the educational attachment figure concerned.

Many children who have no predictability or containment in their lives must feel very much as if they are caught in the middle of an impossible calculation. The unscrambling of such confusion, step by step, with the resulting complete and correct answer, brings with it an enormous and satisfying reward. Blyth (1985) commented on the satisfaction to be derived from activities that have a complete solution.

Giles

We now present an account of a sad 8-year-old boy, with a rejecting mother. There were other major family problems and admission to a unit was arranged to try and prevent his being taken into care. Mother and Giles had lived alone until her re-marriage some five years earlier. Her second husband had two grown-up daughters who lived elsewhere with their mother. Grant, the son of the new marriage, was 3 at the time of the crisis. Intensive help was offered to this family.

Giles was a tall, rather solemn boy, withdrawn and lacking any animation.

He had some irritating nervous habits, one of which was belching on demand. So tight was his rein upon himself that belching, hinting at the inner turmoil deeply hidden within him, seemed to be the only sign that he possessed any feelings.

A subsequent visit to Giles's school revealed a picture of him as a child whose behaviour had been the cause of uneasy concern for his teachers during his first three years there. His work was basically competent although he had recently begun to find mathematics difficult. His teachers were even more concerned about his mother, who seized every possible opportunity to gain their attention to unburden her feelings about her relationship with Giles. It was their doubts about her state of mind and its effect on Giles that enabled them to accept that some outside intervention was appropriate.

Blyth (1985) suggests that, 'Numbers are symbols. And symbols are associated, consciously or unconsciously, with feelings. We symbolise in order to make sense of the world, and our feelings about the world.' Blyth also referred to the state of total confusion and panic that can be the response to the language of mathematics. This could certainly be observed when Giles encountered any sum or exercise that involved money. He would work quietly through a mathematical workbook, gaining some degree of satisfaction as he completed each page competently. Suddenly the situation would change, and this child who was kept in mind with so much difficulty would immediately come into sharp focus. His face would turn scarlet and he would become restless and irritable. He did not become openly disruptive, but he belched loudly and his behaviour provoked feelings of irritation in the adults. He would not (or, more accurately, could not) seek help in this situation.

Money appeared to be germane to Giles's problems in relation to his mother and his natural father. He had not known his father and had, it seemed, a very idealised image of him, a perception in marked contrast to that presented by his mother, who described her former husband as 'a cruel and uncaring man'. She repeatedly told Giles that he was very like his father in character and that his father never gave them any financial support. Giles was not given any pocket-money, nor was he allowed the sort of things that most children like, such as sweets and comics. The parents held very strict views and did not have a television as it was not thought to be constructive, so Giles's life was different from that of most of his peers.

Giles was quite unable to deal with even simple calculations involving money. It was possible to talk to him about why he might be experiencing difficulties with money sums and to empathise with his feelings about them rather than colluding with him to avoid the problem. Giles showed immediate relief from his panic when reference was made to his lack of experience with real money. He started talking about other children who bought their own sweets and comics. He clearly equated the withholding of money with the withholding of love – an equation which seemed to be made at a very deep and profound level. The money sums provided an opportunity for him to experience the attention of an educational attachment figure from a secure base whence he could begin to come to terms with his problems. Facing these sums and coping with them better, he began to be able to seek help. He faded less and less into the background and his belching decreased. As is usual with mathematical work programmes, each activity recurs periodically. When the money calculations recurred Giles again needed support. Working and playing with money was also helpful.

The problems within the family could not be resolved; Giles was totally rejected by his step-father, who refused to see him; he also forbade meetings between Giles and his half-brother. His mother continued to visit him briefly once a week, as he was by this time an in-patient, and a foster family was found for him. The issue of pocket-money proved an important factor in enabling him to start adjusting to his new family. Initially they gave him money to spend as and when necessary, and he was allowed to watch television and have sweets and comics. This new freedom proved too difficult for him to manage: he needed the experience of handling regular pocket-money. The foster family were helped to understand the difficulty and arranged a weekly allowance for him to manage for himself. He responded well to this age-appropriate autonomy in spite of the stark contrast between the two family life-styles. Fortunately it was possible for the community psychiatric nurse attached to the unit to support his mother to give her consent to his new regime, and Giles gained some comfort from her assurances.

After some months Giles's natural father returned from abroad with his new wife specifically to renew contact with his son. Eventually, after a careful period of introduction and preparation, Giles went with everyone's approval to live with his father and step-mother, and made positive progress.

Occasionally a child can express his thoughts about numbers in story form. Darren, a boy of 12, produced the following:

The magic toll-gate

The car and the toll-gate had been given to Tom as a birthday present. He was very pleased with it, and played with it often. The gate opened and he would drive the car through. One day when he did this, the scenery changed. He was on a road with the toll-booth behind him. He drove down the road and came to a town. There was a market going on, so Tom stopped the car and went to see what was going on.

He went up to one of the stores. The man on it shouted 'Adds, multiplies, divides, subtracts, square roots, all available here. Get your maths' signs here!' He moved on, puzzled. 'Angles, degrees, vertices, hours, minutes, seconds, all here,' shouted the woman on the next stall. They all seemed to be selling things to do with maths. The next stall sold numbers. Tom asked the man how he could sell numbers. He said they were special numbers which, when arranged into a sum, moved themselves to make the answer. Tom thought this was a wonderful idea, and bought a pen which had 'number fluid' in it, so he could write the numbers he wanted, instead of having to buy them separately. He tried it out to see if it worked, which it did. He said thank you to the man, got in the car and drove back to the toll-booth. He went through and found himself back in his room. He did his homework, and went to bed. Tomorrow he would explore further, he decided, and see what else he could find.

A description of work with another boy, Keith, was given in detail in Chapter 7, but here is an indication of his difficulty with mathematics. He encountered some simple addition and subtraction sums in his work-book, which had little printed paw-marks indicating where the answer should be written. The actual sums were familiar, but this aspect of presentation was different since previously the answers had to be placed in boxes. Keith found it impossible to manipulate the numbers and place them on paw-marks. The association with the small dog in his story who had been in constant trouble and was removed from his home for making dirty paw-marks was too painful, and he needed a lot of help and support to manage his own feelings of rejection when confronted by this work-book. By recalling the content of Keith's story it was possible for the adults to understand why the 'dirty' paw-marks had such a dramatic effect on him. His sense of achievement when he mastered these feelings, and simultaneously the placing of answers on the paw-marks, was enormous. There can be little doubt that children are often doubly stressed by the content of material and the way it is presented in standard work- and textbooks.

Comment

We do not of course know whether the increasing numbers of children suffering from loss and change in their family constellations have experienced an increase in their numerical confusion. When children are encouraged to make an oral estimate of the outcome of their calculations and actions, they are moving towards an anticipated, reliable and recognisable goal, not one whose posts are unreliable, continually being moved. How often in 'real' life does one have to embark on calculations as complex as long division, which involves a divisor greater than 10? The availability of cheap calculators has made some degree of numeracy accessible to nearly all. The tedium for many schoolchildren subjected to pointless exercises can destroy their interest in a subject which can, at higher levels, reveal the beauty and sophistication of man's thinking. On the other hand a grasp of the basic principles of mathematics is of considerable practical value. An enlightened approach to the subject is needed which will leave a child competent within his own capacity: neither chained to electronic devices for the simplest calculation nor subjected to grinding through hours of frustration and mis-use of the 'best years of his life'.

WRITING SKILLS

In the second part of this chapter we do not address the acquisition of writing skills in any detail, but focus on the work of children struggling to master their feelings about making a commitment to paper. We recognise the serious problem that a lack of writing skills presents to some of the children described in this book. It is not our intention to examine the motor skills involved or the issues arising from handedness. Children frustrated by their inability to express themselves on paper can become disruptive or deviant in their behaviour, particularly if they are intelligent.

Does the skill of writing begin with the child's drawing at a pre-school level? Alston and Taylor (1987) examine the actual skills of handwriting in detail. They trace the precursor of the skill through children's drawing at different developmental stages, using the work of Kellogg (1970) to introduce the manipulative skills required in making marks on paper. It was disappointing that scant attention was given to the effect of 'bad' handwriting on the children themselves, although some reference was made to the self-esteem of senior pupils in an interesting cross-cultural study in San Francisco.

Handwriting can be considered as a technical and motor skill involving hand-eye co-ordination and fine-motor control as well as a creative activity. Although as educational therapists we are concerned with the former two, the latter is the more important, and we should acknowledge children's efforts to master the feelings that may be preventing them from committing themselves to paper.

How do toddlers manage the excitement or anxiety that may accompany the discovery that the marks they make on paper have something to do with themselves as individuals and are an extension of themselves? Their previous experiences have been predominantly tactile, associated with their own or their mother's body, closely allied to reciprocal eye and voice communications. As small infants they will have experimented with their spilled drinks and food, making patterns with their hands and fingers on the table or tray – part of their early exploration, made through the senses, particularly touch. When they start to draw, their sweeping arcs gradually give way to circular movements as their control increases. Perhaps the closing of the circle denotes an experience of 'oneness' – mother and infant – and the experience of being literally contained by mother. In mastering the motor effort required to lift the crayon off the paper as well as making marks, the toddler begins to organise dots, lines and circles (Kellogg 1969).

The first 'recognisable' primitive image produced is almost invariably a form of sun or face, with lines arranged as radii around the circle and 'features' as assorted dots. Perhaps the importance of the infant's awareness of his mother's face contributes to his use of this symbol. Gradually the number of radii are reduced, leaving arms and legs protruding from the head of the 'figure'. It seems as if the mother's arms are an extension of the memory of her eyes, the sound and feel of her. Her facial expression and voice are welded into the memory of being held (in the Winnicottian sense (1965)). Is the early appearance of legs in their drawings linked with unconscious memories of the 'walking' movements present in infants at birth, and with their delight at 'feeling their feet' held supportively on a parent's lap while they make eye contact? In spite of all an infant's physical explorations, feeling tummies, genitals and toes, and the games his parents play, blowing on their baby's stomach, his awareness of his body remains an experience that is not overtly expressed outside himself in drawing or modelling until much later. The emergence of the body in infants' drawings is usually achieved by making a line across the two legs of the 'hair-pin' figure before it becomes an entity in its own right. Early figure drawings seem inextricably linked with the infant's actual awareness of 'mother', her appearance and her significance for him.

The infant's experience of making accidental marks and his increasing ability to control them allows him to extend and explore when opportunities are provided. His representation of faces and figures leads on to the use of letters and numerical figures. Clearly the child who has free and early access to these experiences will be advantaged. As his explorations extend beyond self, his drawings reflect his new discoveries and experiences, his self-image in action or interaction, and the richness or paucity of his imagination. A few children may reveal a perception of themselves as damaged or deformed in some way. Koppitz (1968, 1971) discusses the drawings of abused children.

Learning how to place marks on a piece of paper to show oneself in action or to record an event requires a lot of practice. Each mark must be made in a unique position and juxtaposition, and has an individual size, shape and/or colour; some marks are joined or crossed, some stand alone; each represents some aspect of a child's feelings and experience. For the majority of children this task, especially when self-imposed, is achieved with ease and pleasure, and leads them into mastering the skill of writing. A minority, however, are so preoccupied with inner anxieties that they cannot manage the transition appropriately; the use of letters seems too threatening for them. Even if they have mastered the art of forming individual letters, sequencing them to form words and sentences seems to be an insurmountable task. Most children have difficulty spacing words when they first start writing, but this is only a temporary stage and is soon overcome. Others cannot progress so easily; their writing reflects their own internal confusions, squashed and chaotic or spread across the page with more spaces than words.

Another child we knew found that to leave a space between two words was too frightening because for him the connotation of the word 'space' was rejection. It had been discovered that his father constantly shouted at him, 'I need some space, boy, go to your room.' This meant that he was left alone for long periods, which he came to dread.

From the beginning an infant hears his name, and this symbolically becomes an integral part of ego strength and 'core self' (Stern 1985). Children usually enjoy learning the initial letter of their name as an introduction to handwriting, followed by writing and recognising their forename. But if a child is not sure who he is, then writing his name becomes a major hurdle. When a child is adopted, one of the most important pieces of knowledge that he has to confirm his identity is the name he received when he was born. It is sometimes the only possession he has, but often his 'new' parents decide to change that name in an effort to give him a new start: perhaps wishing to obliterate the child's past, to make him more their 'own'. Children are occasionally given the same name as another child in the family who has died, been killed or was stillborn. (The consequences of name confusion relating to a stillborn child are portrayed in the account of Jackie given in Chapter 9.) Even to have the same name as a parent, if that figure is a feared one, may prove difficult. A different kind of confusion arose for the 7-year-old Adrian who spelt his name 'Adrain'. In a family interview his mother on several occasions referred to him as 'a drain on her'.

In reconstituted families (Robinson 1982), surnames may present explicit worries or less conscious ones, particularly if no explanation is available when the composition of a family changes or members disappear. One boy, Matthew, aged 7, was unable to write his surname. He had two, one from his unknown father and another belonging to his mother and step-father. He was unable to identify himself with either: mentioning the first one was a taboo subject because this name reminded his mother of her firstborn's illegitimacy and her own abandonment at the time of Matthew's birth. He found the second one doubly painful: it was associated with his abuse by his step-father (who was also implicated in the loss of one of his siblings). An older boy, Harry, aged 12, was referred for 'being unable to put his ideas down on paper'. He was one of two siblings whose long-term fostering by relatives contributed to their uncertainties about their surnames, their identities and where they really belonged. At the time of our work with the family his teachers expressed their annoyance about Harry's continued use of two surnames, which caused them considerable confusion as he used both names indiscriminately on his exercise books. After two years' spasmodic work with this family it emerged that the foster children had been told that they were adopted and must therefore change their name. This claim was found to be false when the pressure to become someone else became intolerable and Harry took action by running away. Following various negotiations by the educational therapist and members of the community network, the boy was re-united with his father and grandfather. In several sessions Harry then began practising his true signature in what he called 'proper writing'. Any previous attempts at 'joined-up' writing of any kind had proved very difficult.

We have worked with a number of other children who think their writing is rubbish. The very acts of heavy-handed crossing out, or scribbling over, or using an eraser until a hole appears in the paper, demonstrate clearly the feelings associated with attempts to write. A chalkboard is sometimes used by an educational therapist, so that a child can quickly erase his name if he wishes, and mistakes can be easily rendered invisible. Placing anything on paper can be a major commitment for the children described above. Drawings, as well as attempts at writing, are frequently screwed into a ball or torn up and discarded in angry despair. This behaviour often reflects the children's feelings about their own worthlessness. The 'rubbishing' of a name or other writing can be a child's way of communicating to the therapist how he is feeling about himself, his behaviour and his lack of basic skills.

Tracing is a useful activity, acting as a bridge between chalkboard and paper for a few children. We have noticed that it can give them a feeling of control, but it can also be likened to a much earlier wish to learn by repetition. A toddler playing with material or words in games enjoys the repetition, the confirmation of a constant. The very fact that a pencil has been controlled on paper when tracing brings its own sense of achievement: the concrete evidence is evident. (Does it have something to do with mirroring in the Winnicottian sense (1971)?)

There are numerous ways of introducing writing to children who are not ready to hold a tool in their hands to make marks on a surface of any kind (excluding graffiti). Some children enjoy modelling clay, and using it frequently enables them to express concerns about things other than writing. A group of 11- and 12-year-olds were asked to make words from modelling clay. One boy chose to make an extremely long 'sausage' which he placed in front of his genitals. The educational therapist commented on the size of the model and, by making a direct reference to the word 'penis', enabled the group to have an open discussion about the teasing that one of them was receiving. The tallest boy had become a target of ridicule because although he was large his penis was extremely small, a fact that one of the boys had unpleasantly brought to the notice of others in the showers after games. Following this discussion each boy was able to return to and complete the original task. Younger children familiar with the use of modelling clay can enjoy making letters and linking them to something 'rude', for example 'p' for 'poo'. The privacy of a session allows a child to express feelings about subjects that are not necessarily appropriate to show in other settings or company.

Mervyn, aged 8, had refused to write anything except his first name, which he had written angrily several times on his box. His reading was reluctant and erratic. When an old typewriter was made available to him, his aggressive pressure on the keys of the typewriter gave him pleasure and, more importantly, the courage to use writing to express some of his angry feelings in words. His first sentence was 'You are a pig.' His therapist was then commanded to answer this statement. He then began to explore some of his therapist's feelings towards him by typing enormous sums of money that he said she owed him. She felt that he used this method as one way of discovering whether she could value him. Bringing words, either read or written, under his control in this way enabled Mervyn to make a move towards writing in school, and very slowly he was able to bring his feelings of anger under control too. In one of his sessions, while declaring himself no good at art because 'a boy in my class is the best', he managed to paint a boy swimming. The painting gave the impression of a boy moving forward, showing his head well above the water, but creating many splashes. The figure was described by Mervyn as 'being a winner now he knew how to do it'. He accepted the therapist's suggestion that the swimmer was rather like himself where his reading and writing were concerned. In spite of this, it still appeared too risky to allow himself to show pleasure in his painting when its artistic merit was praised: these feelings too had to be kept under control.

We do not pretend to know why children write with minute writing, in a messy or indecipherable hand, or backwards. Do these actions reflect something of their feelings about themselves? Are they afraid to be understood or do they wish to conceal their feelings for some reason? Has their chaotic experience led to messy presentation, crossing out, and writing that has no semblance of order on the page? (Writing and behaviour may both sometimes be described as being 'all over the place'.) Finally do children reverse letters and numbers to express an unconscious wish to return to an earlier stage of development? Gregory, who had serious reversal problems, said on the day after his seventh birthday, 'The trouble with being 7 is that you have to know more. I wish I was little again, then I wouldn't have to worry about so many things, because I didn't understand them then.' This boy also had many unresolved conflicts relating to a younger sibling. These were likely to have been a contributory factor to his wish to be small again.

Because this book is an introduction to the intervention of educational therapy, the conflicting opinions about dyslexia are not discussed. There is no doubt that some children are severely handicapped by 'seeing' letters and numbers in reverse or have difficulty in placing symbols in sequence or in making use of spaces between them. Their hand-eye co-ordination may be erratic and their laterality not established. Some parents are pleased to adopt the dyslexic label for their children, relieved that the problem is not their fault and that at last their child's problem has been identified and named. Children too may feel more comfortable with a label that they see as preferable to 'lazy' or 'stupid', though others resent the label as making them too different from their peers. It can obviate the need to look further as to why a child is not learning, so may be used as an excuse; it may ensure that greater allowances are made for the child. Perhaps it is easier to tolerate this label than to manage one's fear of the unknown. (This fear was carried to an extreme when a child was referred to a clinic for not being able to read or write. Before his father sat down in the first interview he said, 'He's not mad, you know.') Many children do have severe difficulties, especially those who write letters and numbers in the opposite direction to the rest of us. Perhaps the prime example of a man who has been able to communicate a wealth of ideas to mankind despite reversing his letters was Leonardo da Vinci.

We wonder if writing certain letters incorrectly time after time can have some tenuous link with the unconscious. Our thinking about this was influenced by Strachey's paper in which he considered unconscious factors in reading, a skill he noted that we acquire before writing. He suggested that logically the order should be reversed. Before discussing 'the traces of oral influence to be found in a large number of metaphors applied to reading' Strachey stated that

> the mental energy employed in reading is to some degree derived from certain unconscious trends. In so far as those trends are sublimated, the reading can proceed without meeting with any obstacles raised by other mental forces; if, however, and in so far as, they retain any of the original unsublimated character the reading will meet with the hindrances which would have been put in the way of unmodified trends.
>
> (Strachey 1930)

Can this be applied to writing also?

We have noticed that two vowel sounds cause particular problems in writing as well as in reading. Our thoughts about the lower case 'e' will probably be found difficult to accept. Its shape is reminiscent of that of a foetus. The wish to remain in a dependent state of mind has been shown by several children with severe learning disabilities. We put forward the tentative view that there could be a link between a child's deeply unconscious wish to return to the *in utero* state and his inability to write or remember the lower case 'e'. The following vignette offers no proof of this but we find it relevant. Neil's name contained the letter 'e' which he was just beginning to manage to write. He remained very uncertain whether the marks on the page which were his name had anything to do with who he was now. One day Neil and his therapist were walking in a garden, their room for the therapy session having been mistakenly occupied. Neil exclaimed on seeing a very young fern, tightly coiled. The therapist mused aloud about the completeness of that baby fern, with all its parts ready to unfold, likening it to Neil. She reflected that he had all the components for growth and flourishing and he just needed the right nourishment and warmth to allow for his fruition. He looked at his therapist with wonder and then nodded gravely, continuing the walk. During his next session he began on the extremely slow path of 'unfurling' towards his chronological age, 9.

Our second example is related to the lower case letter 'i', about which we think that our theory will be more readily acceptable. Sally, aged 9, expended a good deal of her energy in trying to remain invisible in school. She was always quiet and very withdrawn in her behaviour, but her work was competent. This behaviour was the antithesis of her loud, dominant and powerful behaviour at home. The family were described as unhappy, but there was particular concern for this daughter, who constantly played one parent off against the other, making frequent gibes about their different racial backgrounds. She was referred for being beyond parental control. Some hint of this child's self-perception could be seen in her story writing. Her stories were endless recordings of day-to-day events strung together without punctuation. She very rarely used the first person, even when the events were about herself; when she did she always used the lower case 'i'. The educational therapist working with this child felt that it was unlikely that she had experienced the 'I am' as described by Winnicott (1986).

Joss, almost 14 years old, had mastered very few basic skills. He found letters unmanageable and indecipherable. His educational therapist thought he resembled an overgrown toddler. His mother had reported in a family interview that he had experienced considerable difficulty in making the transition from home into his first school. She was very protective of him and the clinic team described their relationship as a symbiotic one. His father had been away from home for part of Joss's early life, though the family, which included a younger sibling, was intact at the time of the therapy.

Many of the stories that Joss dictated had the theme of 'little' and 'big'. He seemed to be exploring the nature of the difference within the metaphor of the story. He was in the early stages of puberty and was very much concerned with the changes that were taking place in his body. His difficulty in managing letters seemed to be symptomatic of a wish to remain little. The therapist had the very strong impression that Joss had spent much of his life struggling to hang on to the dependent state of early infancy with his mother in the home. (In typing her notes the therapist inadvertently allowed the 's' of 'his' to run into 'mother' thus making 'smother'.)

Joss dictated the following fantasy about a lower case letter 'r':

The little 'r'

One day, in the Kingdom of Words, the capitals of all the words went missing, and so all the words got jumbled up and into the wrong words.

The King of all Words sent a lot of messengers out to find the lost letters. The messengers came back empty-handed. A little unimportant 'r' went out to look for the capital letters. At first the journey was easy. Then it became hard. The weather was terrible; there was thunder and lightning. But after two days of this it all stopped and it became sunny again, and he went on until he came to a large river. He was drenched, so he decided to make camp for the night.

In the morning, when the 'r' woke up, the bank he was standing on looked quite different. The forest looked a lot denser, but the 'r' went on. It was quite dark at first, but his eyes became accustomed to the dull light. Soon he was quite deep in the forest and was lost, but he went on.

Soon he came to a small house. He knocked on the door. A small old woman came to the door. He asked if the messengers had been this way, but they had not come this way. He said 'Thank you for the information' and went on his way.

As he went into the forest he started to lose his direction and soon all he could see was trees. Then suddenly he came upon a small clearing with a fire which had been put out quickly and was still smouldering. Someone must have been close and moved on fast. He could just make out which way they left and he followed them.

Soon it was dark and he stopped for the night. Soon it became morning, too soon for his liking, but he got up and moved off. He could still see which way they went. He followed. It was only about two o'clock when he came on to a path, but the path only went one way, so he followed the path and soon a light shone through the tops of the trees.

At one point he nearly caught up with the people he was following but they got away. So he decided to be very careful and was cautious. The next day he came upon the camp, so he got into a safe position and spent the night there.

When he woke up he went to a position where he could see the camp from. He got such a surprise when he saw the Capital Letters. He decided to wait until dark and then went into the camp. He went to the tent where he saw the Capitals and set them free.

He got them safely to the King and the King sent the guards to get the outlaws. The King promoted the 'r' to a capital 'R' and the big 'R' lived happily ever after.

The end

Mastering the skills of reading and writing formally mark the transition from infancy into childhood and, implicit in this, towards adulthood. The story that Joss wrote about the little 'r' marked a real change in his life. It opened with the confusion of the letters and the words. To make matters worse all the capitals had gone missing. It is interesting to speculate about this. Joss's mother had 'taught him his letters' using the upper case alphabet. Had this teaching experience at home made it impossible for him to make use of his class teacher as an interim attachment person, in the absence of his mother, in the new and strange situation in school? It does seem that his attachment to his mother was a very anxious one. There were numerous reports of Joss's problems at times of transition: changes arising from breaks in the sessions, and changing teachers and classes in school at the end of the academic year, all provided evidence of the continuation of his symbiotic relationship with his mother.

The therapist comments:

'In spite of all the trials and tribulations, there was a thread of hope running through the Joss story. There seemed to be a possibility of success, a feeling, tentative at times, that the letters could all be assembled together and order made out of chaos. The triumph of the letter "r" over all the adversity was rewarded by promotion, the little "r" became a big "R". The increase in stature of Joss himself that day, seemed to reflect his satisfaction on the completion of his story. All his toddler looks had vanished.'

Also at this time his therapist noted the incipient moustache on his upper lip and recognised the pride that Joss was showing in his acceptance of his adolescence. His progress continued to be erratic, but in spite of this he seemed to have internalised the change; he had updated his view of himself and now felt his own worth had been validated.

In the same way that children, and some adults, have an almost super-stitious attitude to certain numbers, either having an irrational dislike of them or considering them to be 'lucky', we have often wondered about feelings relating to certain letters.

The question of the content of stories can to a large extent be dependent upon a child's manipulative skill when writing. Naturally his imagination may be untapped or inhibited; he may lack the self-discipline required for thinking; he may feel so insignificant that he has nothing to record; any one or all of these factors could affect what a child writes or does not write about. Encouraging the child to dictate his ideas ensures that a child is not deprived of the opportunity to tell stories. Where these stories are typed for him between sessions he feels valued and he can take pride in his work, previously impossible. Reading the familiar text proves possible and enhances his self-esteem.

We have chosen not to consider spelling in isolation. Nevertheless we believe that mis-spellings and problems with reversals and letter order can probably be interpreted at more than one level, i.e. that some may be simple errors but others may be clues to unconscious conflict. For example, a boy with a poor relationship with his father kept reading and writing 'bad' for 'dad'.

Children who have not mastered the concept of symbolism cannot be expected to recognise that a mark on paper such as 'a' represents a particular sound, let alone several different sounds. When the letters 'c' and 'a' and 't' are put together they make another sound. Not only the sounds of the letters have to be memorised but also their order, so that the finished word can be correctly interpreted. Letters which are under control can be moved around in different order: 'c' and 'a' and 't' can become 'act' as well as 'cat'. Children who master the complexities of these simple exercises can enjoy the next stages of the process as their interest in words grows, but for others anxiety and confusion prevail.

For numerous children spelling cannot make sense even when they are not endeavouring to distinguish 'b' from 'd'. Those who write words incorrectly and subsequently try to read them (e.g. 'He is a BaD Dog') are, not surprisingly, rather confused: taken to a child's logical conclusion when he is asked to sound his writing in order to read it, 'bad' written 'BaD' becomes 'beeadee'. Children struggling with spelling sometimes describe their brain as being over-extended, using their hands to demonstrate the size of their problem with all the rules they have learned. They identify their problem as being one of selection, desperate about their inability to identify the appropriate rule.

Part III

CLASSIFICATION OF LEARNING-DISABLED CHILDREN

INTRODUCTION TO
CHAPTERS 9, 10 AND 11

In these three chapters we hope to make a contribution to the understanding of learning disabilities by making specific links between emotional and cognitive learning. Generally, accepted ranges of normal development are linked approximately to children's chronological ages, but children can lose their capacity for learning at any time.

Close observation of the children referred for educational therapy helped us to identify three different types of learning disability. Rutter's (1974) classification of learning-disabled children provided us with an educational construct. He made a necessary differentiation between children who show a 'failure to acquire these (scholastic) skills' (that is reading, writing and mathematics) and those who exhibit a 'later loss of these skills'. In addition to these two educational groups of learning-disabled children we have distinguished a third, those who are resistant to learning.

Decisions based on clinical inference also led us to think about the children's emotional development at the time of the referral. Again we decided to place our 'emotional' categories in three broad classifications. We chose just one study, known as the Strange Situation Study, by Ainsworth and Wittig (1969), previously outlined in Chapter 2, as a basis for our thinking. Ainsworth's study led to the discovery of a range of attachment behaviours in 1-year-old infants at the time of their reunion with their mothers, after having been in the presence of a stranger without mother. Broadly speaking Ainsworth and Wittig placed these children in the following groups:

Group B – secure

The infants who were defined in this study as secure were unlikely to be referred for educational therapy when they reached school age. We shall not concern ourselves with this group here; the interaction of John with his mother (Chapter 3) exemplifies secure attachment behaviour. These secure children may well have specific learning disabilities, but their capacity for learning is unlikely to be impaired.

Groups A and C – insecure

It seemed to us that our referrals might be placed in the group of children whom Ainsworth and Wittig described as being 'anxiously attached' to their mothers. Group A (anxious/avoidant) tended to avoid interacting with mother on her return. In a later study (Ainsworth *et al.* 1978) of these interactions in the home, mothers were observed to be insensitive to their infants' attempts to seek proximity, either blocking or rejecting their approaches. Group C (anxious/ambivalent, sometimes referred to as resistant) were also anxious, but the feelings they expressed towards mother on her return were ambivalent. The later study showed their inability to be comforted. At home their mothers' behaviour was inconsistent.

Group D – insecure

A third group were considered to be unclassifiable at the time of Ainsworth and Wittig's first study. Main *et al.* (1985) studied the same children again at 6 years of age as part of a longitudinal study of the 'individual differences in attachment relationships as they relate to individual differences in mental representation' – that is, Bowlby's (1969) 'internal working models'. Main *et al.* suggested that these unclassified children formed another anxious group which they described as anxious/disorientated, disorganised (Group D). These were the infants whose behaviour was described as dazed and whose postures suggested depression, confusion or apprehension. They made little eye contact when approaching their attachment figures. The experience of the parents of this group included unresolved mourning, possible abuse and other traumas.

We believe that the 'first learning' experience of the Ainsworth and Main groups of children who exhibit anxious attachment behaviour towards attachment figures is most likely to represent the experience of children referred to us. The links between this range of anxious attachment behaviour and the level of their cognitive skills at the time of referral offer one way of examining the process of their 'second-chance learning' with educational therapists. Table 8.1 demonstrates the relationship that we have identified between educational and emotional classifications, although we recognise that there can be no absolute correlation.

We use clinical material to illustrate our hypothesis, devoting a chapter to each of the three groups in the above table. First we look briefly at certain patterns of behaviour in our interaction with individual children. It is perhaps worth recapitulating the features of these patterns: the children's uncertainty about themselves in the present, not only in the here and now of the session but also in the wider context of their 'myriad of systems'; their resistance to remembering the past; their serious doubts and misapprehensions about a

Table 8.1 The relationship between educational and emotional classifications

Scholastic	Emotional
'failure to acquire skills'	'anxious attachment' behaviour that avoids interaction
'later loss of these skills'	'anxious attachment' that is ambivalent to interaction
* resistant to use of skills	'anxiously attached' – disoriented/disorganised

* This classification is our own.

future. It takes several weeks before children can allow themselves to believe that the here and now of each session is real and can be relied upon. Once this 'secure base' has been established, a review or recall of earlier sessions can be contemplated. This is usually a precursor to the child's being able to manage any contemplation of events from his past, where memories may be associated with unbearable pain and lost learning skills. Once access to painful memories has been gained, a tentative belief in the future can be thought about and shared links can be made both backwards and forwards between imagined perceptions and reality.

Once a 'secure base' has been accepted and acknowledged, painful feelings about scholastic 'failure' can be addressed. By the use of material from an earlier phase of development ('educational regression') a restoration of lost skills can be accomplished and 'inwardly digested'. The renewal of a lost appetite for learning becomes possible once the child is able to be in touch with some of the feelings about painful events that took place around the time that a skill was lost, suspended or resisted. The connection between a cognitive task and a state of mind is likely to be put into words by the therapist, but children often make connections themselves and permit the link to be made to previously denied past events or anxiety-provoking future ones; transitions straddle past, present and future as a source of troubled states of mind.

We would like to reiterate some of the observations we have made during our work with individual children and their families and with individual children in school. These observations of the attachment behaviour of children, when they have to leave their parents or teachers to attend sessions and on their reunion with them, have confirmed our use of the three emotional categories of their anxious attachment behaviour. (The parents' interaction with their children in a waiting room in these brief moments is also noted.) Children often give an indication when being collected from a classroom of how they manage the transition from a situation where they have to share the adult with a number of children, that is the class, to having all the attention focused upon them as individuals. Likewise a child's, parent's or teacher's attitude on reunion can also reveal the kind of interactive behaviour that is taking place. Problems related to transition to and from small groups are discussed in Chapter 12. The attachment behaviour of children with their teachers shows us how a child has managed to update, or backdate, his internal working models of attachment figures.

Children's behaviour at the beginning and end of each session offers us an insight into their ability to manage transitions, and we particularly note the way in which they manage holiday and other breaks. There are similarities between a child going into a session, in whatever setting, to the infant in Ainsworth's Strange Situation Study (1969). An educational therapist is a 'stranger' to the child; even when he has met her previously in family interviews, in school or in a special unit, he may still experience her as a stranger. Whether they are accompanied by a family member in a clinic waiting room, or a teacher in a classroom, most children understandably show some anxiety when faced with separation from the known situation to the unknown.

It may seem that we place undue emphasis on the 'emotional' aspect of our classification, and less on the 'scholastic'. This choice is deliberate because a great deal has been written on the more technical aspects of children's acquisition of skills, particularly those concerned with reading. The links between learning and feelings are more difficult to examine and assess. Although there is a danger in classifying learning-disabled children, particularly since there is so much overlap between the groups, we believe that the process helps us to identify the emotional stage where they (and their families) became 'stuck'. It is against this background that we address the feelings related to the lost capacity for learning.

9

CHILDREN WITH NO BASIC SKILLS

The children identified by Ainsworth in her Strange Situation Study (1969) (Group A children, anxious attachment-avoidant) showed little upset when separated from their mothers and on reunion they avoided or rejected their mothers' approaches to them. Their exploratory behaviour did not vary greatly whether they were in the presence of mother or the stranger.

Many of the children who have been unable to acquire basic skills do not seem to have any lasting interest in interacting with their peers, except in a rather fleeting or superficial manner. The presence of an adult seems at times irrelevant to them. Their sense of 'subjective self' (that is self with other) described by Stern (1985) seems slight. Very early in life they abandoned any hope of eliciting the response they sought from their attachment figures, they therefore expended their energy on finding their own ways of managing. Examples of this behaviour in extreme form have been movingly reported by Pontielli (1985). She observed two infants at home from totally different environments and traced the similarities of their patterns of development. Both were subsequently found to have severe learning disabilities.

If part of a child's early learning is to discover that his 'gestures' (Winnicott 1965) cannot be met, he learns to avoid the person from whom he once hoped, longed for, expected a 'gesture' in return, and gives up trying to avoid disappointment. But he learns too that he dare not risk managing without that person, even when he becomes old enough to recognise that his attachment figure does not know how to reflect back to him that he is understood. His worth therefore cannot be validated.

Winnicott (1965) described some children who are rejected in this manner as developing a 'false self'. He said: 'It is not possible to state what takes place by reference to the infant alone' and saw the mother 'failing to meet her infant's gesture'. If this experience is repeated, with the mother imposing her own 'gesture', then the infant becomes compliant in his behaviour. Winnicott considered that her inability to respond to her infant's 'gestures', which indicate his needs, could result in the earliest stages of building a false self. He identified individuals who use their intellect to 'hide their true self' as people who often achieve high academic success at great personal cost. We

147

think that a few extremely vulnerable children adopt a false self as a defence against that which is unthinkable. This is illustrated in the account of the work with Jackie, a 12-year-old girl, later in this chapter.

It is beyond the scope of this book to examine an infant's earliest experience of symbol formation in psychoanalytic terms. But it is essential to acknowledge the obvious – that a child's acceptance of symbols is crucial if he is to increase his understanding of himself interacting with others, as well as to extend his knowledge through reading, writing and mathematics. The children with no basic skills who are referred to us for educational therapy give the impression that they have rarely been held in mind by an attachment figure. This seems to leave them in serious doubt about their own worth, or in extreme cases about whether they even exist at all. If an infant has striven to relate to an attachment figure who remains unavailable, how can an 'idea' of what she represents or symbolises begin to become internalised? If the experience of reality is elusive there is little the infant can find to get started towards symbol-usage. Even if they later manage to cope with reading or counting mechanically, they seem unable to attach meaning to these skills, and so cannot make use of or develop them.

It is important to remind ourselves of another aspect of learning that Bowlby discusses in his conceptualisation of proximity-keeping behaviour. It is worth recalling that in Bowlby's view a child manages to care desperately for an attachment figure, however rejecting that person's behaviour may seem over time. He said, 'indeed an attachment can develop despite repeated punishment from the attachment figure' (1977).

The children identified as belonging to Group A, whose early interaction with their mothers seemed so indifferent, had already given up at 12 or 18 months. Ainsworth in her review of the Strange Situation Study in 1986 said, 'like other infants they very much want close contact with the mother, feel angry because they expect to be rebuffed and are afraid both of a painful rebuff and of expressing the anger they feel'. She called this behaviour a 'defensive strategy'. By rejecting their mother's advances they were already expressing their anger towards her. She had not met their need for comfort at a time when it was most needed.

The children who have reached only minimal levels of attainment in their school learning, and who have formed these anxious attachments to rejecting figures early in their lives, may later adopt very different modes of attachment behaviour. They may develop a retaliatory stance, a reciprocal rejection: the child himself becomes punitive. He ignores his mother's commands and may even resort to hitting her. This anger is allied to fear, and reflects the child's feelings about his mother's behaviour towards him. He fears that his anger will result in the loss of mother if he begins to learn and become too independent of her (in fantasy a child may feel he can actually destroy her). Mother's attitude to scholastic skills contains a double message: what a clever boy he is, followed by resentment of his attempts to learn without her. He is not free to focus on exploratory learning in school.

Other children adopt restless behaviour to minimise their contact with others. This may be to avert rejection or they may have learned to keep busy to avoid thinking about their feelings.

The basic skills of Jackie, a girl of 12, were very limited, although she was referred for educational therapy only for her reading disability. All her attempts to become more secure in her attachment to her mother appear to have been thwarted by her mother's longing for a sibling who had died.

The loss of a stillborn child who is never mourned in our experience has had a long-term effect on the behaviour and learning of some of the siblings born subsequently. These children are so immersed in their efforts to be valued as they believe their dead sibling to be, that their capacity for updating, exploratory behaviour or goal-seeking remains at a minimal level, unless they and the family can be helped to mourn the loss.

THE EFFECT OF LOSS ON LEARNING – THE STILLBORN SIBLING

Beaumont (1988):

'In families where there has been a failure to mourn a stillbirth, subsequent children have difficulties with living and often with learning. Many ambivalent feelings surrounding the incompletely mourned loss can remain in a family, but reside most frequently in the mother; they may be picked up by any or occasionally all of the living children and cause problems for them as they become older. It is this question of ambivalent feelings that I feel we need to understand before focusing on the effect of a specific loss (such as a stillbirth) on children like Jackie.

'Freud (1917) suggested in his classic description of melancholia that the patient had unconsciously lost an object (see Chapter 2) for which he had retained ambivalent feelings of love and hatred. The internalisation of these negative feelings results in a lowering of self-esteem and ideas of self-denigration and self-punishment. Freud suggested that what distinguished melancholia from mourning was a lowering of "self-regard to a degree that finds utterance in self-reproaches and self revilings and culminates in a delusional expectation of punishment". Freud said, "the shadow of the object fell upon the ego". Byng-Hall (1973), in his work with families, adapted the aphorism and suggested that where there had been a death in the family "the image of the lost person can become resurrected in a remaining member of the family". I think that the "remaining member" can then feel guilty about occupying the place of the lost person. Any of the live children, therefore, may have to limit their achievements and spoil their own space, both to assuage this guilt and also to guard against retribution from the dead person. This was certainly true of Jackie: as a replacement child, she appeared to feel guilty about being alive at all and could not contemplate the possibility of enjoying herself. She had to make her whole existence unbearable to prevent herself from being envied by the stillborn child. This is, of course, a problem for the survivors of most disasters, such as those who lived through the holocaust or have survived accidents on any scale, whether the result of human error or by natural causes.

'It has been suggested that following a stillbirth it must be a problem for the mother to hold on to sufficient maternal preoccupation during any subsequent pregnancy. Her whole body and mind was centred on a whole, live, well baby, but if she has produced a dead one instead it must be almost impossible for her to commit herself to the idea of an alive child the next time.

> After a stillbirth there is a double sense of loss for the bereaved mother who has a void where there was evidently a fullness. Even with a live birth the mother feels a sense of loss but the consolation of a surviving 'outside baby' helps the mother to overcome her puzzling and bewildering sadness at losing her 'inside baby'.
>
> (Lewis and Page 1978)

With a stillbirth the mother has to cope with an outer as well as an inner void.

'Any children born after a stillborn infant may feel responsible for the death and damage to the sibling. Sometimes they appear to imagine that they shared the womb together and that the dead baby was killed by getting out first, leading the way into the dangerous world while they hung back in the safety of the womb. Other children imagine death as the envied state: it means returning to Mother Earth and, metaphorically, to the womb. So the child feels that by being alive he has somehow been pushed out and rejected. For a girl like Jackie her desire to get back inside is shown by the intrusiveness of her behaviour. If we consider Klein's view (1931) that the unconscious regards the mother's body as a container of all marvels and all knowledge, and, conversely, that the woman's body can also be a dreaded place of destruction, then, as she says, this could be a basic factor in inhibiting the desire for knowledge:

> it is essential for a favourable development of the desire for knowledge that the mother's body should be felt to be well and unharmed. It represents, in the unconscious, the treasure-house of everything desirable which can only be got from there; therefore, if it is not destroyed, not so much in danger and therefore not so dangerous itself, the wish to take food for the mind from it can more easily be carried out.
>
> (Klein 1931)

'This helped me to understand Jackie's dilemma. She believed that the idealised beloved dead baby was living inside her mother's body and so she wanted to go back there, too. On the other hand, she felt anxious about the contents of the mother's body because it was known to be damaged, thus making any exploration of it frightening. I imagine, therefore, that if the mother's body has proved to be a "place full of destruction" because it produces stillborn infants rather than live, healthy ones, or if it appears too fragile to withstand fantasised attacks from other unborn or born siblings, or the unborn foetus, then the wish to take in food for the mind from it must surely be imbued with all sorts of dreads and inhibitions.

'The replacement child feels guilt about occupying the place of the dead child, and feels envy because of the idealised and loved place the dead baby holds in her mother's mind and (in fantasy) in her body. She feels hatred and sadistic murderousness because she imagines she has killed off the dead baby and is still killing off non-existent subsequent ones. She also feels rejected because she has been pushed out of her mother's mind and body by the beloved dead infant. Jackie's fear of being unable to match a dead ideal, her sadistic destruction of what she and I had created, particularly the written word, and her guilt about living in someone else's shoes, all contributed to the inhibition of her learning. To me she was a person who had acquired "disagreeable and self-defeating ways of interacting" and had learned to exert certain disagreeable pressures (on others) through having suffered them herself.'

JACKIE

'Jackie is the youngest in a family of six children, living at home with her father, mother and elder sister. She was referred to the clinic because of her severe learning difficulties and her immaturity, although she was of average intelligence with no specific physical weakness other than a slight hearing loss. We already knew in the first family assessment interview that no live babies had been born since Jackie. Another girl had died at birth at the end of the fifth pregnancy; however, this was described as a miscarriage and was not discussed further. During this interview it seemed clear that it was in the parents' interest to preserve Jackie as the handicapped "baby" of the family. They emphasised that Jackie had fallen out of her cot and hit her head on a radiator when she was a young baby. She was also described by her mother as accident-prone and uninterested in taking care of herself. It was suggested by my colleague, a psychiatric social worker, that perhaps Jackie's apparent stupidity and rather infantile behaviour was a way of keeping the family together since the losses they had suffered. We suggested that Jackie seemed to accept this role placidly and to enjoy her powerful position of constant babyhood. The parents were unable to enter into any further discussion but agreed to see one member of the team for a brief contract, and agreed that Jackie would see me twice weekly for help with her basic skills.

'In my first individual assessment interview with Jackie I discovered that she could not score on any reading test and was apparently unable to remember any word that we read together, for longer than 30 seconds. She was a short, overweight child with darkish wavy hair, blue eyes, buck teeth and an appealing, friendly smile. She made me feel as if she was a plump, jolly baby, bouncing winsomely and determinedly in her pram, who absolutely refused to make any move towards adulthood. This idea was exacerbated by the way she dressed, which was reminiscent of a fat toddler. She would often appear in baby-pink long johns, white socks, a white vest and a grubby hip-length broderie anglaise petticoat.

'I discussed and explored with Jackie some of the reasons and wishes that people have for not wanting to grow up. Being grown up meant knowing and learning about things that one might not want to understand or hear. Jackie said that you had to read when you grew up. From this she began to make some move towards acknowledging that it was her decision not to read, but to try to remain a baby. In spite of this insight I felt strongly that she was constantly destroying any creative thinking that might be happening between us. She was provocative and stubborn about learning and I would often feel consumed by a desire to shake her. I soon became acutely aware of the murderous feelings her behaviour was eliciting in me. She would sit picking at the side of her mouth until she was disfigured by a red raw spot, and she would wring her hands and mock-wash them like Lady Macbeth.

'In one part of a session Jackie was trying to read from a reading scheme that uses a mainly phonic approach with constant repetition of words and is about the adventures of some little creatures known as the Fuzz Buzz. The sound of her voice belied the fact that she was a 12-year-old.

"Ooh, goodie, Macfuzz," Jackie puffed out her chest and clapped her hands. She opened the book and looked at a picture of a river pouring down a hill.

"Ooooh, it's a weeny, weeny lickle river up there," she exclaimed.

"Is there another way of saying weeny, weeny?" I asked.

There was a long pause – Jackie stuck out her bottom lip and looked sulky.

"Small," she said, "a small river."

"Good," I replied, "that's quite right." She began to read. She stopped at the word "first" and read "at the moment. The river is small at the moment."

"Well done, Jackie. You obviously understand what you are reading. But that word doesn't say 'moment' does it, it says 'at f ....' What word means at the moment but begins with the sound 'f ...? The river was little at f ...?"

"At figgy. The river was little at figgy. That's what it is."

"Jackie, I wonder why you've decided to destroy the meaning. We both know you know the word, but I think you're just showing me you want to stay a non-reading baby. You don't want to be a growing-up 12-year-old."

"I don't know it. I don't ... I don't. At Fred – at fink." Jackie stamped.

"It reminds me of the time when you wouldn't read the word 'letter'. Do you remember, you kept saying the postman delivers parcels, envelopes, stamps – everything except letters?"

152

"I don't know 'letters' and I don't know 'first'." Jackie pouted, stuck out her bottom lip, and read furiously, "The river was little at first."

'Her imaginative play at this time suggested that she was very concerned about the other members of her family. She seemed to feel that there were murderous feelings towards herself and from herself towards her parents and also between her parents. She also continued to feel anxious about growing up. Age was synonymous with infirmity for Jackie. There was, too, a sadistic quality in her feelings towards me. She constantly made me feel that she was attacking any activities we undertook together. She would enter the room with a mixture of a waddle and a pounce, nose in the air, sit down over-purposefully, give a little bounce, clap her hands, open her book, squeal, "I know it," and say something like: "Sugar under cover is yellow jam!" when what was written was, "Shorty started to bark." On these occasions I said nothing, and just waited quietly. Jackie would continue, "That's right – I know it is. Oh no! Shorty ... um ... um ... started ... to ... laugh .... Oh, no, dogs don't laugh ... ha, ha, ha ... bark .... That's it .... Shorty started to bark ...."

'By the end of her first term with me, I thought that Jackie became fearful whenever there were any signs of progress. It was as though she anticipated disaster in every step forward. She seemed to be firmly convinced that success spelt pain and trauma, so it was better to remain a non-reading, non-learning child. She was frightened of failure and also terrified of success.

'A year after I had started seeing her I felt that, although her ability to decipher words had improved, she was sadistically enjoying making rubbish of the text by misreading to such an extent that the result was nonsensical (e.g. "For the rest of the afternoon" became "For the ready of the apinoog"). I suggested then that she rubbished her handwriting, her reading and her speech in the same way, in order to turn everything she did into a meaningless mess. If she continued to do this she could not be envied for being alive. (I made this comment while still unaware of the stillbirth following her mother's fifth pregnancy – the "miscarriage" referred to in the family interview.) At this time she told me that her mother had been ill. I suggested that she must have been very worried when her mother was in hospital. "Yes," she said, "there's been lots of deaths in our family. My mum's kid sister died of cancer and her father died two years after I was born and she had a baby between Peter and Patsy that died." I asked her if she would like to tell me about the baby and she said, "Oh, it was born with half a face; it was in them old-fashioned days and my mum smothered it with a pillow – murder it was, I suppose. Sometimes I think the baby's angry with me because I've got the baby's bedroom, you see, and it comes into my bedroom and messes it up and spoils it. The baby was called Patsy [her elder sister's name] and that makes Patsy very angry, you know. I don't know what I would've been called. Perhaps I wouldn't've been there." She reported this in a matter-of-fact tone of voice, but it made me understand even more clearly about her unwillingness to grow up. I began to recognise that Jackie felt haunted by the feeling that she had replaced the dead, possibly handicapped, baby, and therefore she must not risk allowing her own life to become too perfect.

'The feeling that Jackie was haunted continued. The fact that she could invoke murderous, angry feelings in others seemed to be connected to her feeling that she had, or wished she had, murdered her mother's babies. One day she misread "elbow" in spite of contextual and pictorial clues. She read it as "eggwag" and thus made nonsense of the text. I said, "Jackie, stop it!" (I felt upset by my angry tone.) She looked very alarmed and said, "Oh, sorry, elbow."

'Later, during the same session, I was struck by two of her miscues: "until you find me" became "under my feet" and "hug" became "gun". I wondered to myself whether she felt that her mother actively disliked her and would like to get rid of her, and also whether she felt that she wanted to murder what her mother had made.

'Meanwhile, the theme of haunting remained. During the last session of that term she described her adventures of the previous evening when she was in a friend's house with three other girls including her sister. When they were answering the telephone in the kitchen they heard a scream and a mug fell to the floor, which the girls decided was due to a ghost. I asked Jackie what she thought the ghost was.

"Not the dead baby," she replied aggressively and somewhat melo-dramatically.

"Well, who?" I enquired.

"I don't know, but it takes forty dogs and a vicar to get rid of it."

'I wondered to myself whether she was telling me that her ghost was one that was going to be particularly difficult to exorcise, or maybe she did not want to get rid of it anyway. Perhaps if this was a brief phase of ambivalence it could be a move forward from her previously-expressed destructive feelings.

'Several sessions after this episode Jackie reinforced the impression that she wanted to hold on to her infantile behaviour at all costs. She misread "indeed" as "in baby". When we began to explore this she drew a picture of her mother's bedroom. At the end of the double bed was a rocking chair, and in it a life-sized doll dressed, apparently, in Jackie's christening robes. I wondered with Jackie what the doll made her feel. "Sad," she said, "but my mum likes talking to it and it cheers her up." (I discovered from the other member of the team who visited the family home that this was true.) Later that week she drew a picture of a baby girl ghost which she agreed was her little, dead sister. "I like it. It's not a frightening ghost – I want to keep it forever." When she told me this I felt she was trying to let me know how angry and despairing she felt with her mother for hanging on to the idealised, plastic image of the dead baby. There was nothing she could do to alter her mother's stubborn insistence on hugging this dummy to her.

'A few weeks before I finally said goodbye to Jackie she demonstrated her wish to intrude into the dead baby's space. She was telling me about a recurring dream.

"I always dream the same dream. I dream a murderer's chasing me and my friends tell me to jump off a cliff because he's chasing me."

"That doesn't seem very helpful of your friends," I commented.

"Oh, well, it's only a little cliff. There's a lot of little cliffs where I live."

"In Stockwell?" (a poor, over-crowded district of London).

"Well, you know what I mean. It's quite safe to jump over them."

"I'm wondering why the murderer wanted to murder you."

"Well, I invaded her private property."

"Her?"

"Him, I mean. I invaded his private property. I ran along this half bridge which is broken at the end. It goes over some water and I jumped into the private property. Look, I'll draw it." She drew the picture.

"It looks to me as though you've missed the private property and you're going to fall into the water. Perhaps that's why you keep having accidents."

"No, it's all right, I get into it. Really there's no one in it but the murderer thinks it's hers."

"She's an awfully small murderer. She looks like a baby to me – a baby murderer."

"Oh, here I'll change it," said Jackie, very anxiously.

I said, "It's OK. I think I understand what you're telling me."

'Jackie quietly returned to her book, reading avidly with no mistakes other than reading "strange" as "strangle". She finished the session by asking if she could paint the clay cradle she had started the week before. She said she wanted to paint it white on the outside and bright red inside.

"I think I'll paint the baby black. No, no, I mean white," she added.

'As she jabbed the brush viciously into the cradle I observed a mixture of emotions on her face: the pouting, trembling lip of the rejected toddler who feels ousted by the intrusion of a dead baby into her life, combined with an intensely loving gratitude and possessiveness.

'It seemed to me that Jackie needed to punish herself for her intrusive wishes and the damage she felt she had caused both to the dead baby and to her mother. To return to Klein's idea (1931), since Jackie felt unconsciously that she had damaged her mother's body she was unable to learn, both because she felt responsible and guilty for the damage she had inflicted on it, and also because she feared taking in knowledge from this damaged interior belonging to her mother. It seemed impossible for her to tolerate the idea of the progress she was making with her basic skill learning. She had within the past four months been knocked down by a car, fractured her ankle, had her tonsils out, fallen off the rope in the adventure playground, slipped over in the mud and cut her knee, and on another occasion her heel, on the way to the clinic. Her escort described Jackie crossing the road in front of her: "When the lights are green she starts to cross, but she doesn't go in a straight line. She wobbles towards the trafic almost as if she wants to get run over."

'As well as wishing to punish herself for being alive, did Jackie feel also that the only way her mother would appreciate her was if she remained handicapped in some way by not learning? Or if she was seriously injured in an "accident" would she resemble the dead baby with "half a face" and thus be loved as much as her? Her ambivalence towards her mother was her predicament. She loved her mother dearly, her mother had brought her alive into the world, she had cared materially for her and was continuing to care for her. On the other hand she hated her for her preoccupation with the dead baby, for allowing the baby to die (although, as Jackie herself said, she [Jackie] might not be alive if the baby had lived), for her failure to mourn the death and for her mother's eternal reverie with a dead object.

'On reflection, I think Jackie and I shared many ambivalent feelings toward one another. I felt at times that she must have wondered if I too was preoccupied, not with dead babies, but with the other children that Jackie knew I was seeing. Did I really care or have enough space in my mind for her? If her work did not change she could remain with me, with only her to care for. I often felt angry with her when she destroyed our interaction, or filled the sessions with her rubbish; but, at the same time I was aware of witnessing her pain and hopeless despair.'

The educational therapist who worked with Jackie has chosen to add another dimension to our understanding of the sadness of this girl's life. She thinks it was shared by two famous artists.

'The first, Salvador Dali, who was born after the death of his elder brother, also named Salvador, described his experience in *Unspeakable Confessions* (Parinaud 1977):

> I lived my death before living my life. At the age of 7 my brother died of meningitis, 3 years before I was born. This shook my mother to the very depths of her being. This brother's precociousness, his genius, his grace, his handsomeness were to her so many delights, his disappearance was a terrible shock. She was never to get over it. My parents' despair was assuaged only by my own birth, but their misfortune penetrated every cell of their bodies and within my mother's womb I could already feel their angst. My foetus swam in an infernal placenta. Their anxiety never left me .... Many is the time I have relived the life and death of this elder brother whose traces were everywhere.... I feel he was a kind of test run for myself.

'The second artist to have had a similar experience was discussed by Nagera (1967) in his psychoanalytic study. He explored in detail the effect of being the subsequent child after a stillbirth, and cites another famous example – Vincent van Gogh, who was born exactly a year after the loss of his stillborn brother (also named Vincent). He wrote:

The brother, being stillborn, had never had an identity of his own reality, but for this very reason an ideal one had been created in the phantasy life of the parents. He would have been the perfect child, the compendium of all virtue, ability and kindness. He would have always done everything right, and especially where Vincent failed, the other, the dead Vincent, would have been successful. This extreme degree of idealisation of a dead child explains the high ego-ideals which he set himself, his dread of failing, and his fear of success .... Against such high ego-ideals he would, of course, nearly always fall short.

'Van Gogh committed suicide only a few months after the birth of another Vincent, his brother Theo's child.'

How can the loss of an unknown, unseen sibling possibly be mourned? Even when the loss is of a known sibling there remains a need for an attachment figure who can be available and not overwhelmed by their own grief.

The following two children had not acquired many scholastic skills, though plenty of 'street-wise' ones. They were from very different backgrounds, one from a children's home and one from a two-parent family of mixed racial origins. Both children had lost siblings in fatal accidents, and there had been no emotionally available adult to help either of them to mourn their loss.

One of the children, Marie, aged 9, formed a strong attachment to another sibling who, it is thought, was too preoccupied with her own mourning to be able to support Marie. An educational therapist worked with Marie for nearly two years before Marie could bring memories of her dead sister to several sessions. She eventually constructed a model of a graveyard and made some flowers and a headstone bearing the name of her lost sister, thus allowing herself to begin a process of mourning. The residue of the angry feelings towards the adult thought to be responsible for her sibling's death, however, precluded the expression of grief. It was thought at the time that although her reading improved, Marie's circumstances made it unlikely that any lasting progress, either emotionally or scholastically, would be maintained. Three years later Marie asked for a further visit to her educational therapist. She was offered three sessions, only one of which was taken up. Information from members of the community network over the following two years unfortunately confirmed the prediction about Marie, who became obese and depressed. She stayed at home, refusing any professional help.

A 9-year-old boy, Donald, had witnessed the death of his older sibling (to whom he was closely attached) shortly after starting school. At the time of referral Donald had acquired no basic skills and he was behaving in a manner that made him uncontainable in school. In his educational therapy sessions he spent several weeks drawing maps; these became more and more complicated and yet the roads and rivers never led in any clear direction or to any destination. His therapist reported:

'Donald responded to my suggestion that he might draw maps showing the way to known local buildings like the swimming pool, the school and his home. He struggled to label these buildings. During the next session he drew a different map. This showed where his brother had been killed and included details that were relevant to the death. Finally he added a road leading to the cemetery where his brother had been buried. After Donald had placed the name on a cross in the cemetery he sat very quietly for several minutes. In the weeks following this moving session I was amazed at the speed at which he began to learn. I wondered if he had now given himself permission to go beyond the level of learning that his brother might have reached at the time of his death.'

This may have been a contributory factor, in addition to the difficulties arising from the experience of his parents' separation and being a member of two reconstituted families from an early age (Robinson 1982). It is known that at 14 Donald was continuing to make steady progress in school.

EDUCATIONAL THERAPY WITH JASON IN A SCHOOL SETTING

Casimir (1987, unpublished paper):

Jason

This boy was referred by an educational psychologist for educational therapy as part of his Special Needs Support Programme. The therapist who worked with Jason had a dual role: she provided individual educational therapy for him, and in the classroom she was his learning support teacher.

The therapist described her work with 10-year-old Jason as follows:

'When I first met Jason he was entering his final year in his junior school and was quite unable to learn independently. He had attended an off-site tutorial class for reading for two years but had made "no observable progress". He found number work even more difficult and had resisted all attempts to teach him. His books were empty; his desk was crammed with small toys. I felt his mind was full of anxiety. I was told that he had received five years' intensive speech therapy from the age of 2 when he had entered a nursery school with a "significant language delay". In his first school he was described as "enjoying play, but had difficulty in settling to tasks, was disruptive and had frequent temper tantrums". On his move to the junior school the staff became increasingly worried. Jason presented himself as an affable boy but he was unable to learn. In the class group he avoided tasks and withdrew to the world of his toys. He rejected any one-to-one teaching that wasn't on his own omnipotent terms with refusals and tantrums, demanding only mothering.

He clung tenaciously to spoon feeding and resisted all attempts at weaning on to independent learning. My knowledge of his family life remained sketchy; there was little factual information available to me, only hints about traumas associated with loss and violence when he was very young.

'I began my first session with Jason by reading to him for about 10 minutes, and this was to become the pattern for all future sessions. Jason fed voraciously on the story as a contented baby, almost lying back on his chair. But as soon as I finished reading his behaviour changed. It seemed as though he was trying to express his feelings about his past experience of pain of loss and anger, which were in danger of overwhelming him. I wondered if we would ever reach a degree of gratification that would satisfy this appetite. However, from the first session he responded well to the space and boundaries he was given by vigorously addressing his preoccupations. At my suggestion he dictated a story.

King Yellow, The Scared King

A long time ago there was a king, who had a son called King Yellow. King Yellow was in love with a princess but she did not love him. She loved Prince Hood. Prince Hood's castle was next to King Yellow's. Prince Hood and the princess were planning to get married. King Yellow wanted to stop them. He sent one of his messengers to the princess's castle to give her a message. This is what it said, 'Prince Hood died in war.' The princess read this message and in a few days she died of grief. Then Prince Hood came to look for her up in the mountains and it started to snow. The Prince died of a disease. The ice covered the prince and the princess and when you go up into the mountains you can see an outline of them in the ice.

'In this story Jason introduced the idea of a father who had a scared, unloveable son. This son is rejected by his love object (attachment figure) in favour of a good son. We could interpret this as Jason's bad, angry, omnipotent self as represented by King Yellow. This self is so powerful that it can kill the loved figure and is, hence, scared of its own anger. I thought Prince Hood represented the good part of Jason that tries to repair the damage by mourning. But this good part is, in turn, killed off and preserved under the ice with the love object. Jason, it seemed, had suffered overwhelming loss a long time ago that he had not been able to mourn adequately, leaving him with an angry, destructive and vengeful sense of self to manage.

'At this time I did not, of course, make such a clear interpretation to him but just acknowledged Jason's powerful communication about the pain of loss. I decided to show Jason that I understood what he was saying by choosing *Badger's Parting Gifts* by Susan Varley (1984) to read to him in our next session. This is a poignant children's story that uses woodland creatures to depict death and mourning. Jason clearly derived a great deal from this book which he kept in his box for the rest of the year. After I had read this story

Jason made his own "Badger" out of plasticine. He told me that this badger was dead but his spirit lived in his box. I commented that we can go on feeling sad about people who die for a long time, but that gradually we can learn to grieve and begin to manage these feelings so that we don't feel sad all the time. Jason told me that his great aunt had died when he was 2 and that he had been unable to speak for two years after that. He described how he kept her picture on his wall and I realised that this was the first time that he had been able to talk about his grief. Jason then began dictating another story:

> Once upon a time a boy made a badger out of plasticine. Badger was dead. His spirit passed out of the box and went to heaven. His body was mashed back into a piece of plasticine. The boy missed Badger but he thought of something; he thought of the good things that Badger had left him. Badger sent the boy a print of his hand and a message. This is what it said: 'I have sent you a print of my hand to help you remember me. I will come and visit you in time.' So the boy waited and waited. He was losing his patience. A week later Badger came as a spirit to talk to the boy about something special. This is what he said. 'Soon my spirit will come down into the plasticine and form my body and I will come alive again. Next time I come back I will be alive.' *But*, something happened. Badger's wife died and she went to heaven. So Badger came to tell the boy that he wanted to be with his wife in heaven. The boy was very upset. He was so upset that he told Badger to go and never come back again. Badger was very unhappy because the boy didn't listen to what he was going to say. He was going to say that he would come later for a holiday but the boy didn't listen.

'Jason dictated this story over three sessions. Its similarities to his "King Yellow" story are striking. The written message is used to deceive and betray. The bad, angry, omnipotent part of the boy sends away the good, dead loved one. When Jason had finished dictating this story I wondered aloud if Badger *ever* came back? "No, because he was too frightened of the boy's anger," he replied. Here again the anger is all-powerful and destructive. It also prevents the boy from listening and hence learning something good.

'This was the last story Jason dictated for a long time. He told me quite clearly "not to put the angry parts in a story". Very slowly he absorbed ideas from the stories I read him into his own play and story-telling, but facing the independent task of reading was intolerably difficult. Learning involves relinquishing the old and familiar state of mind and behaviour, before one can take in anything new, and I came to realise that Jason equated giving up or leaving something behind with abandonment; therefore learning was a threat to him. My task seemed to be to enable Jason to move on from his present very immature stage without the fear of abandonment.

'After creating his story the pattern of our session changed. Jason brought his own materials – a collection of small plastic toys and introduced them to me one by one. First there was Guy, the Gorilla, who was named after the

160

gorilla that died at London Zoo. He was a good character who was also very, very angry because he had killed the mummy gorilla. Then there was Dr Lobster, the wise old doctor who could cure all diseases, even cancer. I was given Bluey, the Dolphin, an ordinary but rare dolphin. Lastly, there was Eagle of Death, Prince of Hell. Jason's box became the Crystal Castle inhabited by these creatures, and the stage for much of the dramatic play that followed.

'During every session the characters of Guy and Eagle engaged in vicious fighting, cheating, suffering and betrayal. Guy was supported, morally by Bluey the Dolphin, and physically by Dr Lobster, who tended him when he was hurt. Jason became completely engrossed in this play. It was very painful to watch but Jason let me know very forcefully that it was something I could not share. "You can't feel their pain. Only I can because I created them."

'In the last session before the first holiday break Jason brought a new character for his play, Gnasher, a large, furry, very strong and very hungry dog. In the play, Eagle offers Gnasher 100 sausages if he will capture Guy for him. Gnasher does this, collects his bribe and Guy is imprisoned. However, Gnasher then tells Dr Lobster and Bluey what has happened. They offer him a golden bone, the power of the box, if he will free Guy and imprison Eagle instead. Gnasher performs this task; he then "turns out the sun and returns home to his children with 100 sausages and a golden bone", Eagle is safely in the dungeon and "Guy and Bluey can sleep in the box." Jason was able through this symbolic play to check the disintegration and take some good feeling away with him for the first break.

'The next few months, after the break, were to prove full of difficulties. Jason and his mother, Mrs Evans, had to make a choice of secondary school for him. She discussed this with Jason's class teacher and myself. Shortly after visiting a number of schools and choosing one, Jason's mother came to see me again. It was at this meeting that she shared her own understanding of "how the trouble started". She explained that she went to live with her aunt and uncle who offered her a home when she became pregnant. Shortly after Jason's birth her aunt became seriously ill. She was nursed at home and during this time a strong bond developed between Jason and his great aunt. Jason was 20 months old when she died and the family disintegrated. Mrs Evans's great-uncle evicted her and Jason from the house, and returned to his country of origin. The toddler and his mother stayed with friends for some months until they were housed by the local authority. She found this an extremely difficult time, trying to manage her loss and her toddler on her own for the first time. In recalling these events she felt she had rejected Jason. When he began to attend a nursery school a few months later, aged 2, he had no speech.

'Mrs Evans then told me that she had sought counselling and had become reunited with her uncle, who had returned to England. The birth and development of her second child had restored her confidence and she had gained a place at college. Her concern for Jason however remained.

'In the Autumn term Jason was having to face the prospect of several changes: transition to a much larger school in the near future; an unexpected change of class teacher after the Christmas break; and a further unforeseen change was the remarriage of his great-uncle. The import of these events was reflected in his sessions. He abandoned his play with his animals and made himself two "Lego" models, the "change machines", which inhabited a bleak world where things change and betray each other unpredictably "because they don't trust each other," Jason said. He made them wage war endlessly by making a cacophony of angry sounds, then he began showing me that I was to be held responsible for all these changes in his life.

'After playing for some time Jason turned the smaller machine towards me. He said: "You think it can't do anything, but it is really very powerful. It can destroy the big one." In the ensuing fight the big model lost its good part to the small one, which then attacked this and destroyed the big one. Jason continued to think about mistrust, betrayal and destruction until the end of this first term. He accused me of being an impostor, only pretending to be his educational therapist. At other times he claimed that he was not Jason, but an impostor who had come to destroy Jason's box. I felt that the box was only saved by my intervention. It seemed important that the box should remain intact as a symbol and container of the reality of the sessions, and the many feelings that had been expressed within them. A break was near and I did not want Jason to leave with an internalised image of us both as impostors. At the suggestion of a colleague I took some photographs of Jason with his box and the characters he had created. He gave me one of these pictures and took the other home for his holiday.

'In the sessions following the break Jason chose to make direct reference to his past. When we met after the break it was a cold, snowy January which evoked powerful memories for Jason. He remembered that it was extremely cold at home when his great-aunt had died, when he was 20 months old. He then told me how he "punishes" his young half sister (also 20 months old at the time Jason was recounting these events) by shutting her in a room with his toys and pretending to go away so that she cries – as he had done. Following this Jason referred to his (unknown) father for the first time. He said he thought he had gone away to join the armed forces and had not managed to find his family again. "Maybe he was still searching for Jason," he said.

'This comment by Jason about Jason was the beginning of his working through the thoughts and feelings of his "true self" by somehow distancing himself from the adventures of the character/impostor Jason. He was able to make use of the metaphorical boy in his play and stories, although from time to time this interaction slipped into direct references to the real Jason. He also began to draw to express some of his feelings. His first picture was of "Mr Confident (a little bit)", whom Jason would help to learn.

'It was a visit of the educational psychologist who had referred Jason to test his reading and ability to "Draw a Man" (Goodenough 1926) that helped

Jason to focus on his rage again. This testing took place in our session time for reasons over which I had no control. Jason refused to hear or accept my apology and was furious. Afterwards he asked me, "What would you do if I shot you?" I replied that I could survive his anger. "But would *you* be angry?" he wanted to know. "I would manage these feelings!" I said. We then read the story of *Angry Arthur* by H. Oram (1982), after which Jason began a series of pictures, with captions, which he called "Jason's Anger Against Ms Casimir" [the educational therapist]. We were depicted as two spaceships warring in space. Jason's spaceship attacked and tried to destroy my ship until, finally, I was made to escape in a small rocket, calling out "I'll return."

'I suggested that as this was such a powerful theme we might put his pictures in a book, which he did; the drawings were accompanied by a dialogue and some writing. Within this drama I was forced to take my revenge and we continued to fight until Jason killed me in "The Final Conflict". "You are killed off now – you're dead," Jason screamed, fighting back the tears. I commented on how bad this must feel. This was too direct for Jason. "No, Jason doesn't care. He doesn't feel anything. It serves you right." But I was made to continue speaking from the grave, which Jason attempted to burn. "You see," Jason told me, looking straight into my face, "Jason's anger goes on and on. He doesn't care."

'Jason then appeared to become paralysed by the weight he was carrying of all his destructive, unmanageable anger. He was unable to draw any more. "You draw the next part in red," he commanded. So I drew a picture of myself "filled up with Jason's anger". My question "Where's Jason?" enabled him to continue: "He's keeping himself to himself. He's glad that he is not there. You'll have to get angry with someone else. I'm relaxing in the sun where you can't find me. No more clues." I was reminded of his great-uncle relaxing in the sun of his country of origin. I inserted one more picture of myself saying that I'd managed my angry feelings, I felt relaxed and would look for Jason in the sun.

'Jason then drew an island and continued with the story:

On Palm Tree Island

It's a lovely place; it's warm, relaxing and food is brought to you. You drink mango juice from coconut shells and eat fruit salads. Jason, David and Ms Casimir are swimming in the sea. My mum is getting a sun tan. Jason has no relaxing problems. He got a good job and bought his island. He saved his money when he was small. Now I am 20 Ms Casimir has come to help David. Guy the Gorilla came too. There are no angry feelings on Palm Tree Island. We have got rid of all our angry feelings. But here comes a hungry whale to eat Ms Casimir. Luckily Jason gets out his knife and kills it. I stabbed it with a knife. A good job I helped you, Ms Casimir.

'With the imminence of another holiday break ahead angry feelings began to intrude upon this paradise island. Jason told me, "This is my island. You are in danger because I don't like you, so you must go." I made links between his feelings about the coming break to his words in the story by speaking in role as Ms Casimir, who was both me and a character in his drama. Like many other children, Jason was getting rid of me as a way of defending against his own feelings that I was getting rid of him at the onset of the break. I said: "I don't want to go. I feel shut out. You betrayed me. You said I could come to the island but now you say I must go. I don't know where to go." Jason's response was to draw my spaceship again, this time it was struck by lightning in a storm. He said "I don't care. I'm going home." Having transferred his feelings to me he was able to leave. I felt that this appropriate defence against feelings about our enforced separation, that must have renewed earlier feelings of loss and abandonment, led to a beginning of being able to face them. During this dramatisation Jason began to have more energy for learning. He started to look at the words he was reading and tried to think about what they might say. He could use the sound of the first letter in a word as a clue, and he wrote some short stories. His progress was extremely slow and he needed help at the level one might give to a much younger child's first attempts at creative writing.

'Having seen that we both survived the break, Jason plunged straight back into his anger, greeting me with an emphatic "Goodbye." In class he was very resistant to my support for his class activity learning and in our sessions his vehemence was very hard to contain. He brought a new character for his play, a small plastic dinosaur which he called Tridor. Tridor had "lost his parents when he was young and was out to revenge himself on the murderers". The Eagle of Death told Tridor that it was Guy and Bluey who killed them. Tridor and Guy battled until Guy and Bluey were buried in a sand tray. Jason said they were "stuck". He then left this story until the last session of that term. In retrospect I think this play became too close to his own reality for him to be able to continue it.

'I decided to read Jason an ongoing story, *James and the Giant Peach*, by Roald Dahl (1961), a few chapters at a time, as a way of providing continuity. I thought that a story in book form would enable events to be held in mind and that future events might be predicted. The story is about James, a small boy inhabiting a hostile world, who was able to escape from, and triumph over, his adversaries. Jason took in ideas directly from this story for use in his own play. He brought a small figure called Yoda and began the drama of Yoda and the Magic Box and followed them on a journey over the rainbow to another paradise island where it was hot and exotic fruit grew. This play was both serious but yet relaxed and in sharp contrast to the very difficult Jason that I was encountering for most of each session. He continually tried to push me into an open confrontation. "I don't like you! I don't care about you!" he shouted and on one occasion he threatened me with a pair of school scissors.

My job, it seemed, was to contain his anxiety and anger and to continue helping him to express it by use of the metaphor, despite his resistance. During one session he chose to play "squiggles" and produced a series of pictures that expressed his feelings about our interaction again revealing his anger and pain and feelings of desolation.

'At this period Mrs Evans asked to talk to me at school because she felt Jason was behaving more like a 2-year-old at home, exhibiting temper tantrums and difficult behaviour. I discovered that she had had to spend a few days in hospital with her daughter. When they returned home this child's father spent some time with them. We both agreed that all this had proved too great a test for Jason's fragile maturity; it was yet another re-enactment of his abandonment, this time by his "new" family.

'I was not sure how Jason would react to my meeting with his mother, especially as it was near the end of term. However, he was able to use the ending to think about the very painful loss of his own father. He returned to his play with Tridor, the dinosaur that had lost his parents. Tridor was now grown up and had lost his son. A new character, Tiger, claimed that he had killed Tridor's son and a vicious battle ensued in which Tridor killed Tiger. But in his dying moments Tiger admitted that he did not kill the son but took him away and hid him in the mountains. Tridor then "unstuck" the other characters, Guy and Bluey from the sand (where they had been all term). They searched for many years for the lost son who was waiting, wondering if his father would ever come. For Jason the ending was almost unbearable – father and son are reunited and fill a plasticine bowl with their tears. Jason ended this session early with a long silence, and as he left said, "I'll see you next term." Thus he was able to tolerate the break and manage old losses with less of his previous anger and despair.

'For the summer term I chose *Charlotte's Web*, by E.B. White (1952), as our story with its appropriate theme – the power of the written word to convey messages as well as its handling of death. I also asked Jason to choose three words from the story each week to make his own sentence. Jason's first sentence was "Bad pig has stopped crying," which coincided with a dramatic improvement in his attitude to classwork. He began to work out words using his rudimentary phonic knowledge, when reading to me; he attempted some workbooks for his class teacher and started to participate in lessons, raising his hand to give answers and comments. Acknowledging this progress, Jason's class teacher sensitively removed the toys from Jason's desk, put them in a bag and suggested that he was now ready to take them home. Jason accepted this message – that it was time to move on to becoming a 10-year-old.

'When we came to the chapter in *Charlotte's Web* entitled "The Miracle", Jason wrote the sentence "It was a miracle when I was born." He followed this by a statement: "When I was born I spoke immediately. I said 'dada' and then I cried but I didn't make any noise. The nurse had to tell my mum that

I was crying. They couldn't hear me at first but then they heard [here he made a series of pre-verbal sounds]. Now they understand me." These moving autobiographical words needed no comment from me.

'In the last session of this very short half term Jason was again able to use the break to think about how loss had contributed to his feelings of impotence by transferring these feelings on to me. He took the plasticine and made three figures that were, he said, a "pop group" who sang a song to me. Jason then made another pop group that he handed to me. He said, "Now your group must sing the song." I protested that I didn't know the words or the tune. "Learn it then," Jason said, "I'm not going to help you." "But I can't," I replied. "You can. If you can't I'll destroy Bluey." With this Jason flung the plastic figure of Bluey, the dolphin, my character, into the rubbish bin. I was rubbish because I couldn't learn the words. Jason left Bluey in the bin, which I felt meant he was leaving the 'rubbish' part of himself behind.

'When Jason returned to school for his final half term in the Junior School, he had "ending" firmly in the forefront of his mind. He was very anxious about his transfer to his next school and I told him that I would make a visit to discuss his educational needs with his new teachers there. He then decided to clear out his box and keep the things that he wanted in a folder so that "when he destroyed the box, at the end, I could keep the valuables as a memory".

'In our last sessions we read the part of *Charlotte's Web* where the spider dies. Jason found this very painful and hurled the book across the room shouting that he hated Charlotte. We talked about the way Wilbur (another character) managed his feelings in the story – remembering the good things Charlotte had left him and making new plans for the future. "You gave me the box," Jason commented. "Well, I let you discover the stories in the box for yourself," I replied. "Yes," he said. "It was Jason's creation." The last sentence he chose to make was taken directly from the text of *Charlotte's Web* which was, "She was a good friend and a good writer."

'At my first meeting with the educational psychologist we had discussed the possibility of my moving into the secondary school with Jason, to offer him support over the transfer period. Jason had very mixed feelings about this plan. Clearly, he felt relieved but he also felt angry – that such a difficult part of himself would be following him into his new school. "Why do you have to come? You'll be saying I need help forever!" He stormed around the room, refusing to do anything and becoming extremely abusive. We looked back at the "squiggles" that he had done and found the "Creature who had his power safely in his tail". Jason then became calm and serious and began to tell me "a story that must not be written down": It was about a girl who wanted to leave home to "explore on her own". She was eaten by a witch but saved by a wizard.

'Jason used the last few weeks of our sessions to play out and dictate the story of "Jason's Creation". It is written in a style exactly as he wished.

Starring:
The Evil Eagle
The Power of Good, Dr Lobster
The Strength of Good, Guy the Gorilla
The Undefeatable Badger
The Faithful Bluey, assistant to Dr Lobster
Tridor the Rescuer

It was a nice warm, sunny day and Guy the Gorilla thought he would go for a walk on the island. BUT the Evil Eagle and his invisible guards caught Guy and beat him up with sticks and hard stones and threw him in the dungeon. Eagle sent a message to Badger's cave. This is what it said: I've got Guy trapped in my dungeon. If you want him come and get him. Dr Lobster came to rescue Guy but he lost the fight with Eagle. 10, 9, 8 ... EXPLOSION. Tridor smashed through the dungeon wall and set them free. Eagle was M A D. The battle between Eagle and Tridor begins but Tridor is shot in the side by one of the invisible guards. Badger uses his special powers to get everyone back to the castle. Dr Lobster looks at Tridor's wound. Tridor does not give up that easily. The allies return to get their revenge but lose again and are imprisoned. Tridor, with a new strength, bursts open the dungeon and kills Eagle. BUT, Eagle rose again. This is not the end. When you find out how bad Eagle is you will never forgive him. He is so mean and bloodthirsty that he killed Bluey. Eagle makes a fake Bluey and fools them that Bluey is still alive. 'The allies are going to get their revenge.' Tridor digs his way in – SMASH – the bars of thunder light fall on Guy and with his strength he destroys Eagle. The allies could never find Bluey. He left his memory. But Eagle rises again and disappears to a castle on the Equator. All of a sudden there is a CRASH and a BANG and thunder and lightning. In 10 seconds everything returns to normal. Eagle is DEAD FOR GOOD. 'Who did that?' asked Guy. Badger replies, 'The FORCE OF GOOD, Jason himself.'

'Jason planned his final session very carefully. He decided there would be a ceremony to mark the death and destruction of his box. The characters were assembled for the ritual and they all wept their tears into the plasticine bowl he had made. Jason then began slowly to break up the box. As he worked he became more vigorous until, finally, he tore it apart and put it into the bin. "Now only the spirit of the box is left. It will go with me to the secondary school." I recalled Badger's Spirit and how the boy had felt betrayed and not seen Badger again. "Oh no, the boy has got him out of his system, he's forgotten that," Jason answered.

'The school were able to arrange for me to spend the last day with Jason, and he handled himself with a new maturity and confidence. He took part in the "Leavers' Assembly" and read out his "memory" of the school, which included a reference to one of the teachers he had had when he was 8 years old. He had assembled his thoughts and played them on tape to all the children in the school, the staff group, and the parents. On saying goodbye to his class teacher he asked, "Why do things have to die?" "Because the body stops repairing itself," was the reply. "Luckily for us their spirit lives on," said Jason and went on his way.

'At the time of this major transition Jason's approach to basic skill tasks was different; he was now struggling to master them rather than putting all his energies into avoiding them. His head teacher commented that he had grown about 10 years in the past one.'

Jason in the secondary school

Jason transferred to his new school with his therapist as planned by the educational psychologist and herself, with the agreement of Jason and his mother, and the co-operation of the head of the Special Needs Programme. The therapist gives a brief résumé of their work of two terms in the new setting.

'I saw Jason twice a week, supporting him in a range of subject lessons as well as continuing our educational therapy sessions which had been negotiated with the school staff. He adjusted to the many necessary changes of room and teachers with his new-found confidence. I could see he was popular with his peers, and was seen as "co-operative and enthusiastic, despite his difficulties", by his teachers (with the exception of his mathematics teacher who felt "unable to make allowances for children like Jason in class"). However, he was placed in a small group, where he was encouraged to follow an individual mathematics programme. He was described by the teacher of this group as "keenly competitive and reading successfully". He discovered an interest in home economics, where he led a class project in which his recipe and design for a new brand of confectionery was voted the best. This has led to his ambition to own a restaurant serving the food of the country where his great-aunt and uncle had been born.

'In our sessions Jason made it clear from the outset that we were here "to work and not talk about feelings". He used his energies primarily to improve his reading skills, by making a concerted effort to master the school reading scheme and to make use of phonics for spelling. I was interested that in spite of his opening remarks in our first session, he showed how much of our previous year's work he held in mind. There were references to the old characters and stories: Guy the Gorilla and Eagle remained in his folder for the occasions when he needed them for inspiration to dictate other stories.

'Our final session was managed by his dictating a poignant story that was illustrated and entitled "Waiting for/Wanting Ms Casimir to Go". This story was strongly reminiscent of the one about his anger against the character of Ms Casimir, again using the metaphor of two warring spaceships. The major change was that this time Jason was able to express his anger and mourn the loss in a much more manageable and contained manner. He was able too to use the story of Amos and Boris (described in Chapter 5) to think directly about parting and sadness. He quoted exactly from this story: "They know that they might never meet again. They knew they would never forget each other. Jason said thoughtfully that "it had been a good two years – he had learned to read and to beat me at games by thinking ahead, and most important of all he had developed his own fuel." I reflected this back: "Your own fuel?" "Yes, it would never run out, it had a special ingredient for reproducing itself."'

Jason's capacity for rediscovery of himself seems to us to have been quite remarkable; not only his capacity for facing the pain associated with his early learning, but also his capacity for getting in touch with his feelings about the attachments that were important to him. His mother may have felt she had rejected her son, but he seemed able to transfer a memory of some good-enough mothering. He was able to form an attachment to another attachment figure, his great-aunt. But he not only suffered the loss of his great-aunt when she died, he also lost his unknown father and his closeness to his mother. These losses all occurred in his first two years of life, followed shortly afterwards by the loss of his home and his great-uncle.

We have seen in this chapter the kind of desperation that these children show in their attempts to influence interactions with people who are or have become important to them. Included in their despair lies an anger that results in the rejection they greatly fear, but paradoxically invite, by their own behaviour. For children like Jackie the prognosis we think is not hopeful. She does not seem to have ever been part of a good-enough experience of attachment to a trusted figure, because that figure was unable to be emotionally available to her. Her mother's learning had become suspended at the time of the loss of her dead infant, so that she could no longer move towards another experience of attachment behaviour that encompassed good-enough mothering for Jackie.

The difficulties inherent in trying to re-awaken an appetite for learning with this group of children are not easily overcome. They present a kind of helplessness that provides a shield for their hidden anger or sadness. If these defences can be appropriately lowered to reveal the child's true feelings, and these feelings can be tolerated, he can be helped to express them.

10

CHILDREN WITH SUSPENDED LEARNING – LATER LOSS OF SKILLS

The children in this chapter are known to be able, having worked at a level commensurate with their intelligence, but sometimes suddenly, sometimes gradually, their attainment level drops. An apparently inexplicable loss of motivation or a more gradual suspension of 'scholastic skills' is usually associated with adolescents, but the learning of younger children may also become suspended or 'stuck' in school. Changes in the patterns of learning in previously competent children can be associated with transitions that for some children assume gargantuan proportions. (Adults tend to accept transitions as normal life events and they rarely connect any disruption to a child's learning to such changes – or their effects are underestimated.) There are some however whose suspended learning cannot be readily associated with any obvious event or current experience.

We have differentiated these children from those who had never managed to acquire basic scholastic skills by placing them in Yule and Rutter's classification of children who exhibit 'a later loss of these skills', that is reading, writing and mathematics (Yule and Rutter 1985).

The patterns of interaction between these children and their mothers observed in family interviews reflect the behaviour of the Group C children in the Ainsworth Strange Situation Study (1969). Like the children in the previous chapter, they appear to be anxiously-attached, but the behaviour of this group frequently reveals their ambivalence towards their attachment figures. In the Ainsworth study the behaviour of the 1-year-olds vacillated between seeking proximity to mother, wanting to be close to her, and at the same time showing how angry they were with her. They were 'intensely upset by the separations' and 'wary' of the stranger. We have often observed in family interviews that children with suspended learning frequently sit as close to their mothers as possible and then reject them if they address another member of the family or the therapist. Sophie, nearly 12 years old, seemed to be trying to wrap herself around her mother, and made several attempts to sit on her lap. If her mother's attention was given to anyone else Sophie pouted and turned her back on her mother, tried to find sweets in her mother's handbag or interrupted her by tugging her arm.

170

In 1985, Ainsworth considered the effects that the patterns of infant/mother attachments had on a child's development. Not surprisingly her study yielded substantial evidence that a mother's behaviour in interaction with her baby had significant influence on her baby's behaviour and on the 'pathway along which his development proceeded'. Ainsworth identified the qualitative differences in the interactions. The ambivalence of the infant's behaviour towards his mother is related to his internal working model of an attachment figure who offers inconsistent responses to his needs. Sophie's mother responded inconsistently to her on several occasions. In the interview referred to above she pushed Sophie away when she tried to climb on her lap and reprimanded her, then followed this with a loving reference to her daughter's behaviour. We have observed this type of interaction repeatedly in family interviews. Barry, aged 6, attempting to gain his mother's attention, offers yet another example of this behaviour. He interrupted her five times in a repeated crescendo; he tapped her, put his arms round her neck, and then gave up. His mother continued to ignore him, a clear example of non-assuaged attachment behaviour. He started playing again, making as much noise as he could. When the therapist commented on Barry's further attempts to gain mother's attention, his mother eventually commented on his activity. Barry's response was 'No, Mum' and he angrily turned his back on her.

Ambivalent behaviour continues to be much in evidence in individual educational therapy sessions. These children seem to have little expectation that adults' behaviour will be reliable or even truthful, and they think that their therapist will not be able to understand anxious or angry feelings if they are revealed. When we assume the role of educational attachment figures we give children an opportunity to update positively their internal working models of adult behaviour. (This is not to say that negative feelings are denied.) Very few of these children are reported as being able to separate readily from their mothers on entry into school, and they tend to have symbiotic relationships with them. The child can often be observed having difficulty separating from his mother in the waiting room as his therapist collects him, and similar anxious behaviour can be seen again towards the end of a session.

Anxiety about change seems to be enough to halt the learning process. A mother's decision to seek a place in higher education precipitated a crisis for Seamus, aged 9. Until then he had managed well enough in school both academically and socially, though he and his mother had some difficulties in separating from one another each day. Seamus often had stomach aches and stayed at home. This was thought to be due in part to the difficulties surrounding the break-up of his parents' marriage some three years earlier, but also to his mother's ambivalence towards formal education. In spite of this she had a good relationship with his teachers, who gave her many opportunities to become involved in school activities. Her criticisms of the system were accepted and genuine pleasure was expressed by the school staff when she decided to go to college. Seamus's reaction to this decision was dramatic: all his learning became suspended and he stopped going to school or even out of the house. His mother described him as a 'growth on her side'.

When Seamus was referred to a children's psychiatric unit for help, his capacity for playing and learning had been suspended for around a year. He was admitted to the unit on a weekly basis and the members of the multi-disciplinary team decided that he should receive individual educational therapy once a week, in addition to his daily programme on the unit.

Seamus

The therapist described Seamus in his first session:

'He shuffled slowly into the room and flopped on a chair. He resembled an oversized, sleepy baby, huddled in a foetal position. His long hair, cut roughly round in pudding-basin fashion, fell right down over his face, like the coat of an Old English Sheepdog. He seemed unavailable. He was given a clear message of expectation from his therapist that together they would find a way to recover his 'lost' scholastic skills.'

For several sessions there was little or no possibility of movement for either child or therapist as Seamus struggled to get her to take on a mothering role. He was a large, lumpy boy and his tenth birthday was looming: the thought of being 'one and zero' overwhelmed him. It was only possible to acknowledge and stay with his distress at growing inexorably older when his avowed wish was to remain a baby, preferably not even a 1-year-old.

Once he got started, Seamus was able to work directly in the metaphor by dictating and illustrating a story about a helpless, 'rubbished' kitten who was lost and couldn't find his mother. This kitten faced one disaster after another, always being swept along without any chance of influencing the direction in which he was being taken. Seamus used the metaphor of the kitten to examine his own feelings about abandonment and loss. This led to a re-evaluation of his worth within the therapy. Gradually over the months the kitten became stronger and began to discover ways in which he could influence the outcome of events, until finally he had control over his life as a young cat. The relationship between this cat and his owner became a positive one; both were able to maintain appropriate boundaries for themselves.

Seamus appeared to use the achievements of the kitten, as well as his own interactional experiences, to update his inner working models. He survived his tenth birthday and returned to school after 9 months in the unit. He continued to receive educational therapy for a further 3 months after his reintegration into his old school. His learning had been reactivated and his social skills, previously very poor, were greatly improved. He successfully negotiated the transition to secondary school when the time came and his mother started her training without further problems. The fact that Seamus was able to use the working space positively confirms, we think, that his capacity for learning was not lost as early as that of the children without any basic skills described in Chapter 9.

The sudden suspension of a child's learning can be provoked by a family crisis; it may also be associated with a current event that triggers a painful conscious or unconscious memory from the past. If the problem continues and becomes intolerable the child's pain may be expressed by a total collapse, as happened with Seamus. Children's feelings are often expressed psycho-somatically: difficult-to-diagnose illnesses, abdominal pains, asthma attacks, headaches, enuresis and encopresis are common causes for concern. Other children show their distress by a series of 'accidents' (Wagenheim 1960). Occasionally a psychosomatic symptom can become physically intolerable.

Evan

This boy, aged 10, stopped learning in school. In the opinion of his head teacher (who had known the family for some years) this was to draw attention to a family crisis. A child psychiatrist and an educational therapist from the local clinic team were invited by the head teacher to meet Evan's mother at the school. The team were told that Evan had been meeting his father in secret on several occasions since the father's release from prison. It was known that Evan anticipated trouble for his mother and siblings but that at the same time he wished to remain loyal to his father. The head teacher asked the clinic team to focus on Evan's educational needs, because he was due to transfer to secondary school in the following year. Educational therapy was arranged for Evan, but clinic attendance was not thought to be appropriate for his family, who were receiving long-term support from social services.

Shortly after this interview Evan's father threw a brick through a window of the family home. This behaviour not only increased Evan's anxiety for the safety of his mother but reawakened past memories of violence between his parents. Did Evan's emotional pain find release in physical pain? The urgent need to remove his appendix appeared to coincide with the crisis.

Following this event many changes took place. The education authority agreed to a year's delay in the transfer of Evan to secondary school; new arrangements for access to his children were made for father; and Evan allowed himself to resume his learning. In a final follow-up interview with the clinic team, Evan was reported by his mother and his former head teacher to be a confident and articulate 13-year-old.

The following accounts are of educational therapy with two boys, aged 7 and 15 years. Both came from backgrounds where many changes had to be encompassed, and illustrate how they unconsciously used their suspended learning.

Anthony

Anthony was described as a cheerful-looking boy, rather tall for a 7-year-old, with an adult manner of speaking. His intelligence level was placed at low-average. He was referred by a family doctor to a children's psychiatric unit because his behaviour was 'unmanageable' at home. His school performance had suddenly deteriorated, although this was not a part of the reason for referral. The family background had been a troubled one for many years, with Anthony's father coming and going at irregular intervals.

Shortly after one of his father's extended visits Anthony started a serious fire in the family home. From this time he continued his fire-setting activities, which culminated in his behaviour getting beyond parental control and his admission to a psychiatric unit. A member of the assessment interview team noted with concern Anthony's lack of feeling about these dangerous actions. He was described as laughing in a 'manic way'. Because we wish to focus on this boy interacting with his educational therapist we have not included any comments on the parallel work with the family.

Anthony attended the unit on a weekly basis, returning home for weekends. He spent each morning in the educational unit classroom and was also seen by his educational therapist for an individual session once a week. The team thought that this concentration of educational input was an essential way of strengthening Anthony's self-esteem and confidence in his ability to manage when he returned to his own school. He was very anxious and confused for his first month in the unit. One of the staff described his behaviour: 'He seemed full of nervous tics, and frequently laughed inappropriately. He could not relate to his peers, and kept his head down most of the day. He gave the impression of feeling quite "uncontained".'

Anthony's behaviour in the individual sessions was similar to his behaviour in the small unit group. His educational therapist helped him to dictate a sentence each week until gradually this became a story. The practical activity of punching holes and assembling a simple book seemed to steady him, but it was the actual and metaphorical use of a swing that enabled him to share some of his pain and confusion.

'In his very first session Anthony attempted to make a model of a swing. His movements were clumsy and awkward. He explained what he was doing as he struggled to suspend two very thick pieces of plasticine from a precariously balanced crossbar. Inevitably each time he tried the side posts bent. I commented that the posts didn't seem quite strong enough. He was unable to take action, and seemed to be devoid of any strength. I did not remark on this feeling of helplessness but said that we sometimes find it hard to work out the best way to manage something. He looked directly at me and held the contact. I felt that he was surprised but reassured that his dilemma had been acknowledged. He then added two small pieces of plasticine as token straps to the ropes of the swing and said firmly, "It's engineering." I repeated the statement, which he confirmed as he calmly put his model away. The following week he constructed another swing: this time from cardboard and glue, with an equally unsuccessful outcome.

'In the next session he announced that he would make a swing out of paper. He took pen and paper, drew a swing and cut it out. He then took out his glue, again saying that he loved sticking things, and stuck the paper swing to the previous session's cardboard one. I mused about swinging and the sensations experienced in the constant motion and contrasted the extremes of movement. Anthony vehemently said, "I hate the feeling when Lawrence pushes me on the swing." This was followed immediately by another statement: "I hate saying good-bye, why do children have to go from here?" His manner became agitated and tearful. I said that good-byes are difficult and painful especially when you cannot know if people will return. His normally red face became quite ashen and he looked desperately at me. He said repeatedly how he hated saying good-bye. I was thinking about the uncertainties and confusions in this child's life, his father's unpredictable disappearances and the recent loss of his grandfather, who had been an important attachment figure for him. Currently he was having to tolerate moving between his family home and his weekly residence in the unit. He must have been aware too of the farewells we made to other children in the unit. While I was thinking about the wretchedness of Anthony's life experience, he was dabbing violently with the glue brush on scrap paper, on his fingers and all over the table. I mused aloud about the qualities of glue and how it could hold things firmly in place to keep them from becoming lost. He said he wished that he could have glue to keep him safe. I accepted his statement and said that we would both work hard to find ways of helping him to feel safer inside himself. He told me that he needed help and added, sighing, "I do feel safe here." We sat quietly for a few moments and then he told me that he didn't want to go home that night. (The plans for his return to his family for the weekend were very uncertain.) I made a direct reference to family struggles about saying good-bye. Anthony replied, "It's hard to say hello too." I was reminded of Anthony's fire-setting shortly after his father's last return. We sat quietly together again, until we had to say good-bye at the end of the session. I acknowledged once more the difficulties of saying hellos and good-byes. He nodded and seemed calm. I was left pondering the links between the emotional tensions of greetings and departures to the experience of being on a swing.

'On his return after a holiday break Anthony took plasticine to construct another model. As before he was unable to use the medium correctly. He just tore strips off and pressed the ends down to make them stand. He had no idea of moulding or rolling the material. Once again he told me he was making a swing. I just stated "another swing". "Yes" he said "I get very frightened when they go really high and ...." He appeared to bite his words back and chose not to complete the sentence. (I could not help thinking about his fire-setting activities, wondering if he too had made the connection.) I commented that swinging could be calming or so exciting that it became a frightening experience. He made eye contact immediately, as though again surprised that I had understood. I went on to think aloud about things that could be bad and good almost at the same time and how hard it was to manage such mixed feelings. I talked too of the excitement that could be felt when one was doing something "bad". He searched my face and told me how hard he was finding it to manage, adding quietly that things were bad at home. I accepted this admission but made no comment. Instead I referred back to swings, and the good and bad bits of swinging, and its lack of stillness. I suggested that we could search for some stillness and – like the swing – come to rest in the middle, between the high and the low. His reaction was to pick up the glue brush and say "I love sticking things, I don't know why." I reflected this back to him as a question, "You don't know why?" Anthony repeated our words from the previous term, "They stay where they're put, so you can find them again".'

Anthony was swinging in the unit garden when he was collected for his tenth session. The therapist continued:

'He saw me approaching and leapt off the swing from a high position. "That's the first time I've managed to jump off a swing," he announced with pride. Once inside the room I took up his remark about his achievement on the swing. With careful consideration he told me that he was managing to do a lot of things now. I said that it seemed possible for frightening things to be exciting as long as we felt they could be controlled (again thinking of the fire-setting). He looked at me as though he recognised what I was saying. I felt it necessary to say that getting the right balance needed careful consideration. He almost hummed with pleasure when I made this statement.

'Two weeks later he managed to operate the swing. I made a link to his learning and how he was now managing that. "That's right. I wish there was a certificate for managing not to get things all muddled, like you get for swimming. I don't get into such a lot of muddles nowadays!" My comment was again in question form, "A certificate like the one you get for swimming?" "So everyone can see," he replied. I went on to say that everyone could see that he was often calm and sensible now; even when he was angry he had found a way to manage these feelings without hurting people. I suggested that he did not need a certificate to remind him how he was managing, because all his struggles had helped him to know this inside himself. His response was very thoughtful, "You see, I'm growing up." When I told him I agreed, he gave a satisfied smile and began assembling his latest story and illustration for his book. We made occasional use of the swing metaphor during the rest of our work together.'

176

This intervention was very short, only 6 months. Anthony returned to his family, but the travelling distance was then too great for him to continue working with his educational therapist. It was known that he did well in school after his reintegration, but continuing family difficulties made it impossible to predict any lasting change.

Gordon

Gordon was almost 16 years old when he suddenly lost the use of his mathematical skills for no obvious reason. Did the imminence of his entry into the adult world of work, which he thought he would have to face alone, trigger some incipient memory of childhood experience? At the time of his transition from his family home into the care of the local authority he had had to face a different world, alone. The loss of his mathematical skills puzzled and worried both Gordon and his teachers. His social worker was more concerned about the effect of this loss on Gordon's behaviour outside school. He had been in trouble with the law on and off since he was a very small boy. The social worker and his other community care-workers expressed their fear that as an adolescent Gordon's earlier impulsive behaviour might be re-enacted and lead him into trouble again.

The educational therapist to whom Gordon had been referred admitted her own anxious feelings prior to her first session with him, because she regarded herself as practically innumerate. She described her first meeting with Gordon in the clinic waiting room.

'I saw this small fair-haired boy who looked more like 12 than almost 16 years old. As he rose to greet me his eye contact was strong and I gained the impression that he was trying to assume an adult manner to disguise his anxiety. His demeanour was serious and his face was very pale. The pseudo-adult role he seemed to have adopted was continued. He walked with a slight swagger, as we walked down the corridor to the therapy room, hand in pocket making polite conversation about the weather and the building. When we entered the room Gordon sat on the only armchair, one hand dangling over the arm as though he was holding a "fag". I remember thinking that "cigarette" seemed the wrong word to use when I recalled Gordon's behaviour.'

The therapist described her first decision:

'I felt I had to respond to the only part of himself that Gordon seemed able to offer at that moment. I said in what I afterwards regarded as a rather pompous manner, "I understand that you are having some difficulty with your mathematical concepts at the moment." I was rather surprised at his reaction, which was a relieved "Yeah" as he sank back into the chair, his body resting in a concave position. I was aware that I too felt relieved that some of the facade was lowered.'

His very defensive behaviour had made the therapist aware of her own defensive feelings, but now she felt able to respond more naturally.

'I suggested that at 15 Gordon probably knew more maths than I did, as this was not my best subject.'

This 'admission' appeared to free both the adolescent and the therapist.

'I engaged Gordon in a discussion based on the reality of his current concerns about where he felt he was "stuck" mathematically speaking. Gordon volunteered the information that he was unable to understand area, a mathematical concept that he was being taught in school. Momentarily I thought that Gordon understood the meaning of various mathematical terms but then realised that he was passively pretending he knew in order to maintain the defensive adult role that he hoped was disguising his anxious feelings. I also discovered that Gordon was very uncertain about the meaning of the word "angle" but only from a mathematical point of view. Semantically his understanding was obvious, when it transpired that he was familiar with the colloquial and sporting connotations of the word "angle".'

The therapist introduced some educational material that she felt might engage Gordon on two levels. The first used his interest in words and the second used material in a concrete way to help him regress educationally. The material proffered was a puzzle made of wood and brightly painted. The puzzle pieces had to be grouped into colours, and when fitted together made shapes – circles, rhomboids etc. When completed each shape had words like 'circumference' and 'diagonal' printed across them. The material was introduced to Gordon in the following manner:

'I realise that jigsaw puzzles are the kind of thing you probably did in your first school, Gordon, but I thought perhaps if we go back, we might be able to discover where you feel you became stuck. My guess is that you have probably just forgotten some of the basic mathematical concepts.'

By the use of adult language and the presentation of the material in a face-saving way, Gordon was able to accept the task. He had no reading problems and enjoyed words like 'horizontal', entering into an intelligent age-appropriate discussion about horizons, a word that on an unconscious level was already becoming important to him. The therapist thought that his willingness to construct the puzzles was helping him to begin work on some of his feelings, again perhaps at an unconscious level, relating to his separation from his family. It is rare that any educational therapist will impart any information that she has about the child's family history directly to the child in question. Normally she will wait until the child, overtly or covertly, introduces feelings about his unique situation.

During the next session Gordon spoke at length about his present position in school. He said, 'Teachers assume that you already possess far more knowledge than you've actually acquired or have forgotten.' He was reflecting back the therapist's words from the first session. A sophisticated and amusing dramatisation of the masters in his school followed and he made the point that 'they never seem to see you as an individual. What do they know about me? It's just the same at ....' Gordon again dramatised his experience in the community home where he was living to describe the lack of acknowledgement that his individuality received. These dramatisations led him to make a forceful statement about the lack of communication between people who made decisions for children without consulting them.

Mathematical activities provided the basis for many wide-ranging discussions in subsequent sessions. Gordon became very serious and anxious when he spoke about leaving school at the end of the year without any qualifying examinations, and he expressed concern about his chances of gaining employment. For the first time he admitted that he really would like to become a journalist. The therapist knew this was his father's profession, but Gordon did not volunteer this information at that time.

The educational therapist suggested that Gordon might make an appointment with his year tutor to discuss his wish to become a journalist. She also offered to visit the school to make an independent assessment of his work. Gordon accepted her offer and was amazed when the results were reported back to him, hearing that each member of staff had in fact perceived him as an individual, giving a very definite account of his behaviour and achievements. 'You just don't know what people think of you, do you?' he said. For several weeks after this discovery Gordon behaved in a totally different manner. The meaning and use of words became an overriding interest in every session, the direct result of the school visit. The realisation that his ambition to become a journalist was no longer an impossible dream seemed too frightening a possibility. He began to behave like the adolescent he was, choosing to use his sessions to test out his relationship with his therapist by the use of socially unacceptable language. While continuing to make use of drama as a means of expressing feelings about himself and his peers, he also made constant impossible demands by attempting to smoke, for example. The use of four-letter words was frequent. The therapist responded by suggesting that he had found a new way to communicate with her. This promoted a discussion about the acceptance of certain words in different social settings: school, his 'home' or in the company of his social worker. For the first time Gordon mentioned his father, who had always stressed the importance of speaking 'proper'.

In contrast to his earlier positive view of self that had begun to emerge, Gordon swung into a mood of great sadness (the pendulum swing of adolescence). The therapist had introduced the word subtraction and asked Gordon if he could recall learning this concept when he was younger. His response was to recall his experiences in his first school. This led to a most moving account of himself at home, including recollections of taking considerable responsibility for his two younger siblings at times of family financial distress. He recalled the time when his after-school activities at 5 or 6 years old were mostly directed towards avoiding the law. 'I don't want to sound boastful like, but I was somebody. I was the leader of this gang.' Then he described himself: 'I was able to talk an' act big, all the other kids looked up to me, but then when you got indoors you just seemed to shrink, and you're all little again.'

Gordon's awareness and ability to verbalise his feelings about himself at a time when his mother was first beginning to fail in health and his father left home, (although Gordon did not speak of these facts) led the therapist to make use of the words 'inner resources'. Gordon thought for some minutes before responding to the therapist's statement about what she thought were his inner resources. He recounted the history of another boy in the 'home', comparing his own early family life and the security it had offered in spite of the blacker side to that of his friend. His recognition and insight into another boy's internal world seemed to awaken a new perspective on himself. There was a certain amount of denial by Gordon of the undoubtedly very hazardous childhood he had experienced, which included numerous incidents when he had been expected to act unlawfully. However, the internal working models that he had of his interactions with his attachment figures from pre-school days seemed to have given him some feeling of security. About half way through the second term of once weekly sessions Gordon began to 'introduce' his family to the therapist. His idealisation of his father, a journalist, was coupled with concern for his ill mother, and curiosity and concern for the welfare of his two younger siblings. (He visited his mother occasionally and had contact with his father by telephone or letter. He knew his father had re-married and that his siblings lived with him.)

Towards the end of his first year of educational therapy a case conference was called to discuss plans for Gordon's educational and domestic future. Remembering Gordon's feelings about children having a right to speak to adults and state their own point of view about their future, the therapist and his social worker arranged with other members of the community network for Gordon to be present for part of the conference. Gordon was 16 by this time. His anxiety about the conference was exacerbated by the cancellation of a session by the therapist and a row with his girl-friend, and was made worse by the fact that he had not received a birthday card from his father. As a result of this anxiety Gordon got drunk and made some slight cuts on his wrists. The explanation about the 'cuts' that he offered to the 'home' was that they were part of a blood pact with his girl-friend prior to their quarrel.

In the subsequent session the reality of these events was faced. (They had been discussed at a conference when both Gordon, his therapist and social worker were present.) Reflecting on their work together, different aspects of Gordon's behaviour in the here and now as well as in the past were considered. How might these experiences affect the future? The reference to his first school, where he was a leader of a gang, was linked to his need to show the 'big' aspect of himself, that is to demonstrate to authority figures that by getting drunk he could behave like an adult and manage his behaviour. His attempt to harm himself and his girl-friend was part of this need to prove himself, and at the same time perhaps expressed a wish to punish himself. This act could in turn be linked to another, much earlier, need to be looked after by the 'home'. The wish to punish himself was also linked to anger with his therapist for cancelling a session at his time of need for support. This exacerbated his ambivalent feelings about his father, who had forgotten his birthday. At the same time he admitted he would have liked his father to have shown enough concern to visit him after his attempt at self-mutilation. Being let down by two people at a time when his future was being planned put him in touch with an earlier experience as a small boy. This was also at a time when a future was being planned for him, i.e. removal from his family. The whole question of self-esteem and facing the here and now prompted Gordon to look at his father's 'feet of clay', such an essential corrective for all adolescents.

Gordon slowly and painfully examined his discovery of his own collusion with his father's deception of various authorities, and his ability to empathise with his mother's inability to cope. Sharing his feelings with an emotionally available adult enabled him to leave his past experience with regret and gratitude for what he saw in retrospect had contributed to his being the person that he was now, in the present. Gordon was to remain for some time caught up in the adolescent pendulum, so common in this age-group, oscillating between trying to be adult with girl-friends and drinking, but also behaving like an unhappy and disappointed little boy needing assuagement of his anxious feelings.

Sharing so many intimate details of his past and present made it difficult for Gordon to continue his sessions. The question of feeling disloyal to his family was taken up with him. Understandably, based on his past knowledge of adults failing him, he frequently expressed doubts about how much he could trust his therapist. She took up her own difficulty of not knowing how their work might continue, commenting that by coming late to sessions Gordon was perhaps feeling he no longer needed help. The following week he arrived on time. The therapist reviewed the work they had done together and then said that she would like to read him a short excerpt from a book about a boy who had reminded her of him. The passage she read was from *Cider with Rosie* by Laurie Lee (1959). It recalls with humour a boy's first day in school and his chagrin when he does not receive the present he was expecting. The two meanings of the word 'present' in the story leads to the boy's misunderstanding. This reading enabled Gordon to recapitulate his own experience with the therapist through the events that took place for the boy in the book: warm beginnings with his family, fights and doubts in early schooldays, unhappiness and trouble to come and all the encounters and changes and pain of growing up. This led to a discussion about the author and about writing as a career, and the acknowledgement that mathematics was no longer a problem for Gordon.

Details of the work undertaken by his therapist with members of the community network supporting Gordon are not included in this account. Although he was kept informed of these meetings, it seemed inevitable that his fantasies about them contributed to his doubts about his therapist. This raises a question about the role of an educational therapist. Some prefer to work exclusively with the child, while other members of the team undertake school visits or family/social service interviews. Others discuss their own involvement with members of the community network as part of the work with the child. This may be done for purely practical reasons, such as a lack of team resources, or because it is seen as an integral part of enabling a child to experience one or two adults working together to support him both emotionally and scholastically. We have found the timing of school visits, social work or family interviews to be crucial as far as the child's capacity for trust is concerned. If they take place before he can trust his therapist, then he may experience any arrangement with suspicion, as adults conspiring against him, which can be entirely counter-productive.

In his last term with his educational therapist, Gordon managed several major changes. The two that were the most significant were direct contact with his father, arranged by his social worker, and visits to his mother, initiated by himself. In his sessions he discussed his plans to ask his father (in whose care they had been placed) for a reunion with his two younger siblings. He spoke of them at length and again recalled that it had been his responsibility to hide them and keep them quiet when the authorities called at his home. He made some very thoughtful and rather wistful comments about the reality of meeting them now, and how much they would have changed in the intervening years. He negotiated a meeting with them with his father and subsequently visited them in their new home. His therapist reported:

'I was very moved by his accounts of this meeting, so poignant but facing the reality in a mature way. Gordon's visits to his mother he found reassuring. Actually being able to see for himself that her health was more robust, that her environment was comfortable and that she was so clearly managing her life to her own satisfaction was another factor that freed him to re-assess his own future.'

Gordon's teachers felt that his seeking a college place was a viable proposition for him and he brought an application form to a session. He had the greatest difficulty in holding the idea in mind. He became anxious when his therapist asked how he intended answering the question on the form: 'What reason do you give for wanting to enter this college?' He became very embarrassed and remained silent for a minute or two. He finally said, 'What I really want to put is that I want a second chance to learn, but they might think that was silly.' 'But what do *you* feel?' 'I'll put it,' he said. Once this task was accomplished, Gordon settled into a quiet period of discussions that lasted for several sessions. He expressed many thoughtful ideas about current social and political issues. His feelings about the report of a young man's suicide following his attendance at the showing of a particularly violent film were put forward. 'It's a horrible film, but if it's going to have that effect on someone I reckon he's halfway there before he got inside the cinema.'

Preparation for the ending of Gordon's educational therapy seemed to run in parallel with the ending of childhood and early adolescent adventures. The final sessions addressed his preoccupation with the advent of college entry after the summer break. It was agreed to have two follow-up sessions during the college half-term break. One of the subjects he had chosen to study, albeit with some apprehension, was mathematics. He had confirmation of his ambition to become a journalist with his acceptance on a more advanced English course but also with the publication of a short article in a house magazine that was circulated to other 'houses' financed by the same financial group. The article was autobiographical and not without humour. This led to a long-term ambition to write a book on ways to help others who had 'lost' their families. It would discuss decisions that were based on his experience but would offer very different solutions to the problems.

'In our follow-up sessions I discovered that college entry was something of a shock for Gordon. His insight helped him to recognise that his behaviour in the first few weeks was similar to that of himself as a 5-year-old gang leader. He felt that having achieved entry he again "was somebody". However, his first disillusionment was his discovery that the courses he had been entered for were set at a standard higher than he had anticipated. Earlier in his sessions he had frequently complained that teachers in school treated him like a child, so the initial stages of college life presented a challenge to him when he found he had to carry out the tasks set by using his own initiative. The salutary effect of being treated like an adult by his tutors, however, enabled him to extend his goal-seeking appropriately. He was accepted on to an advanced course in the following year, and became tremendously excited when the idea of a degree course became a possibility.'

Gordon's learning epitomises the process of educational therapy for us. He accepted a secure base, formed an updated attachment to his educational therapist and showed his capacity for exploratory play in many ways, but particularly with his enjoyment of words. He could allow himself to move from the here and now, regress educationally and examine the loss and pain of his past. His ability to return to many here-and-now sessions and situations outside them led to a realistic examination of his future. Blos (1979) in the *Adolescent Process* summarised a state of mind that Gordon successfully overcame to face his new reality: 'If memory fails to become firmly and clearly structured through the acquisition of word symbols then no workable organization of memory exists for an adaptive evaluation of current reality.'

The children in this classification of suspended scholastic learning and ambivalent emotional development have very rarely, in our experience, remained in the position in which they had seemed temporarily paralysed. Our assuagement of over-anxious feelings about being able to recover lost skills is, we feel, a contributory factor to recovery of those skills. Once they feel secure enough to accept their ambivalent feelings and are prepared to make tentative links between certain events that took place at the time they stopped learning scholastically, most are able to resume their goal-seeking behaviour. Younger children, however, who are not yet ready or able to move into age-appropriate independence, are unlikely to recover unless members of their family are able to perceive and accept the links we have mentioned on the child's behalf.

In these and numerous other examples of children with suspended learning we note that the majority have fathers who appear to be emotionally unavailable. This reminded us of some work by Elizur (1986), who studied the coping reaction of parents from 'normal' families when their children, who were already 'exhibiting signs of maladjustment', entered their first school. He evaluated their adjustment to the new environment over a period of two years, and found that the 'coping' behaviour or strategies of mother alone were insufficient to alleviate a child's difficulty in adjusting to school. Indeed, he saw the problem increasing where future transitions were likely to evoke distressed behaviour in the child: 'a family organisation characterised by a strong mother–child bond and a peripheral father may become dysfunctional'. He stated that a greater involvement by father not only helps the child, but can also change the mother–child relationship. We share Elizur's view of the significance of the father's role, which has been confirmed in our work with families of learning-disabled children. However, we would not confine this view to children who have lost their skills.

11

CHILDREN WHO ARE RESISTANT TO LEARNING

Our third category of children who are resistant to learning is the most puzzling group of the three that we have identified. They have no learning disability as such; nor have they lost their capacity for learning. They appear to resist learning: they can learn, but they won't. Their goal-seeking behaviour seems to be directed away from achieving success. Their intentions appear to be to alienate adults, siblings and sometimes peers. Their demands for attention may prevent others from learning. If the child takes on the role of class clown some of his peers will respond to him. They may react differently if he is a bully or behaves 'oddly', but the majority of children are tolerant of each other and become upset only if one child's actions persistently prevent them from getting on. Much of a resistant child's energy is directed at preventing himself from conforming.

Families frequently report that these children refuse to respond to family codes of behaviour. (This does not refer to normal adolescent statements about conforming.) They appear to be angry, sad or depressed, and we place them, emotionally speaking, in the group defined as 'disoriented and disorganised' by Main *et al.* (1985). The behaviour of some of this group remains chaotic in school (the boy with the kaleidoscope in Chapter 7 exemplified this behaviour). We feel that most of these children have been unable to build a memory of an attachment figure who is emotionally available to them, although they may receive tantalising glimpses of gestures from this figure. Main *et al.* suggested that many of the parents of this group have suffered losses or other traumas that remain unresolved. If these children unconsciously recognise that their attachment figure cannot cope they may themselves adopt the role of care-giver, which Bowlby refers to as an 'inversion of the parental role' (1973).

A parent may threaten to withhold love or even to abandon the child; the command may be covertly or overtly expressed. The child's response may be to take control of the chaos either by adopting this mode of behaviour themselves, or by developing a rigidity of thinking. Both these behaviours are likely to override the child's goal-seeking and his enjoyment of playful activity: if they take control, exploratory behaviour becomes inhibited. Giving himself permission to reveal what he knows has to be denied. Those who keep feelings and actions under rigid control may become obsessive in their scholastic skills, but avoid close contact with teachers and peers.

We find that children who resist learning present parents and professionals with an enigmatic profile. They seem to be trapped in a position where it is impossible for them to function at an age-appropriate emotional or intellectual level that corresponds to their abilities. There seems to be a connection between their predicament and the confusing messages constantly given to them by their parents, which can result in uncertainty about any goal-seeking behaviour. A child can be inhibited by parental denigration or mockery, and even more by a parent's active dislike of him. In our work with families we have found that the parents of other children in this group have unresolved grief or unresolved conflictual feelings about their own attachment figures. We give two very brief examples. The Cohens' family life was dominated by the dead maternal grandmother. They felt she haunted the family, albeit benignly. Her 'presence' was thought to be having an adverse effect on the learning of the middle child. It was not until mother was helped to relinquish her need for the grandmother's ethereal presence that her daughter gave herself permission to resume her learning.

We have already mentioned Mrs Andrews, who brought large bags of food into a clinic waiting room each week and fed her 'good' but not her 'bad' boy. She resisted mourning the 'loss' of her former husband (who had remarried) and appeared to remain in the angry phase of the mourning process. So much of her energy was expended in expressing her resentment towards her former husband that she remained unavailable to her younger son. He in turn behaved in such a chaotic manner in school that he was quite unable to settle to any task.

When the parents themselves are resistant to change, their children may not be able to allow themselves to take advantage of any specialised intervention, such as educational therapy.

It seems possible to link the onset of resistance to a stage where a child would normally be developing an awareness of the views and needs of others; a time when he discovers his own mind as distinct from that of another, usually his attachment figure – Stern's 'subjective self' (1985). It is then that the infant begins to understand the meaning of 'shared intentions'. Stern calls the continuation of this process 'affective attunement', which we understand to be close to the concept of mirroring or empathic responsiveness described by Winnicott (1971). The following examples will illustrate the concept of resistant learning.

Nathan

Nathan was 10 years old. He was the eldest of three children in an intact family. Because his father was only home at weekends, Nathan was expected to be the man about the house in father's absence in addition to maintaining a very hectic programme of after-school activities. When he was not assuming these 'adult' roles he behaved like a very awkward toddler and had many tantrums which were difficult to contain both at home and at school. Though he had no discernible learning disabilities he was unable to achieve any scholastic task adequately, his work being poorly presented and his attention constantly wandering. He spent most of his time in a fantasy world where he was a world-ranking sportsman.

Nathan was referred for educational therapy at the suggestion of his teacher who said he had become increasingly sad and isolated in class. The therapist described her initial reaction to him:

'When he arrived for his first session he had his anorak zipped right up to his nose and his hood pulled down to meet it. It was not possible to see his eyes. His limbs were curiously stick-like and his movements restless and jerky. He climbed up the stairs one at a time like a toddler despite considering himself an accomplished sportsman. He appeared very apprehensive and guarded, fiercely defended.'

He continued struggling to resist all efforts to help him in the therapy; all his energy was taken up with maintaining his defences. Although it was possible for his therapist to develop some interactional behaviour with him in the sessions it was never very meaningful. He constantly chose to draw, dictate stories or play games around a single theme – that of sport. Superficially this seemed to be a healthy preoccupation for a 10-year-old, but each sport that he favoured involved the use of protective gear – e.g. American football, jousting and cricket – reflecting his defensive manner and appearance.

Nathan's ability to make any attachment was damaged, and if he was able to get in touch with his feelings they would erupt in what can only be described as a primeval scream which arose from hidden depths within him.

Nathan's inability to express his feelings in a conventional way was demonstrated when his therapist was ill.

'On my return he greeted me politely (his mother had said in the first family interview that he always said what people wanted to hear), but he managed to express his displeasure by farting repeatedly. I mused about how angry he must have felt with me for being away. He (unusually) made eye-contact, nodded sadly, relaxed and began to work more appropriately.'

After a period of two years the process of ending the therapy proved to be the most important part of the work. Nathan was able to allow himself to face some of the realities previously unacknowledged. He started to talk about the feelings of sportsmen when things went wrong for them, how they had to keep their feelings to themselves, 'to be good sportsmen'. The therapist said

'We were able to look together at the more demonstrative behaviour of the players and their expression of their feelings. Nathan was able to share the difficulties that he experienced when playing team games because of his terrible anguish and anger if his performance was not perfect. He was able to describe how he couldn't trust his team mates enough to pass the ball to them. When the therapy was finally completed he could be seen leaping up the stairs wearing only shorts and a tee shirt for his sessions; his anorak was left at home.'

But only minimal changes had been observed in school, although Nathan's parents reported that he was happier and his behaviour had become more equable at home.

Samuel

Samuel was 6 and his background was different from Nathan's. He was a natural learner but he could not allow himself to work. He had suffered repeated rejections in his short life, and was in his fifth foster home in two years when he was admitted to a children's psychiatric unit, where he started educational therapy. It seems certain that his mother had been able to give him a good-enough start to life in spite of the confusion and conflict between her and the child's father. He was a lively little boy who always showed an interest in things; but, as soon as he recognised what was happening, he would spoil or destroy the activity or game he was playing. He repeatedly embarked on a calm and happy-seeming game with the farm animals (his current foster parents were farmers) from his box, only to destroy it with a desperation that was hard to observe, let alone experience. When he had been receiving educational therapy for about six months his fifth foster placement broke down abruptly. Samuel was then reunited with his grandparents and other siblings (four children altogether). A major investment of help and support was made by the unit staff and social workers to make the placement possible.
    The educational therapist described the sessions at this time:

'Following the traumatic upheavals that again rocked Samuel's world he did not open his box. Instead he repeatedly played violent games with paper aeroplanes. His behaviour was terribly restless, hurling his planes around the room in his despair. Sometimes he played alone and sometimes he involved me in dog-fights. All I could do was reassure him that this was his space to use as he needed. I accepted and empathised with his distress while trying to provide the space in which he could express his feelings, carefully maintaining the boundaries of safety, time and place.
    'Later he gave up using the aeroplanes and started hurling himself around, climbing on the furniture with his feet seldom if ever touching ground. I was acutely aware of the lack of educational content in our sessions but decided

to accept his behaviour until he finally turned to the typewriter. He used to type the key-board sequence of letters over and over again. He used the space bar repeatedly and I mused about the use of space. This comment seemed to free him to move again and he began moving the furniture around in every session, repeatedly making "dens". He took enormous care to include a "bed", a "fire" to keep him warm, a "kitchen" where he could prepare "food", and a "toilet" area. I mused about his need to make a house for himself. "This is my home," he said. He appeared to use the time to reassure himself that he could look after himself.

'He began to ask me to read a story in his den each week. He chose *Amos and Boris* (Steig 1972). (This simple, poignant tale about a friendship between a mouse and a whale has already been described on p. 105.) I felt Samuel was struggling to derive comfort from this story as a way of coming to terms with his many losses. He began wearing a mouse hat and tail as he sat listening to the story, saying that he was the mouse and I was the whale.

'Progress was slow and Samuel went through a period when he made quantities of confetti with the hole punch, scattering and eating the pieces. He opened his box just wide enough to get the Sellotape out and used a great deal of it, sticking up furniture, confetti and sheets of paper as if his life depended on it. He rolled it into balls and played catch with me. I never ceased to be amazed at the uses he found for it.

'I became increasingly aware that he never opened his box except to get the Sellotape. It seemed to be a container for all those things that reminded him of his past life and of his farming foster parents. I struggled to find ways of managing this, sharing my thoughts with him about how painful the memories must be for him. He neither agreed nor disagreed but put his box on the floor, ostensibly to make room on the table for a game. Instead he started making another "home", the first for some time. He stood on the box. I decided that I should give him permission to open it, reassuring him that it would be all right if he did, and that I would help him to manage. At this he became very wild and started to jump on the box (which was made of sturdy cardboard) over and over again. Finally he slowed down and I said that I thought that was enough. Very quietly he lifted off the rather battered lid and took the contents out one by one. Together we collected them and the box remains and put them in a large bag, I locked them in my cupboard as the session ended.

'The following week Samuel and I repaired his box with the Sellotape and he seemed free to return to the more common pattern of an educational therapy session. He dictated stories, played with his cars and animals, played paper games, and listened to a wide selection of stories. His grandparents were finding him easier to care for and although he could still be very awkward at home and in school he was making good academic progress. The educational therapy came to an end after 2½ years. Probably for the first time in his life it was possible to prepare Samuel for a separation. During this process he reviewed many earlier traumatic separations that he had experienced. The final session included a re-reading of *Amos and Boris* (Steig 1972) at his request.'

We have referred elsewhere to a concept of 'backdating' as the reverse of Bowlby's concept of 'updating' (1973, 1980). Our own observations of these disorientated children suggests that their experiences lead to the backdating of their internal working models, which reinforces their unsatisfactory behaviour. They seem to exist in a permanently 'hovering' state of mind in which they glimpse the possibility of change, only to be returned to an earlier state of mind where there is no hope (in response to a rapid change of adult behaviour). They live in a state of conflict, caught between their natural thrust towards healthy development and a need to deny this by rubbishing everything they do. They receive confused messages from the people who are important to them. Many of these children become very disruptive in the classroom: unable to tolerate praise, they spoil their work and their social interactions with adults and children alike, ensuring that they are unlikeable.

Two boys who came within the superior range of intelligence and from middle-class, well-educated backgrounds experienced problems with the control of their own behaviour and their brains. They both behaved in a restless manner in class, causing disruptions by their incessant questions of peers and teachers. At home they became over-excited at the time of any social event. Both these boys described their brains as too powerful and beyond control. The younger boy, after making painstaking efforts to write, suddenly destroyed his work. He then described his brain as 'whizzing around very fast, in yellow stripes'. The older boy, Ralph, described his brain (also at a time of angry scribbling over some spellings he had just completed) as 'hurtling around into a black hole', a subject about which he spoke with considerable knowledge.

Both boys were undoubtedly able, but much of their emotional energy seemed to be spent in not learning, while their intellectual energy was channelled in two directions. First, to fill their own and others' space and time with rapid talk about fantastic schemes, often with a scientific base: second, to pursue elaborate deviations and distractions that actually prevented any tasks from being achieved. Adults found they became trapped into colluding with these requests.

Going by our empirical evidence, we consider that this small group of resistant children frequently show how insecure, disorganised and disorientated they appear to be in their attachment behaviour. They are children who often have a desperate need for structure in their lives – fiercely resisted in a formal learning situation, but an almost obsessive interest in a therapeutic setting. An activity of discovery and construction can itself become so exciting that it gets beyond control. We can only speculate as to whether it is the realisation that consistency and constancy exist that becomes too tantalising a thought to contemplate calmly. It is likely that these children make connections between experimental findings and their possible relevance to human behaviour. Their behaviour frequently confounds adults and peers with an element of eccentricity inappropriate to their age and the setting. They are unaware of the effect their behaviour has on others, and when it is brought to their attention it puts them into a state of disbelief. Emotional outbursts or silent tears seem to offer the only way for them to express their fears, frustration and chagrin at being misunderstood. Is their disorganised, disorientated behaviour and presentation of work a defence against 'getting it wrong again', as a mother described her son's behaviour? Or is their behaviour unconsciously (or at times consciously) punitive towards others for getting it wrong again, that is, misunderstanding the child's disorientation and inability to act in an organised way, and so missing his underlying desperate need to be understood? In other words, are they prevented from learning by their anger? Are they unconsciously punishing themselves by not giving themselves permission to use the ability they know they possess? Is this because they feel that others perceive them as 'bad'? Do they do this in order to confirm their parents' perception of them – paradoxically the image they most want changed? Or is their behaviour linked to a need to punish their parents for disliking them while showing affection and approval to their siblings? The work with Ralph (see p. 192–7) makes any of these a possibility.

In addition to describing their attachment behaviour as disorganised and disorientated, Main *et al.* (1985) also used the word 'dazed' when describing a child's behaviour on being reunited with his primary care-giver. We understand this to mean the severe form of switched-off behaviour adopted by some children as a defence against further hurt.

We have referred to the adoption of a 'clown' role as another form of resistant-to-learning behaviour seen in schools. This behaviour makes teachers angry and can eventually alienate the child's peers, but what it may mean for the child concerned is rarely examined. His punishment is frequent removal from the class or group, again confirming that he is unacceptable, because he has not been helped to understand that it is only his behaviour that is unacceptable. It is almost as if children who behave in this way cannot allow time for learning. Do they fear that if they give up their not-knowing (how to receive messages from words or numbers), they will discover some information that is even more difficult to take in or digest?

We have already referred (in Chapter 8) to the possibility that a more serious kind of not-knowing exists. The title of Bowlby's paper (1979) 'On knowing what you are not supposed to know and feeling what you are not supposed to feel', gives a clear indication of the kind of secrets we think some of the children in this classification may have to carry. Bowlby says, 'There is evidence from several sources that parents sometimes press their children to shut off from further conscious processing, information the children already have about events that the parents wish they had never observed.' To give just two examples from our own work: Margaret came from a family where a sibling had been murdered, but when this was beginning to become 'known' (acknowledged in her conscious memory) it was too threatening for her to be able to tolerate. As the realisation that she knew what she was not supposed to know came closer, she became depressed and obese. The other child, a boy of 9, kept the 'secret' about the mysterious death of his sibling. These two children proceeded 'to conform to their parents' wishes by excluding them from further processing such information as they have; and that having done so, they cease consciously to be aware that they have ever observed such scenes, formed such impressions or had such experiences' (Bowlby 1979).

To give up the not-knowing about a family secret, or something less potentially harmful, like learning to read, involves change, a step into the unknown. To learn means taking on and moving towards different responsibilities. Resistance to change, which we think can be both desired and dreaded by these children, reflects the wishes of so many of their parents. The parents' desire to maintain a homeostatic way of family life, particularly when they wish to maintain a socially conforming 'family face' (Heard and Barrett 1977), can lead to the child alone being pushed forward to be 'changed'. The label of 'misfit' does not match the image most parents wish to present. When the behaviour of their children confuses others, this apparently gains them a certain contrary satisfaction. As we can see from the following account of the work with Ralph, 'satisfaction' belies not only the sadness and anger of the boy but also that of his parents. Before studying some aspects of Ralph's behaviour when interacting with an educational therapist, we propose evaluating some of his parents' resistance to learning.

The Sopwith family interviews were usually attended by Ralph, both parents, two younger siblings and two educational therapists once a month. The contrast between behaviour and statements was to remain a feature of the interviews. There was frequent denial that feelings could inhibit or facilitate learning. One of the therapists suggested that although their son was probably functioning at a higher intellectual level than the four adults present, yet emotionally he was functioning at the level of his younger sibling not yet at school. She continued:

'In a later interview Mr Sopwith became very angry when he recounted his son's "wrecking" of a family celebration by his "infantile" behaviour. Despite the obviously upset state of their son during this account, mother joined in the attack, describing his behaviour as "over the top – he stuffed his face with food and started acting the clown". When we commented on Ralph's distress, we were advised to ignore the tears as this was quite a common occurrence. Following a painful silence we expressed our concern that none of the adults could find a way of helping Ralph with his distress, and how sad this made us feel. At this point the youngest sibling came over to Ralph and offered him some modelling clay. We were very moved by this demonstration of sibling support and understanding.'

One of the recurring criticisms of Ralph was his interest in a science-fiction programme on television that his father felt was too young for a boy of his intelligence. This interest led him to spend time in the local library reading about the characters in the programme, which meant he arrived home late from school. Mrs Sopwith supported him in the sessions for the first time and said that she felt he tried very hard to please his father, who responded by admitting that he could relate to Ralph only on an intellectual level. He then wondered why Ralph could not be more like his little brother. We remarked that this might be part of the trouble, as both parents had just recalled Ralph trying to behave at a pre-school level which had resulted in a family occasion being 'wrecked'. At this early stage of the intervention the family were unwilling to accept our comment that Ralph might be holding the mistaken belief that if he behaved like a 3-year-old he would receive the same approval as his younger sibling.

It was not until almost the end of the individual once-weekly educational therapy with Ralph, described below, that some of the parental resistance to learning began to lessen. Mr Sopwith had revised his opinion of the television programme that his son followed so avidly when he discovered that several of his colleagues also found it interesting. The therapist who worked with the family continued:

'There were other references to earlier comments that had been made about our understanding of this boy which had been previously denied, particularly by his father. Ralph had made a model of a moonscape with his therapist which he chose on one occasion to show to his parents at a family interview. The model was dominated by two breast-shaped mountains, which inspired Mr Sopwith to make a reference to Greek mythology.'

We were unable to understand this reference and said so. It was suggested at a subsequent meeting with the parents that the model was indirectly showing Ralph's age-appropriate interest in the opposite sex. This suggestion was vigorously denied by Mr Sopwith at this time, but much later he said that he realised that our reference to this model had indeed been right, and that at 14 his son was naturally more interested in sexual matters than Greek mythology.

It was known throughout this work that Ralph attended the same school that his father had done, and Mr Sopwith had frequently implied that he had done very well at this school. He felt that his son could never reach a very high standard, although he might do well at university 'if it weren't for the examinations in between'. In the final family interview, the therapists commented:

193

'We were taken by surprise when Mr Sopwith admitted to his own mediocrity at school and the fact that he had not been "university material". An even greater surprise came in the last few minutes of this interview. We felt we had not succeeded in enlisting the support of these parents to give Ralph more age-appropriate autonomy, although he was demonstrably managing this for himself. He had been offered the option of returning for a brief contract if problems arose in the future, and this was again mooted. Mr Sopwith ignored both of us and turned to his son. "Well, it's a kind offer, Ralph, but really I think it's up to you now. If at any time in the next year you feel the need for help with school work, or just need someone to talk to, then you can ring Mrs Jones and make an appointment; there's no need to ask your mother or me".'

Throughout this work Ralph had been extremely well supported by one of his teachers, who became his 'specific attachment person'. Even so, this alone had not been sufficient support for Ralph. She worked closely with the clinic team, and was instrumental in helping other members of staff to revise previously held opinions of the boy. Ralph came close to recognising the effects that his impulsive behaviour could have on others. He began to differentiate the appropriateness of the 3-year-old impulsive behaviour that amused people from that of an adolescent which angered them and caused upset to himself.

We have not detailed the painstaking work with Mrs Sopwith, who used the telephone to communicate her feelings. Although initially she also resisted learning about change, possibly out of loyalty to her husband's views, she learned to respond more independently, and gradually recognised that family events were becoming more pleasurable, and that she could trust Ralph. She became more open and able to examine the painful feelings associated with change from her own childhood.

Ralph

The educational therapist working with Ralph gives an indication of the depth of his feelings about himself and learning. He seemed too to be trapped in the pendulum swing of adolescence.

'Ralph gave the impression of having chosen the role of the absent-minded professor. He wore his clothes as though they bore no relation to his body and his glasses were permanently balanced on the end of his nose. He spoke very quickly when invited to do so, but hesitantly when expected to examine situations involving his feelings.

'I knew that his psychological assessment placed him in the top band of the intelligence range. The educational psychologist remarked that Ralph had found some of the tests intellectually challenging, but in other unstructured tests he became anxious and managed less well, despite having been told that there were no right and wrong answers. He often behaved in an impulsive manner which hindered his performance. His reading age was just above his chronological age, but the assessment confirmed the school's concern about his spelling and writing. He saw no connection between reading and spelling.'

(It is interesting to note that the 7-year-old mentioned at the beginning of this section, had this problem in reverse: he could spell phonetically, even words with double sounds – "oo", "ar", etc. – but absolutely resisted reading such words.)

'In our first session Ralph examined the contents of his box, but said that it was unlikely that he would ever need them. I began our work by offering Ralph spelling and writing exercises. These provided a structure in which he could learn how to order things. Each session included an unstructured time, which allowed him to face the feeling of helplessness that this engendered. He agonised over decisions and then became upset at the "waste" of a session if he had escaped into his world of convoluted thinking about holes and space by drawing or talking to himself. It was not until I thought Ralph was able to play in my presence in the Winnicottian sense that this unstructured time became less threatening.'

Bauer (1972–3) advocated that when educational therapy was practised successfully one of the teaching tasks was to reinforce the child's external reality. He saw the 'ego-dysfunctional child' as one who 'appears to move from reality into fantasy and back'. He also felt that if certain goals are achieved through the use of this intervention the child would need his 'internal refuge less often as his mastery over the external world increases'.

The therapist continued:

'During an exploration of some words that he was finding it difficult to spell, I praised Ralph for his reading skill. He admitted to guessing words, he had been "very slow in learning to read". A colour-coding game was introduced to help him to master spelling "rules". When he began to practise these rules Ralph took some paint colour samples out of his bag to help correct the spelling. He expressed surprise that the time passed so quickly when I told him that the end of the session was near. He rearranged the contents of his box and asked me to keep it safely for him until the following week. This was the first indication of how important a symbol of containment the box was to become.

'I soon discovered that Ralph's performance in basic skill work was influenced by the meaning of the words he had to spell, and that this perhaps partially explained his resistance to learning them. I noticed that he could not read or spell or write the word "shoot", and placed the word "fool" (which he claimed he could not read) at the bottom of the list. He said he could not read "spoil" or "destroy", although he had no difficulty in managing other words in these "oo", "oi" and "oy" groups.

'When the words "spoil" and "destroy" were put into a sentence, he still could not read them from the obvious contextual clues, so I read the sentence aloud. Ralph immediately rushed into writing a barely legible new word-list. I commented that I thought he seemed bent on running away from the sentence, and that perhaps some of the words held a special meaning for him. He slowed his writing pace, and then began to rummage through his felt pens, saying they had been "messed up by somebody". He returned to his list and said "everything is in a pattern these days". He then started talking about the word "spoil", and made reference to the silent battles he had at home when things were removed from his room and destroyed without his permission. He then went on to talk about an overloaded circuit that had brought a city to a halt. He accepted my comment that sometimes we fear we might become so angry that a fuse would be blown that could destroy things forever, or that if we fought too fiercely we might spoil something special and bring it to a halt.

'When games of Scrabble, Pelmanism and word jigsaws were introduced he expressed his surprise that he could enjoy games with words. His interest in colour and order remained, and he asked permission to rearrange the colour sequence of his felt pens, an oft-repeated activity. After several months he began to mix paints on a palette but he never placed the paint on paper. It seemed as if putting the mess permanently on paper was too threatening a reminder of the "mess" he felt he was in; if the mess remained on the palette it was easily removed.

'Ralph could enter into interactional play but he still became anxious when letters in Scrabble seemed beyond his control. When he was unable to find the letter "y" he described it as a calamity. He said "Yes, I'm making patterns again" when he began to place letters upside down or used them as mirror-image letters. When a session was missed through a misunderstanding by his parents, I felt delighted by what I regarded as a healthy adolescent outburst. "I knew it. I was right, that's typical of them, they got it wrong again!" This outburst also led to his first acknowledgement of being in an upset state of mind at the beginning of the next session. The exploration of the attraction properties of a magnet helped Ralph to discover and discuss feelings of ambivalence.

'Doubt had been cast in one of the joint family meetings on the authorship of a piece of Ralph's writing. "It looks too good" was the remark his mother made. I supported his effort and commented on the difficulty of seeing things in a new way when they had been the same for a long period. In the subsequent individual session Ralph refused to discuss this family meeting with me. He became more and more insistent on playing a game involving plastic letters. Suddenly he "switched off" and began moving the letters around the table.

He placed the capital letters of I O U in that order. I felt he was perhaps expressing some indebtedness to me for my support in the family meeting. He continued to doodle with the letters and talked a great deal about letters having to fit in with others, which I thought was an indirect reference to himself having to fit in and comply with his family's wishes and rules.

'Following this session his feelings about me seeing other children were taken up. He was concerned that I might not have space to fit him in if I saw too many other children. Even if he was fitted in, would I be able to care for and accept him as much as the others? This exchange took place just prior to a break.

'The content of our sessions changed after this break, and Ralph made many drawings of weapons. On one occasion just before the end of a session he insisted that he had time to draw a face, half of which was smiling, half with a confused expression. He readily agreed that the man was like himself, having mixed feelings about staying and going at the end of each session. He was now able to show his enjoyment of the play on words; for example, he made the word "zip", saying later in the game he had "zipped into the lead".

'When I had to cancel a session he resisted talking about what this meant to him. He repeatedly said it did not matter, and that talking could not alter the situation. "It's all spoilt now so forget it." Expressing my own sadness and anger at having to cancel the session led to a discussion of a shared plan for ending our work together in 3 months' time.

'Ralph's dismissal of the contents of his box at the beginning of the intervention was in marked contrast to his feelings about them at the end. In the last session he carefully packed up his models, looked at his spelling lists and drawings, then spent some time sealing the box and tying it with string. It seemed as though he had placed much of the unmanageable part of himself inside for safe keeping. I wondered if this was in the hope that he could be free to make use of the "changed" states of mind that now seemed available to him. I talked about the need to seal the past in his box, but reminded him that the past would retain a range of feelings that could not be eradicated, but could be used as a reference point from which to consider the present, and perhaps even the future.

'In the final family interview, when Ralph was told by his father that he could make his own arrangements for returning to the clinic without consulting his parents, Ralph turned to me and smilingly said, "I don't think I shall be needing that box any more, Mrs Sergo".'

Part IV
GROUP WORK

12

EDUCATIONAL THERAPY WITH GROUPS OF CHILDREN IN DIFFERENT SETTINGS

Figure 12.1 Group dynamic

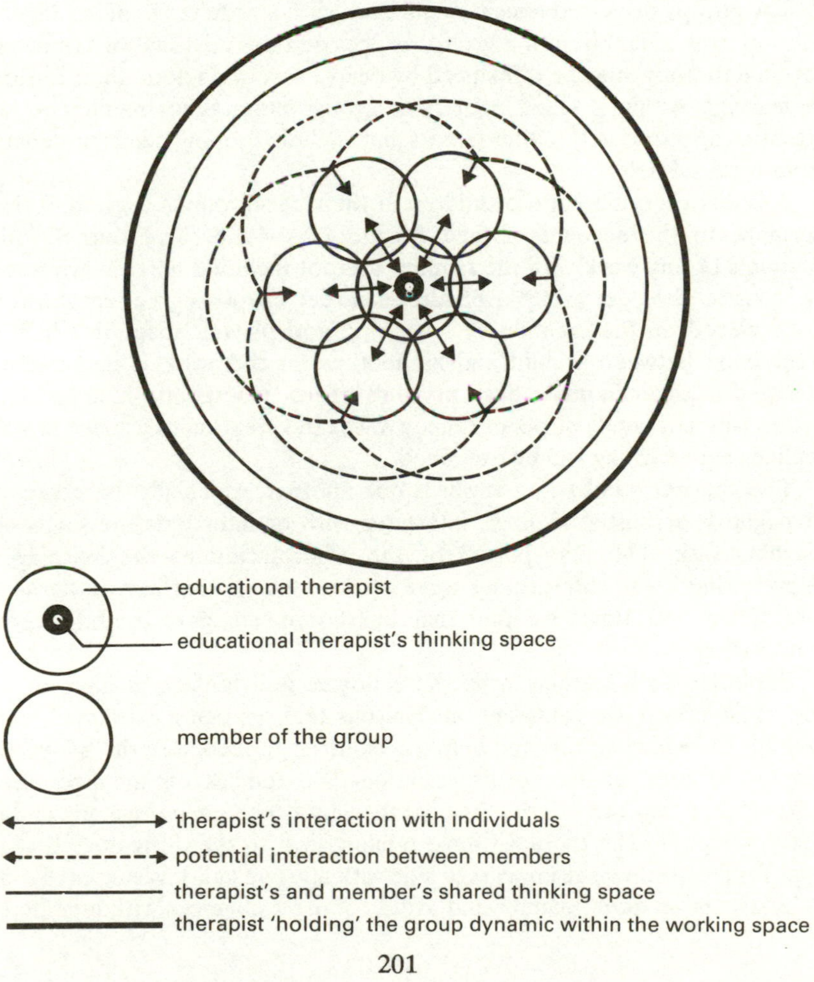

educational therapist

educational therapist's thinking space

member of the group

→ therapist's interaction with individuals

◀-----------▶ potential interaction between members

———— therapist's and member's shared thinking space

━━━━ therapist 'holding' the group dynamic within the working space

In this chapter we consider one or more educational therapists working with peer groups of between three and six children in a variety of settings. We attempt to show that, even when a setting appears to militate against it, the concept of undertaking educational work in a therapeutic manner remains tenable.

The dynamic of an educational therapist and a small group of children is unique, whether this be a peer group or a family group. Patterns of interaction with either of these groups have a process that is similar to the educational therapist/schoolchild dynamic. Inevitably every group will be influenced by the experience that each member brings to it, including that of the therapist. As in individual educational therapy, the primary task is the establishment of a secure base for the group, and a working space within which feelings can be explored.

We give detailed accounts of educational therapists working in a school and in a children's unit attached to a child and family consultation clinic.

The groups discussed consist of children with a wide range of intelligence. The referral of children to a group, as opposed to individual or family educational therapy, may be influenced by one of several factors: their difficulty in learning within a class; poor peer group interaction; inability to seek attention appropriately. Other factors may include training needs or demands from local schools.

A brief description of the children or their backgrounds is given, if this is germane to the account of their functioning within the group. Detailed accounts of any work with the families are not included here, as we wanted to focus on the peer group dynamic. In earlier chapters great emphasis has been placed on the creation of a working and playing space in which the interaction between a child and his mother, or therapist, is negotiated or changed to accommodate each person's needs, moods and feelings. Interaction within a family or peer group involves the creation of a space in which feelings and learning can be examined.

The children's behaviour towards one another, especially the expression of negative or hostile feelings, interferes with or interrupts the focus on a learning task. The part played by the adult facilitates the learning, by commenting on or interpreting some of the feelings that may underlie the interactions. At times we find that our comments have inhibited group functioning.

Exploring and 'learning with' the children, individually, in pairs or with the whole group, we comment on rivalrous feelings being expressed, either verbally or behaviourally, and help the children to recognise the 'ploys' they employ to gain the therapist's attention. We remark on the peer group support that they are offering one another, and then encourage any child to acknowledge it. The therapist must remain alert to the difficulties that can arise for the group if she appears to side with any one child. We try at all times to behave in an adult manner and avoid collusive alliances with members of the group. If one child is rejected by the others we aim to deal with this by working in the metaphor, for example by using the story of the Ugly Duckling with younger children. Introducing a game where four participants, or two pairs, are required, can highlight this problem for older children. They may try to engage the therapist as a fourth member or partner, thus excluding the child whom the other three for some reason reject. Older and younger groups can then usually respond to a straightforward discussion about ostracism.

Children accept that talking is a worthwhile learning activity once group cohesion is established. The fact that even 'silly' remarks are taken seriously by the therapist seems to surprise and reassure most children, and they in turn begin to find the meaning that underlies an ostensibly frivolous comment. As in individual educational therapy, an adult's capacity for listening and seeing beyond the face value of opinions contributes to the functioning of the group.

Children are helped to understand some of their unconscious behaviour; for example, they may try to project some of their own feelings, which they are unable to handle, on to one member of the group. This unconscious behaviour can result in one child being forced to take on an inappropriate role, which might be that of a much younger child, the 'baby' of the group. This is not to say that this child may or may not take on this role to meet some unconscious need of his own, but the whole group needs to understand this dynamic, if they are to learn how to interact age-appropriately as peers.

A variety of tasks for individual children, pairs, or a whole group, is selected by the therapist to show the possibilities of working in different ways. These tasks may be chosen to invite co-operative learning or a better state of independent thinking, or to help a child to tolerate the reality that any one member's skills can be fairly assessed only by reference to previous performance. In addition to learning with, teaching, and providing a space for each child, we aim to develop a group space in which we can think about the group dynamic. Feelings about the absence of any member are taken up with the remaining children in order to help them to understand the effect that this is having on their interactions. Another important aspect of acknowledging the absence of a child is that it confirms for the others that one is held in mind and a place always awaits one's return. The overall aim of the therapist is to try to find a balanced mode of group functioning.

If a group is seen sessionally outside a school setting (often at a clinic), the re-integration of several children into the classroom is problematic from at least three viewpoints: first, for the classroom teacher, who may well be already engaged in teaching an activity or task to the whole class; second, for the class, a disruption in the middle of their introduction to a new activity or task; third, for the educational therapy group, who have to adjust from being members of a small group to being (re-)assimilated into a large class. Some children, and occasionally a class teacher, may resent this change; others may find it a welcome relief. Certain children cannot tolerate the small-group situation and prefer the relative anonymity of a class to the exposure and more intimate atmosphere of a small group, where the adult is tantalisingly available and yet has to be shared – which can be too painful an experience for them to manage. This is especially true for those who have been unable to gain the attention they seek from their attachment figure at home. The smallness of the group can unconsciously remind a child of unresolved feelings of rivalry towards his mother and siblings, which can be particularly significant for those children who know that their younger siblings, being too young to go to school, are at home with mother. The resultant behaviour for the returning group can be attention-seeking, by making unreasonable demands on peers or teacher, extreme disruption, or withdrawal into self-cosseting (all of which have been reported by class teachers).

We have found that the similarities between working with peer and family groups are manifold. Both reveal a complex process that moves with tremendous speed. In this chapter we have chosen two groups which give some idea of the educational therapist/peer group dynamic.

We begin with an account of the establishment of a group in a mixed (co-educational) school, previously designated for children labelled educationally sub-normal. The majority were children of very low ability, although some, whose behaviour had been described as 'disturbed', were of average intelligence but had nevertheless been admitted to the school from time to time. As the school had a long-standing relationship with the local child-guidance clinic, help was requested for several 'difficult' children, said to be 'non-achievers'. Four girls, aged 10 or 12 years, were selected by the head teacher. He was unable to state the nature of their problems because 'there were a hundred and one others who also needed help but, if you can teach them anything, this will be progress'.

A GROUP IN A SCHOOL SETTING: PREPARATION

Salmon and Franco (1989):

Following long and slow negotiations which involved getting parental permission, the head and the clinic team finally reached agreement on a starting date for the group. It was decided to allocate two educational therapists to work with the group, because all the children came from one-parent families and had limited experience of adults interacting co-operatively. It was agreed that a brief contract of one term would be offered to assess these children, with the option of a second term. In spite of some reservations on the part of the head teacher, arrangements were made for twice-termly interviews with the school staff and the children's families, but these are not included in the following account.

The two therapists set themselves a diagnostic task, primarily to help them to discover something about the referred children's approach to tasks, their current skills and their capacity for play, work and interaction. This was in part influenced by the head teacher's reservations about the wisdom of seeing the children at all when it was actually time for the group to begin. It was, therefore, decided that an on-going assessment of the group would ascertain how the children functioned socially: as individuals, in relation to peers, and in relation to adults; and that an educational evaluation would reveal: how they approached a task, how they dealt with difficulties, and which methods suited each girl's ability. The therapists felt that their first task was to establish a 'secure base'. In reality, during the assessment period, this proved a major difficulty due to three room changes and several interruptions.

The group

Jenny, aged 12, was described by her teachers as 'exasperating'; Patty, aged 10, was 'aggressive but shy'; Sara, aged 11 (one of the more able children) was 'disliked'; Josie, also aged 11, was 'withdrawn'.

The first assessment session

'The classroom allotted to us was already occupied and this provoked a considerable amount of confusion for all of us. It took some time for the teacher in residence to remove her class. After some difficulty we were able to get the girls to settle down.

'It was assumed that as each girl had achieved so little, scholastically, her self-image was likely to be a poor one. We therefore began to deal with the group's corporeal image. One girl, Sara, was absent and the other three formed an uncomfortable group with us.'

(We note that the therapists associate themselves with the discomfort.)

'We talked about the difficulties of not knowing how to begin. (With hindsight we realised how much the setting had to do with this. By inviting the group to sit in a circle with us we added to their discomfiture.) We re-introduced ourselves and said we would be working together to find out how we did things and how we felt about ourselves, each week, in this room, at the same time of day. One of us acknowledged how difficult it was to begin working together when we did not know one another. How would they like to begin?

'Jenny suggested saying their names. Did they know why they had been chosen? Jenny again answered, saying that it was because they "don't do too good in school". With a lot of gentle encouragement we asked the girls about their interests. Jenny again answered readily, Josie less so, being often fidgety and looking uncomfortable. Patty was silent. We offered them their boxes and folders for their work. Jenny eagerly said she would write; Josie, with some reluctance, said she would draw; Patty, finally, also agreed to draw.

'All three continued to interact with us individually as they sat at their desks, so that it was difficult to maintain the unity of the group. One of us commented that when Jenny asked if their surnames should be written on the folder we felt that she was sharing in the directing of the group. We returned to our circle and invited the girls to show and discuss their writing or drawing with the rest of us. Jenny immediately asked questions about Josie's work. Josie was unable to respond spontaneously to us; but answered any of our questions to Patty on her behalf. After Jenny had read her story about a cat, all three were invited to model one and to form the word "cat" in plasticine. Jenny and Josie then formed a pair, further isolating Patty, who continued to draw, away from the others. Jenny sang, "Patty put the kettle on" (parodying a nursery rhyme) when Patty continued to ignore our statement that the session would end in 5 minutes.

'This group was interrupted by other children entering the classroom asking for their class teacher on at least six occasions during this hour. It was impossible for the group to disregard these interruptions, and Jenny engaged them in bantering conversation each time. The therapists decided at this stage to acknowledge the interruptions but to wait until the other children had left before trying to re-engage the group.

'Sara had returned from her holiday by the second session, but the girl's class teacher was away. The teacher taking her place expressed to us her dislike of two members of the group, Jenny and Sara, the latter having been punished for not completing a piece of work. She described the class as being "high". When we reached the room where we worked, these two girls were there with the two boys who had interrupted the first session. A team of builders was working outside repairing the school and when pieces of wood came flying through the window we decided to close it, even though it was a very warm day. The boys were asked to leave and the two girls rushed off to find Patty and Josie. We finally settled after moving and placing the furniture we would need in a corner of the room. Remembering our experience of the first session, we felt that it was important to establish an actual group boundary within the classroom that was familiar to the girls. When our circle had been formed Jenny told Sara that her name had been mentioned on the previous week, and asked us if we would be doing the same work again. We introduced ourselves to Sara and invited her to tell us something about her holiday.

'The girls were then reminded of the discussions they had all had about themselves in the first session. It was suggested that they could begin by looking at faces. One of the therapists said she would talk about her appearance; this was followed by the other, commenting on behaviour and the feelings that can be revealed by facial expression.

'We gave them a mirror and encouraged them to talk about their own features. All responded by looking at one another and commenting on colour or number of features, until the discussion led to the senses appertaining to each feature. The girls were then given their folders and asked to write a short

206

story about themselves. This may seem an unrealistic task for children thought to be of limited intelligence but we had in mind only one or two sentences using simple language. Looking at their exercise books and their models from the first session seemed to give them pleasure. Jenny began by attempting to take over our role again by telling the others how to spell but, with encouragement, allowed the other three to work at their own pace. Patty worked very slowly with her face close to the paper. Jenny said that she had glasses and Patty agreed. Josie needed step-by-step help, Jenny and Sara finished first. During the drawing of their eyes their behaviour became exploratory as they added eyebrows and lashes, and Sara noticed that her eyes also had the colour red around them.

'During this activity, the teacher who was replacing the regular class teacher of the girls came in and opened Sara's desk, taking some books from it. Sara said, "That's my desk," and stared hard at this teacher. It seemed to us that Sara in some way felt violated by this silent intrusion. It upset the other three and it took some time to regain their attention. When the teacher had left we acknowledged how hard it was to concentrate when you did not know why someone was looking in your desk.

'The next task we gave the girls was to sort out a small set of Concept cards (a series of photographed common objects that can be used in numerous ways) and give us a sentence to describe each picture. We had selected certain cards so that the pictures had some obvious feature, such as colour, in common, but none of the children was able to manage the deductive thinking required. Perhaps the noisy hammering by the workmen outside the window and another two interruptions by the same two boys while this game was taking place disrupted the girls' concentration. However, we commented on our feelings about the disruptions to our thinking; the girls nodded their agreement. Once the effect was acknowledged and accepted they were able to continue with the activity, at first rather tentatively, but when they understood the scope for sorting the cards into sets their behaviour became more exploratory.'

Subsequent assessment sessions

'Because the group had enjoyed the activity using the senses we continued it in the next two sessions. Cards with simple sentences had been prepared which the children had to place in logical sequence beginning with "My name is ...." Patty for the first time took some initiative by constructing a sentence in her own way: "I am Patty." Other sentences such as "I smell with my nose" were added in the form of a card game. They had to collect sets of senses – rather like the game of Happy Families. Patty was much slower than the other three; her interest could be maintained only if she could change fairly rapidly from one task to another. One of us helped her to collect sets while the rest of us played the game, so that the differences in speed of understanding were minimised.

'On another occasion the focus was on the sense of taste. The girls were given lipstick and asked to make lip prints, which they cut out and glued into their exercise books, adding the word "lips" or "mouth" as they chose.

'The group, although more co-operative with one another and relating in a relaxed manner to us, found it extremely difficult to speak articulately. We used the fact that one of us did not speak English as a first language, and frequently enlisted the girls' help when pronouncing words. The Concept card game gave them an opportunity to add to their confidence in speaking clearly in front of others. Placing a hand on a card when it was face up on the table, the child had to say how the picture related to one of the senses; for example, if it was a picture of an apple, "I use my mouth to taste an apple," or "I can smell an apple." They became very excited when they understood the game and, with the exception of Patty who held back, enjoyed collecting cards when an appropriate sentence was given.

'During the free-choice time following this game, Patty could play only in response to an offer from Jenny; they modelled snakes; Josie continued to match the cards; Sara placed her animals in family groups, except for a lion and some hens which, she told us, were waiting to get into the three pens she had made. In spite of staying within the metaphor, Sara was unwilling to tell us more about the animals and was, we felt, uncertain about how to attach meaning to the play; so we accepted it without comment.

'On arrival for the next session we were told that we would have to use another room, and at the same time were informed that Sara and Jenny had been given money by the builder's workmen, which the staff had confiscated.

'We unlocked the door to our new room and were immediately joined by a boy, who was bundled out by Sara. All the girls began to re-arrange the furniture as it had been in the other classroom. Another boy then entered, demanding to know what we were going to do; we said that we were sorry that it was not possible for him to join the group and he left. Once settled, we asked the girls if they liked stories. Sara volunteered to tell the story of Goldilocks and the Three Bears. This took so much time that the other three became restless and interrupted several times. The situation was exacerbated by the loud hammering coming from the roof above, but it provided us with an opportunity to introduce the question of the workmen and the gift of money. Shortly after we began the discussion we were interrupted by two teachers who apologised and withdrew.

'Sara and Jenny spoke openly about the money. Sara said John the workman liked her and had seen her leaving her house and again on her way to school. She said her father had telephoned the school to express his annoyance that the money was Sara's and should not have been taken from her, although he added that she shouldn't have accepted the money. In future he would deal with it himself. Jenny was quite unable to express any opinion. We tried to help them to think about ways to resist temptation, and wondered aloud whether it was right to take money from people unknown to you. There was a certain feeling of excitement and fear coming from the group during this discussion, as though they were aware of the implications of talking to strangers. Their subsequent behaviours perhaps reflected these states of mind. During the next activity, when all four were unusually chatty, each in turn asked to go to the toilet. Their conversation became noisy with Patty playing an active part. She and Jenny spoke in strange gruff voices. They talked about workmen, boy-friends, knickers and farting. One of us commented that although we had not written about our bodies today they still seemed to be very important.

'At the start of a game of Pairs, we were interrupted again, this time by a helper with a cup of coffee which she placed on a table. When Patty began to win, Sara was able to express her anger by pretending to grab her. The other two were distracted by the smell of the coffee and found it increasingly difficult to maintain their interest in the game. Patty became excited by her success and as we were packing up, asked for the toilet again. We asked her to wait but, just as we were being told by the others that she could not, she urinated on the floor. All four girls accepted what had happened in a very matter-of-fact manner and said that it was a common occurrence. We apologised to Patty, and accepted the remonstrations of the other three.

'It was decided in view of the rather unsatisfactory discussion about the workmen to focus on the sense of touch in the next session. (It was never made clear why the head teacher appeared not to have spoken either to their employers or to the men themselves about the incident.) Josie was absent, and the other three were asked to draw around their hands and then to make finger-prints. The word "palm" was introduced; it was the first time any interest in a word had been expressed. This activity did not lead to further direct discussion about the workmen, but a theme about change emerged, overtly related to managing feelings about changing classes and leaving school, though we felt that covertly they were expressing interest and anxieties about their bodily changes. Jenny in particular was very obviously pubertal; physical development was less discernible in the other three.

'A continuation of the tactile theme began another session, when each girl was given a small bag containing objects with contrasting textures, which they were encouraged to identify by touch alone. Sara spent a considerable amount of time stroking a small furry animal. She was reluctant to relinquish it until the therapists commented that the animal seemed to be wanting to be cuddled and that perhaps we all needed demonstrative affection sometimes.

'This discussion about another aspect of the tactile sense veered off to a most unexpected topic, that of glue-sniffing. When Sara referred to the word "temptation", and the difficulties that arose when trying to resist it, further revelations were made. All the girls except Patty expressed concern about taking part in something you were told was exciting but might be dangerous. We were interested in this mirroring of our statement of a few weeks previously. They described one incident with some older children in detail, with a mixture of bravado and fear. We realised that this was part of their testing out our adult view of what was, or was not, permissible behaviour at various ages. After saying that when they became adults they could do as they wished, they told us about their pleasure in being silly, at which point they started giggling, perhaps to relieve the anxiety that had arisen from the serious discussion.

'Later, interest in words was renewed when another game of Pairs was played and a picture of a palm tree was shown. Pleasure at the recognition that the word "palm" had other meanings was in contrast to the tension engendered by the game. Each one strove to be successful, showing resentment towards another's success. We mused aloud to one another about the group dynamic as a way of helping them all to understand what was happening. Patty knew that the others did not want her to win, so she tried to make a "wrong" choice, the course of action that she thought would place her in a disadvantageous position. The others were pleased by this but it was acknowledged that everyone wanted to win and that even adults sometimes found it difficult to be in a losing position. In spite of having employed tactics intended to make her the loser, Patty eventually won, and this was accepted by the group.

'As the time approached for us to end our "assessment" period we felt very anxious, and regretted not having made a firm decision at the beginning by offering the school a straightforward proposal to work with the group for a longer period. We submitted a report of our work to the staff members directly concerned with the group before meeting them and the head teacher for a decision to be made about the cessation or continuation of its activities.'

The educational therapists' assessment of the four girls functioning in the group was as follows:

'The most striking feature of this group is the way in which they deal with competence. They like the idea of success but find it difficult to manage when they do achieve any task. It is even more difficult for all of them to recognise and tolerate the success of another group member. Whenever they feel unable to accomplish any tasks together their interest wanes, because they do not appear to have been able to develop any strategies to help them to co-operate with others. At the same time, working individually presents problems if there are any distractions. Group cohesion fluctuates.

'The girls lack an understanding of their anxieties and lack a capacity to exercise internal control of them. Their anxieties are often displaced on to each other in the form of disruptive or aggressive behaviour. Individually we perceive them like this:

'Josie coped initially by behaving in a withdrawn manner; when she took a more active part it was by trying to establish a relationship with us by playing the role of "good girl". In the one-to-one relationship with an adult she appears to adopt a more mature manner than when interacting with her peers.

After her absences, her effort to re-integrate herself was to ally herself with one of us. When this did not succeed she made direct attacks on a weaker peer.

'Sara, in spite of missing the first session, was able to integrate herself with ease. She is a participating member in group discussion, can offer new ideas and works independently, only occasionally seeking help. We see her as being separate from the rest of the group, which we attribute to her wish to identify with adolescent behaviour. We are concerned that she is finding it difficult to resist pressure from older children to join in activities that she knows would merit adult disapproval. She cannot verbalise aggressive feelings.

'Patty has great difficulty in relating to adults and tended initially to follow blindly the activities of her peers. She works very slowly, but we think she uses this as a way of insisting that her needs are met. Mastering her feelings, especially when she is being successful, remains a problem. Working with her peers creatively is almost impossible; even working alone cannot be managed unless conditions are very favourable (for example, aggressive behaviour from peers brings about withdrawal).

'Jenny quickly showed a wish to please adults, although denying this. The uncertainty of her individuality or her understanding of her own feelings or wishes gave rise to her taking cues from and even imitating her peers. Her creative work showed her concrete thinking and lack of imagination. Superficially, she has the best performance; she deals with problems when engaged in a task by chattering and giggling to distract the other members. We see this as her attempt to avoid failure.'

Reporting back to the staff group

'Having completed our assessment period with the children we arranged a meeting with the head teacher to discuss the result. The difficulties we had encountered in forming a cohesive peer group seemed to be reflected in some of the difficulties inherent in the staff, whose members appeared not to have formed a cohesive group. One teacher, when asked if she was coming to the meeting said, "not now"; another "saw no point", as he worked with the girls only once a week; two more stayed briefly to offer opinions on the individual children. What was to have been a staff group decision as to whether the educational therapy group should continue was now left to the head and class teacher. The head teacher now withdrew his initial reservations regarding meetings with parents. He thought that the parents could be taught how to handle the four girls – not quite our intention. The class teacher asked us to justify several statements from the report and then spoke more warmly of Sara than hitherto, but expressed irritation at Josie's absences, and felt that Patty would always need help and that Jenny's obstinacy could be most exasperating.

'It was agreed that we would tell the girls that given their parents' consent the group activity would continue. We both felt that the decision to allow us to continue had been that of the class teacher. Without her approval we did not think the head teacher would have agreed to the proposal.'

The continuation of the educational therapy group

'It was very difficult after one term for us to place a boundary around our assessment, which we knew to be the practice of the clinic department we were representing. Many of the themes from the assessment period became recurring ones. The question of rivalrous and aggressive feelings were dealt with through puppet play, the girls being encouraged to express their feelings indirectly and orally. Patty continued to be placed in the role of the baby or weak member of the group and Sara frequently denigrated her efforts. Unfortunately, Josie fell in the kitchen at home and broke her leg, resulting in a long absence from school. Jenny still occasionally took on the role of group leader, but also became defiant when not allowed to have her own way, for example wanting to take objects away from the sessions.

'Sara had one session alone because of the absence through illness of the two remaining members. The theme of change and anxieties about growing up were discussed by way of her reference to having a bus pass (which meant she could travel alone to and from school): this led to a discussion about independence. Sara's reference to a current murder story enabled the fears that accompany independence to be acknowledged. We remarked on the strangeness of Sara's present situation, one child with two adults, when she underlined several words in her book. One of us said that she was, perhaps, showing her need to be supported like the words.

'We felt that we had not managed the Easter and half-term breaks very well. The girls, while not exactly denying the breaks, behaved as though they were irrelevant. They certainly gave no impression of experiencing any difference between our assessment work during the first term and the continuation of our intervention over the following two terms. Perhaps our own uncertainty about the future of the group's existence had prevented our working successfully on the first ending. We felt rather apprehensive about our last few sessions. How were we going to help the girls to believe in the final ending?

'In several of the final sessions Patty was reluctant to enter into any activities and Sara suggested it was because she missed Josie. (It was not until our family interviews that we realised the extent and importance of this friendship.) Jenny continued to have great difficulty in accepting that she could not take things home with her. On one occasion near the end of the work she hid an object. When it was discovered she said she would not come the following week, and became tearful and angry. Although she appeared to understand her need for concrete evidence of the sessions, she still repeated her request in each subsequent session. We were always puzzled by Sara's presence in the group, and indeed in the school. Her reading and writing skills were revealed as being at a more competent level than that of her classroom peers. No satisfactory explanation for her attendance at the school was ever given.

'All three children made small story-books, but Patty could not manage to assemble hers. We could not understand her anxious behaviour until we realised that she wanted the book as a gift for the absent Josie, and the execution of the task assumed great importance for her. Because Patty was slow but could respond to individual adult attention we referred her for individual educational therapy in the term following the end of the group work. Josie's long stay in hospital precluded our making an accurate prediction for her, although it was felt that she would need a great deal of support for her re-integration into a new class after the summer break. (Her mother reported how much her daughter missed seeing "those ladies" and how much her reading had improved.)'

The final session

'The final session was dominated in one sense by the missing Josie. The other three made cards for her, and the therapists sat the girls in the circle to talk about the ending. We said that we had already talked about our sadness that Josie could not be here to say good-bye, but that now it was time to think about Sara, Jenny and Patty. Sara reacted seriously, but Jenny tried to deny the reality by talking about what they could do next week. We spoke about thinking about each other next week, "holding each other in mind", and remembering all that we had learned together. Patty interrupted by saying that she wanted to collect up some papers to send to Josie. We asked her to put them away. She shrieked, "Why?" and we replied that it was now time to think about her, Patty. Sara and Jenny were able to say good-bye, although Jenny added, "See yer, Miss", implying that this was not the end. Patty, the least intelligent and most immature of the group, surprised us by saying good-bye to us both, and when she reached the door she turned and said, "It feels strange."

'Our farewells to the head teacher were dominated by the emphasis that he placed on his wish for the continuation of the groups next year. The class teacher expressed surprise that we were leaving and gave us her views on the deterioration of the school. She conceded that Sara was "better", but made no reference to the other three. We felt that we had not succeeded in helping the four girls to form a group, partly because each girl showed a propensity to relate to either one or the other of us exclusively, except perhaps when they were engaged in a shared activity.'

The therapists expressed their own feelings of ambivalence about the ending of the group work.

Because we wish the focus of this chapter to remain on the group dynamic, we have not examined the girls' family backgrounds and their earlier attachment patterns either at home or in school. Instead, we refer to a chapter by Richardson (1975) called 'Harnessing the Emotional Forces in the Group'. Her thinking seems applicable to the group dynamics that were described, although she was studying the pupil–teacher interaction in a classroom. To understand this Richardson used the theory of Bion (1962), who discovered in his work with training groups that any group's real problem was to do with what he called 'basic assumptions', or the unconscious emotional life of the membership. Richardson states at the beginning of her paper that

'a good teacher will have one main objective: to help his pupils to learn for themselves. For the one inescapable truth about the whole educational enterprise is that every child must, ultimately, accept responsibility for his own learning, whether he is an acknowledged leader in his form or its most retiring member.'

Following a statement that most children wish to achieve, but that this is dependent on the use they are able to make of the opportunities afforded to them, Richardson asks us to consider an underlying factor of group behaviour: 'Yet, as members of groups, their behaviour is continually dominated at the primitive unconscious level by emotional needs that may have little to do with growing up or learning'.

The group behaviours defined by Bion (1962) as the 'dependent culture, the pairing culture and the fight-flight culture' Richardson saw as applicable to educational situations such as the classroom. She said:

In the dependent culture the danger for the group is that it relies too implicitly on the leader and becomes frustrated because the leader cannot rise to the expectations people have of him. And so the teacher, as the dependent leader, must contrive to be reliable while continually urging the class to question his omniscience, challenge his opinions and realistically accept his human limitations. And at times he will create situations in which members of his class take his role, and become accepted as alternative leaders in a basically dependent culture, using their own expertise as he uses his when he is the accepted leader.

The latter part of this statement applies, perhaps, to the leading role that Jenny attempted to take in the group, described above. Had Josie continued to attend this group we imagine that she and Patty would have formed a 'pairing culture' where, Richardson said:

the danger is that the group rests in the lazy hope that two members will continue indefinitely to carry responsibility ... resulting in the frustration of individual endeavour. Here the teacher's role is to break up the task and give each pair or small group [she was referring to a class] a manageable part of it to tackle.

This means that the group as a whole no longer invest all their hope in one pair.

The 'fight-flight culture' is likely to have been experienced by many professionals working with classes of children or adults. The first danger is one where the group's hostility can undermine or, at worst, destroy a teacher – an all too common occurrence, especially in inner-city schools. The power of a group can also result in its self-destruction, which Richardson suggests takes place when the group behaviour leads to

> unleashing of its own hostile impulses or withdrawal from the situation altogether. And so the role of the teacher is to channel the aggression into an attack on ignorance and apathy, so that the class rediscovers its powers of co-operation in a learning situation and uses its leaders in a constructive way.

It is necessary for teachers to have some understanding of these 'basic assumptions' so that ways can be found in which to prevent the group from being overwhelmed by destructive forces, 'so that new forces can come into play and be used by the group in an increasingly mature and responsible fashion'.

In spite of the misgivings of the two therapists working with the group described, we felt that the girls showed a degree of maturity and behaved responsibly when it came to their management of themselves at the end of the work, especially when we recall how each had previously been perceived by their school staff.

In the following account we describe the work of an educational therapist with a group of emotionally and behaviourally disturbed children in a unit attached to a child and family consultation clinic, a very different setting. All the children and their families attending the unit were initially referred to the outpatient clinic.

THE CHILDREN'S UNIT

The unit is staffed by a multi-disciplinary team and is housed in an annexe of the local hospital. A variety of full- and part-time treatment programmes are offered to children up to 12 years of age and their families, ranging from family therapy to specific help with management techniques.

There are usually eight full-time children attending the unit classroom on a daily basis and their ages are between 5 and 12 years. Their intellectual levels are usually within the 'normal' range, but the majority have lost their capacity for learning. Some have specific learning disabilities. They remain on roll at their local school and, where possible, attend there each Friday to maintain links. The majority return to mainstream school, while others need special educational provision due to their continuing emotional and behavioural disturbance.

The unit staff work with the children and their families (or other primary care-givers) while making a full assessment of their needs and offering short-term treatment (typically between 6 and 9 months). Most of the children referred are members of complex and confused families, who require more intensive help than out-patient clinic attendance can offer. The performance of children of school age is inevitably affected by what is happening to them elsewhere and all three categories of anxious attachment are represented in the full-time unit group.

The unit teacher is an educational therapist. Although she meets parents, sees children individually for educational therapy and liaises with all members of the educational system, the account that follows concerns only her work with the full-time children (some of whom are resident from Monday to Friday).

'I have overall responsibility for each child's education and have to ensure that they get a "balanced and digestible diet" of educational "food".

'I work closely with my welfare assistant and together we review sessions and openly discuss our own feelings and the children's behaviour.

'The children start each school session in the main classroom. All the rooms lead off this area: one contains a sand tray, a large low sink for water play and experiments, painting easels, clay, carpentry equipment and a "home corner". Another room houses the "library" with an area for quiet reading, language, computer and other individual and group work. A large doll's house occupies one corner of this room, screened by a tall cupboard for some privacy.

'A third room is free of furniture, containing just two cushions. The space is used for floor games and activities such as cars and road layouts, brick constructions, farm and zoo animals, offering an opportunity for both individual and co-operative floor play. The room also provides a quiet space for children who are angry or upset. They can use the two cushions (known as the "kicking" cushion and the "tears" cushion) to express their feelings non-verbally until they are ready to speak openly about them. They can choose to use the space in this way or, occasionally, they are sent there for "time out". If a child becomes overwhelmed by his feelings within the classroom, he will be physically held to keep him and others safe and, equally importantly, to reassure him that his feelings of distress can and will be contained for him.

'Our aim is to offer ourselves as educational attachment figures and, by consistent care-giving within our professional boundaries, to provide these extremely vulnerable children with a secure base and facilitating environment. We place ourselves in the same position at the beginning of every day

216

and every session, and every child has his own personal space and tray for his work. The arrangement of the tables, and who sits with whom, is constantly under review. Children are carefully prepared for any changes, which are kept to a minimum.

'Because the unit is open all the year round, admission and discharge are regular features of daily life. Preparation of the group for a new child is vital. Our policy of open discussion helps the children to find some space in their minds to think about the newcomer and recognise that his arrival will mean change. They need time to work through their own feelings before they can contemplate the adjustments that must be made. The ages of the new children and the nature of their difficulties, as well as those of the individuals in the established group, are carefully considered. (For example, it is essential to work out the safest place to put a potentially violent child.) It is essential that existing members of the group know that they will continue to receive the support and reassurance that they need. We make use of the continual arrivals and separations by linking them to past and future transitions.

'The arrival of a new child generally follows the departure of another, and both events change the "pecking order" in the group. Interestingly the existing children allow the necessary space for the new child and almost invariably are initially generously supportive and model appropriate behaviour. We think that this experience puts them in touch with their own feelings of being accepted on entering the unit themselves. We use these opportunities to review their progress positively. "Do you remember, Shane, how hard you found it to sit still when you arrived here?"

'The process of assessment involves careful observation of how each child responds to our expectations and those of his peer group. He will be required to sit quietly on his chair and attempt the tasks presented to him. We make minimal scholastic demands of a new child at first, allowing him to choose a tray (the work container) and make a name label for it. How he tackles this task helps us to understand something of his level of confidence and competence. He is then given paper and asked to draw a picture of himself. Although some children find this a difficult and upsetting request it is an important part of our early assessment. Next the child will be asked to either draw or write about his family and provide such personal details as he knows (e.g. his address, birthday, name of school, and so on). Finally he is asked to make a list of his likes and dislikes; again, if he cannot write, either he can draw or we write to his dictation. How he manages gives us an indication of his approach to tasks, his self-esteem and his achievement levels. This introductory procedure allows us to provide support and encouragement and, more importantly, offers an opportunity to demonstrate our acceptance of the child for himself, regardless of his scholastic skills.

'Because family work continues as a closely integrated part of each child's treatment programme, we are constantly made aware of the many changes in their family lives. We know that events outside the unit are likely to have an effect on each child, particularly events that involve loss. He has probably had to tolerate many sudden changes. Throughout our work and as part of the weaning process, preparing the child for leaving us, we make numerous and regular links between past, present, and future events within the unit. This preparation provides an opportunity for each child to experience a planned separation, very often the first time this will have happened. Particular attention is given to breaks, even minor ones, during the working day. Any break represents a change and is stressful for these children, who have already suffered as a result of changes and separations. The level of anxiety associated with any transitions can be acute.

'We try to provide all the children with strategies for coping with change, enabling them to update their internal working models in a positive way. This involves helping them to make a gradual transition from the unit to either a new or a known school environment. Our follow-up support includes continued liaison with other members of the community network, for example, educational psychologists, special needs support teachers and social workers. We also offer on-going family and individual therapy, which includes continuing educational therapy sessions.

'The normal primary school curriculum provides a scholastic structure within which we address each child's emotional development, observing their behaviour and trying to understand how they approach learning. The introduction of the National Curriculum in Britain as a result of the 1988 Education Reform Act is highlighting the close relationship that we see between a child's emotional state and his scholastic achievement levels.

'We find that learning to sit calmly and comfortably gives the children an experience of stillness that allows them to feel contained, so when they arrive in the classroom we expect them to sit in their own place with their hands on their laps. This is particularly important for confused, "unheld" children who can begin to feel in control of themselves in their own space and learn to respect the space of others. Their physical distress and energy can be "earthed" in this way. Once the group are as calm as possible the children are asked to fetch their trays. If the group behaviour is "high" they do this one at a time; if the group is calm they are free to act independently.

'In our experience helping children with minor transitions, that is changing from one activity to another, enables them to manage major ones better. We recognise the threat of a new beginning posed by every ending [as it did for Luke in Chapter 4], as well as the benefit of a "fresh start". We use charts to record and mark the beginning and ending of each task. This procedure ensures that we give close individual attention to every child at the time of each change. The calendar aspect of the charts helps us all to acknowledge the time scale of the admission, to prepare for breaks and subsequent transitions, and it is utilised when endings are in sight. Once, when I commented to my colleague, "I'm noticing how well Dale is sitting while he's writing today – do you remember how difficult he used to find it?" Dale swung around to face me, making excellent eye-contact, beaming, "Not now I don't!" and all the children straightened up.

'Recently, after two children joined us, a member of the established group had a major outburst, needing time-out to keep him and others safe. This was the first incident of the kind that the new children had witnessed. One of them, a girl, suddenly burst out, very shocked and distressed. "Whatever did the other children and teachers think of me when I was like that in my old school?" Together we thought about this insight into her own behaviour and reminded her that one of the things she was learning about now, in the unit, was how to manage herself. Perhaps because we so often make links for the children, they quickly learn to do the same.

'As adults we use every opportunity to model new ways of working together, negotiating, and conducting our own problem solving. If we don't know how to tackle a particular situation or incident we openly discuss the possibilities, for example: "I've noticed how hard it is for Mandy to manage today. Do you think it might help her if she moved into the library? I know she has a lot on her mind just now." We try to help the children to differentiate between the things over which they have control (that is, how they manage their tasks and their interactions with others) and those events and the behaviour of others over which they have less control. It is important to help the children to accept that some changes have to be resolved at an adult level.

'Step-by-step preparation is made for the ending of each session, starting with a verbal reminder of the time. Then the children put their work away and sit once more quietly with their hands on their laps. When they are as calm and composed as they can be we think together about the session that is ending. Each child comes out to me in turn, and the others are expected to allow each other to have his own personal attention without distraction. Together we reflect on how the session has gone – a "mini" review. The emphasis is on how well the child has managed the things that have been difficult. If he has had a tantrum we think about how well the time-out period was used (if it was necessary) for him to regain control and to feel more settled. If the work was new or difficult he will be praised for coping with the fears and frustrations that he experienced. The focus is very rarely on "good work" as such. The children show considerable insight into their own behaviour and discover ways of sharing their new-found understanding. They develop a sense of personal job satisfaction. The highest praise of all is a silent handshake.

'Reading, writing and painting provide us with the therapeutic basis of our work. As the children become more confident and feel more secure they are able to benefit constructively from mathematical and other problem-solving tasks. Eventually they feel free enough to make constructive use of scientific and topic-based exploratory work, previously possible only with intensive individual help.

'A very high value is placed on stories, whether we are reading to the children or hearing them read. It is possible to keep in close touch with a child's feelings by paying close attention to his miscues and the metaphorical content of the story. I have become increasingly aware of the problem of managing this well enough for those of our children whose reading skills enable them to read alone. They seem to need the support of an adult to help them manage the content when they find it stressful. We try to be sensitively aware of the implications of all written material that the children use, including their mathematics and other text/work books. When the content triggers off a memory of an event from the past, not necessarily at a conscious level, a child may suddenly exhibit resistance to the work in hand and become upset. [The description of Keith's difficulty with the 'dirty' paw prints in his mathematical work book in Chapter 8 is an example of this.]

'To emphasise the predictability of the children's classroom experience, every working morning starts with a written task. On Mondays the children are asked to record any weekend events that they wish. This offers them the opportunity to share their feelings with us, either directly or indirectly. On subsequent mornings they are free to write imaginatively or about how they feel. The younger children draw a picture and dictate sentences, some of which they might copy, trace or write over, whichever best enhances their skill.

'The older children, including those who have habitually refused or avoided writing in their schools of origin, are expected to write for themselves; the amount of support and encouragement to make this possible varies. Surprisingly the children rarely fail to respond to this expectation, although getting started can present problems. Some resist our offers of help, or they may rubbish or destroy their attempts. Almost invariably we find that such difficulties arise because their feelings about the material they have written or the ideas that they have for stories are too distressing or "dangerous" to manage. We acknowledge these feelings, however they are expressed, as a way of demonstrating our understanding of them.

'The daily writing activity allows us to share each child's efforts with him. Indeed, this often proves to be essential in order to decipher the various scripts. In addition to giving the children spellings we ask for good guesses when they cannot spell or express themselves with ease. We accept all their efforts, however messy. We play incidental games with words that are proving elusive, introducing an element of fun into what has previously been a daunting experience. We have selected three examples of unit children's stories, beginning with Letty, aged 4, who dictated the following:

The little girl killed the little baby, the little girl killed mummy as well. Goodbye and I'm going to buy some sweets, baby. All right, bye bye. I'll see you tomorrow, bye bye, bye bye. Away in a manger no crib for a bed ... hm, hm, hm, and the little baby killed mummy as well and that's .... Once upon a time there was a little girl going to visit her mum. Little Red Riding Hood bought some milk and sugar. Oh, that's the little Red Riding Hood ... bought it for mother. The mu ... the ... the witch killed little Red Riding

Hood .... Once upon a time there was a little baby .... The little baby killed monster, the monster killed the baby. Be quiet baby, I love you now. Be quiet, be quiet, be quiet, be quiet, be quiet, baby no [angry voice]. Go to byen [sic]. I'm not going to sleep. Goodbye, goodbye, see you in the morning. Once upon a time there was a girl, down the seaside with no-one else and she had her baby down there and sister went in the water with her towel and she got it wet and the water was deep. She went in the sea and went dead and that's the end. And ... but back of the sea ... and the water was deep and that's the end.

'As a result of the stories that Letty dictated we learned that she had been a "replacement" child (not previously known). She was conceived immediately after the cot-death of a 1-year-old girl.

'Another child whose writing revealed thoughts about her fragile state of mind was Kim, aged 9. She was of mixed parentage and had been adopted when she was about 9 months old by a Caucasian family who were members of a very strict religious sect. Another adopted child had died as a toddler 4 years previously. The adoptive parents emphasised that both children were specifically chosen because "no one else wanted them". Kim had become totally withdrawn and mute at home and was admitted to the unit; the relationship between her and her adoptive parents was described as "icily cold". She wrote the following poem:

The mirror

There was a mirror
Shiny and bold,
But when I touched it
It was hard and cold.

I called it my twin
But never would it let me in
One day I saw a maid behind me,
But when I looked
I thought my eyes were deceiving me.

She lit a fire and
It was really there.
She singed the best carpet
And I called her a tire.

Next day I saw her again
Throwing silver glitter like rain.
I could not see her, it was a ghost!
A real live ghost!

221

I screamed and made my throat sore.
The ghost spoke
And said I was a bore
We moved house;
And the only haunt we had
Was a friendly mouse.

So that was the end
Of our haunted house,
As I watched the demolition men
Knock down our haunted house.
The end

'The third example was written by a boy of 9, Sean, who had experienced repeated rejections. Shortly after his admission to the unit he removed a magnet from the classroom, subsequently "discovering it" (as he said) in the garden. He was helped to return it and we thought the matter was concluded; not however for Sean, who wrote stories and painted pictures around the theme of robbers, magnets and prison over the next three days. These are two of the stories he wrote:

One day I saw a robber who had stole (sic) a car. I quickly got a extra strong magnet that took me to the stolen car. I had a bucket with me, I took it out of the car and the robber got caught.
    One day I went out with a strong magnet you can turn off and on. A thief climbed up a pipe with magnets so I quickly turned on the magnet and the magnet pulled the thief towards me so I took him to the police station.

'I mused aloud about the problem he seemed to be having with magnets, I wondered whether he had found not being punished for taking the classroom magnet too difficult to manage. Until this moment Sean's behaviour had been awkward and sullen, but in response to my statement he turned and made excellent eye contact with me, nodded and visibly relaxed.

'In order that each child can have some personal space apart from the group we offer them privacy while they are painting and dictating whatever they wish about their pictures. Again, all their efforts are accepted and valued regardless of any artistic merit. This is an intimate time and is often used by the children to share worries. Their paintings frequently seem to mirror their inner anxiety and turmoil, and they use them to explore their conflicting feelings within the metaphor. When it seems appropriate we may reflect on "How lonely that tree looks" or "That must be very frightening for him", giving the child a message that we are working hard to understand the picture, until he is ready to acknowledge and link true feelings to the expression of them on paper.

222

'We decided to give a brief description of six children before giving an account of their interactions during a morning session in the unit classroom.'

Brian

'Brian was just 12, and found it very hard to face the reality of growing up. He was unusual in that he had an IQ of 65 (WISC [R] 1976) and initially we were concerned about how he would manage to fit into a group of more able children. This proved not to be a problem. He had been placed in care two years earlier when his family broke up. He had no contact with his natural parents. Our aim in admitting him was to help him find ways of managing his distress and anger, and to come to terms with the long-term rejection he had experienced. He had been with us for 11 months and was being prepared for long-term fostering (previously impossible). He was a wiry, red-haired boy who became very violent when upset. At the time of reporting he resembled a 7-year-old. He had been spending weekends with his long-term foster parents and was being introduced to his new special senior school prior to leaving us within a few weeks.'

Amanda

'Amanda was 11 years old. She came from an intact family and was the eldest of four children. She had never managed to settle in her mainstream school, having been unable to separate from her mother. She had always been a restless, "naughty" girl in the classroom. The school made two major complaints about her behaviour: she was "highly manipulative" and had "violent outbursts". Her parents were reluctant to seek help until the need to choose a secondary school for Amanda precipitated a crisis. The parents had reached the point in their work with my colleagues where they had gained sufficient confidence to begin to look at the whole family dynamic, and to acknowledge that this was not just a school problem. Amanda was a tall girl with long dark hair that frequently concealed her face. She had never been assessed by either the school or the educational psychologist because of "her refusal to co-operate". After a stormy start in the unit she became reassured by the predictable expectations and constant availability of the adults. She made rapid scholastic progress, showing herself to be a conscientious worker. Her manipulation of adults and peers had reached a highly sophisticated level and continued to present problems.'

Henry

'A the time of the session described below, Henry was due to leave us six weeks later to go to a local boys' special secondary school, even though he was not yet 11 years old, the usual age of transfer. He was a heavily built boy of 10+, though he resembled a podgy toddler rather than an obese schoolboy. His appearance was menacing, particularly when he felt threatened. He had been rejected repeatedly by family and foster homes and had attended innumerable schools. It was in the schools that his problems were most severe, but invariably the breakdowns there led to the collapse of his foster placement. He was finally placed with an older, very stable foster family with considerable experience of difficult teenagers. In spite of their undemanding support the inevitable happened and their local school reluctantly had to suspend him. The complaint was that he would never stay in his place. "His bottom never touches the chair for a moment." He was constantly disruptive and violent, and his teachers in mainstream school were unable to contain him.

'Henry's first stay with the unit was for six months. We felt that he needed a bridging support to enable him to manage a gradual return to mainstream school, which is where we felt he really belonged. He was placed in a special educational resource centre (a small unit within a mainstream school, with the appropriate opportunities for gradual integration) and was supported there until his teacher felt he was settled. Tragically, during the first half-term break two members of his foster family were killed in a car accident, and two others were seriously hurt. From this time everything in school began to go wrong for Henry. When he learned, right at the end of term, that the teacher with whom he had formed an attachment was leaving he was devastated. He and his foster family struggled to get through the summer break, only for him to start the new term with suspensions for violence. By this time Henry was totally out of control once more and was re-referred to the clinic. It was then that the education department asked if we would re-admit him on a temporary basis while a special school placement was made for him. The traumas that the foster parents had experienced over the months made it possible for them to accept help for themselves which they had previously resisted, and they were able to acknowledge their own grief. They patiently stood by Henry while we supported them with weekly home visits.'

Belinda

'Belinda was 9, of mixed parentage, the eldest of three children. She was an attractive girl with a dark complexion. Her referral to the unit was based on great concern over her depressed state, frequent nightmares, and attempts at self-destruction. She was preoccupied with her colour. Apart from her natural grandfather, the rest of her family were white. Her mother's second husband, father to the two younger children, was no longer a member of the household. During the time Belinda had been with us a former boy-friend of her mother's had joined the family. He was supportive to mother and together, with the help of the unit team, they had worked on some of the problems that Belinda was having with her siblings. In the unit classroom she tended to be withdrawn, maintaining a "good-girl" image, reluctant to seek help. Her written work and the dictations to accompany her paintings reflected her preoccupation with the extremes of good and bad, happy and sad, black and white. Belinda had shown that she could take advantage of the unit experience, and the change in the family dynamic appeared to have helped her feel slightly more secure. She was being prepared for her return to her own school for the last two weeks of term, so her discharge was imminent. Her feelings were as ambivalent about this forthcoming event as about all other aspects of her life.'

Colin

'A 9-year-old, Colin, was another member of the group. He was a wiry, street-wise boy whose eyes held a "knowing", rather piercing, expression. Prior to his arrival at the unit he had lived for a time with his mother, younger brother, and half-brother, until rejected by her and her co-habitee. Then he was returned to father, a stepmother, and another half-brother aged 1. He had attended six schools, none of which had been able to either contain him or teach him any basic skills. His life had been beset by desertions and he was constantly terrified that his father should be hurt or vanish from his life. His physical needs were not well met and he was left largely to his own devices for long periods. He was good with his hands, and had a lively enquiring mind. Colin often accompanied his father in his many outdoor pursuits. He was extremely knowledgeable about the adult world of the lorry-driving fraternity; there was very little that he didn't know about the mechanism of heavy vehicles. He was, however, difficult at home.

'Colin was tense and restless in the extreme, and unused to coping with the predictability and presence of caring adults. During his two months' attendance he had found the unit programme difficult and had presented many behavioural and management problems. He was initially resistant to any learning – scholastic or otherwise – but once he was able to respond to us he began reading with rapidly increasing competence and writing his own short stories. His progress was erratic and was not maintained, however, perhaps due to the elusiveness of his family who showed little interest in his achievements and whose attendance remained spasmodic.'

Andrew

'Andrew, an 8-year-old boy, can only be described as a very sad shadow. Quite tall for his age, with mousy hair, he had very pale colouring which often seemed to become transparent. He had been admitted to the unit on a daily basis earlier in the year in an attempt to improve the relationships between him, his mother and his stepfather. Andrew was the focus for the family problems. The problems escalated and he became an in-patient. He was preoccupied with being hurt and placed himself at risk when he expressed his anger and distress. He did this by provoking his peers, who retaliated physically. He gave the impression of clinging to the classroom and its predictability with a sense of desperation. His stories were full of violence and disaster.'

A morning session

The educational therapist follows her introduction of the children with an account of one morning session to illustrate the group dynamic.

'The morning in question started as usual with a "handover" meeting from medical to educational staff to up-date information about the children. We then joined the children for a "community meeting", to outline the programme for the day, an important part of our preparation process. The children can discuss any topics they choose. The meeting on this particular morning was centred on the theme of "leaving". We noted the absence of Amanda.

'The children came into the classroom quite calmly, with the exception of Colin, who was waving his arms and humming loudly. They all sat down in their places with their hands on their laps, including Colin. Although the children were affected by Colin's singing, they looked calm and expectant. (Children in the unit become very accepting and tolerant of one another, and behaviour such as Colin's can help remind them of their own progress.) When they got up to fetch their work trays they tucked their chairs carefully under the table. We think that the completion of movements is important to these highly disorganised children. It allows them to build up an experience of their own constructive controls. (The habit of this small action can alter a teacher's perception of a child's behaviour when he returns to his own school.) Back in their places they check their pencils: if they need sharpening they put up their hands. They appear to find the repetition of these simple instructions and their responses very reassuring, confirming a recognition of, and respect for, their own space and that of others. Surprisingly few children resist these formalities: those who do are given positive help from their peers to "remember" what is required of them. This example of constructive group interaction is extremely valuable, particularly on the arrival of a new child.

'Although Colin was singing, the other four children started their writing – stories out of their own heads. I suggested that Colin should have a count of five to settle, otherwise he would need to have time-out. He was unable to respond and needed to be taken to the quiet room. He was anything but quiet but he managed to stay there, for which he was praised. The others were able to pursue their tasks and we made comments to support them individually: "I'm noticing how well you are managing, Brian, even though there's so much noise" and "I'm remembering how hard it was for you, Henry, when you first came, if there was any disturbance. Is it a little easier now?" and to my

226

colleague "It's really useful for the children to get practice at working when there is a noise, because there are always lots of distractions in ordinary schools." We encouraged the children to help one another, and reassured Colin that we were available for him too, verbalising this at an adult level.

'Picking up the topic raised in the community meeting, we initiated a discussion about the impending school visits for those who would soon be leaving. Henry anxiously interrupted to remind us that, as he was only 10, he would be the youngest boy in his school; we acknowledged his concern. Belinda said she was going to a friend's party at the weekend, and would be able to tell her friends that she was starting back in her school in two weeks' time. She said that "a lot of her" wished she was staying in the unit. We talked together about saying good-byes, remembering that Andrew, Brian, and Henry had all experienced sudden separations without any preparation. We reflected on the way we work on endings together in the unit, and the children looked less anxious.

'The noise coming from "time-out" had continued unabated. I was struggling to think of a solution to my hasty action of placing Colin there, because I knew that he was due to go to a music therapy session at 9.30. (He was always apprehensive about this, though he made good use of the time once there.) I decided to leave him until he was collected and went quietly to him to explain. He paused briefly while I spoke and looked less fraught. Standing by the door of the quiet room I verbalised my thought for everybody that perhaps the children were all able to work quietly because Colin was acting out on everyone else's behalf. The children stopped working and looked directly at me, and Colin settled quietly on the "tears" cushion. I praised him for managing to calm himself and told him that the music therapist would be collecting him in 3 minutes' time. He sighed and relaxed.

'My colleague pointed out that Henry often asked for the spelling of a word immediately after Brian had done so. I asked Henry if he had noticed this, and then complimented him on the changes in his writing skills. We remembered together how he had found it almost impossible to manage in the past. He looked very pleased as he acknowledged his progress. Brian by this time had written several lines, an unusual achievement. As he would be going home after school for an extended weekend, he was asked which of the week's stories he would like printed out (typed). I reminded my colleague, for the benefit of the group, that I would be out tomorrow taking Brian to visit his new school, so could she make sure that the other children chose which story they would like printed? I wrote a note, to display on my desk, as a reminder of this. (Preparing the children for my absence was important and the selection of the stories for printing would help them to keep me in mind.)

'Colin went off calmly with the music therapist for his session; the rest of the children were asked to think about ending their stories. Belinda was due to go to the clinic for an individual play therapy session. She said that she was going to extend her story on her return (perhaps confirming for herself that she would return?), and then made an oblique comment that "they write five pages at my school". I asked her to fit the story into the time left so that she could start something different on her return. Before she went we thought together about her morning and reflected on how well she had managed to organise herself to give her story a beginning, middle, and end in spite of the short time available. As usual, her face was expressionless, but her bodily movement suggested that she was pleased. She returned to her place briefly until she was collected; we exchanged good-byes and she said, "See you after break." We were pleased that she could make this prediction with such certainty.

'Andrew completed his story and brought it out to be checked. He had written about "five idiotic poofters [sic], naked except for socks, vests and hand-cuffs". The hero of the story "shot off to the police. Soon they were in prison and I got a medal for bravery, but it went on so I ended with six medals." His story was quietly accepted, his chart was marked off and he was asked to start on his maths. (We often reflect on the content of a story but on this occasion I was unable to think of a way to comment.)

'Henry and Brian were reminded of the time, and Brian was asked to bring his book to me. He had produced a long, well-written, coherent story (measured against his usual standards), and showed his pleasure by stretching his body as if to appear and feel taller. I offered him a choice between his having extra time to finish the story himself or dictating the rest for me to write. He firmly opted to finish it himself, bursting with pride. I wondered whether he could manage or whether the self-imposed pressure would prove too much. It was an important moment for him and I made myself keep quiet. He managed, brought his book again and I shook his hand.

'Henry, too, continued to write, but he could never write without opening his bowels part way through the task. On his return he always showed his resentment of any attention given to other children in his absence, so he received extra individual attention to review the week, look at the past, and consider the future. We felt we must give him a clear message that however he behaves in his new school he cannot expect to return to the unit again.

'Andrew's mathematics was being checked and I was aware of his tense facial muscles as we talked about his struggle to type sums of money required for a shopping list (an exercise from his mathematics workbook). Together we recognised that, although many things have changed for him, his feelings of anxiety about money have not. His problem of stealing money and small items from shops had not been entirely resolved. Tackling these money sums provided an opportunity to help him recognise his own growing resources.

'At 10.00 the children were asked to leave their work and collect their library books. As discharge dates come closer, we incorporate planned changes into the programme in order to help the children to prepare for their return to a less predictable classroom routine. It was at this moment that Colin returned, unsettled once more. He was asked to sit on his chair and did so, humming loudly, while the others went into the library, making space for each other on the large floor cushion. When they were settled I firmly told Colin to come over to my desk. He turned and twice called me "fat cow". I ignored this, stood him in front of me and put my hands on his upper arms, gently but firmly. I told him that I understood that he was feeling very upset but that we could help him to settle himself down. He was tense and tried to free himself from my hands, but suddenly I felt a relaxing of his muscles. He looked tearful, and I asked him to take a deep breath, breathe out, and then shake his arms gently by his sides. Having begun to recover he collected his tray, sat in a dejected manner and wrote a line; "There was a car that had no driver to take him where he wanted to go ..." I read this and said to him quietly, "I think perhaps today you seem a bit like a car without a driver." He looked at me, nodded and sighed. He picked up his pencil and completed the story about a driver "that took the car where he wanted to go so he was happy".

'The other children returned from the library and resumed their work. Henry went to paint. Brian looked cross and sulked, as he had been asked to complete a mathematical task; but his high motivation enabled him to overcome his mood. Henry returned from his painting to tackle his mathematics. As usual he found it very difficult to get started. He began chewing nervously at his pencil and looked confused. The calculation was simple multiplication, straightforward and well within his scope. Henry has great difficulty in thinking about increasing numbers. I was very aware of the regular additions to his natural family (three more boys since he had been taken into care). He saw them only very occasionally. When he returned after the break he was able to settle to the sums with enthusiasm and complete them correctly. He remarked upon the effect that the break had upon him. I suggested that, if he ever became stuck in the middle of his mathematics lessons when he was back at school, he might try giving himself a little break, by sitting with his hands on his lap for a minute or two.

'It was time to prepare for the end of the session, the transition into break. The children were asked to stop working and put their hands on their laps again. No distracting noise disturbed the group as they settled expectantly. They seemed really to appreciate the opportunity to think together about how the session had gone. Each child came out to my desk in turn while we focused on him or her, before returning to his or her place.

'Andrew came first. "How do you think the session went?" I asked him. He said that he had found it difficult to settle to his first two tasks but that it had then got easier. He was praised for managing the first tasks so well, in spite of the noise and the money sums (referring back to the earlier discussion). Henry chose to come next and we noted his ability to settle to writing tasks but his inability to manage his mathematics in the same way. He was complimented on managing to find his space in library time and he beamed (this had been a major problem for him earlier). Brian felt really good about himself and, as he came out, a smile of acknowledgement was all he really needed. I noted the difficulty he had had initially with his mathematics. I praised him briefly and he grinned and strode back to his place. The children were reminded that they knew best just which bits they had managed to do well, and that they must be really pleased at just how much they could manage.

'Colin then stood up. He was rather anxious and could not make steady eye contact. He was quietly praised for managing to settle himself before and after music, and his need for adult help to calm himself was acknowledged. We talked together about how we could help him to manage from the beginning of the morning, recognising for him that being unsettled and "silly" made him feel badly about himself. He then made good eye contact and was praised for managing to work steadily once he had got started. All the children were then asked to line up at the door. They were collected at once and left for break.

'Break for us is an important time when we discuss the observations we have made and the interactions we have experienced. We share our feelings and make plans for the next session. Each session is complete in its own right; we always start afresh every time. There is, however, a sense of continuity which is important for us to maintain as we aim to establish a memory of an individual and a group experience, looking back and forward, constantly making links. We believe that everything we do in the classroom has a symbolic significance for the children, and we offer them a daily chance to explore and express their feelings within the metaphor. We try to provide calm containment for violent feelings and physical outbursts so as to enable the children to feel safe. We help them to tolerate frustration without being over-protective. We see them struggling to manage their own internal pressures as they respond to the external pressure they feel we are exerting on them. The amount of support and encouragement we offer is carefully adjusted to ensure their success. We work together, too, on the process of weaning and endings that can be made right. Much of the working through is shared, but we find that when these children understand that we are emotionally available to them they develop their own insights into what is happening to their internal worlds.

'Learning together is essential for adult and child alike if the work is to be constructive. The interaction of all the members of the group complements and strengthens the growth of each individual in this "second chance" learning opportunity. For some it seems almost to be a last chance.'

The agreed openness between the adults seems to be a major contributory factor to the children's increasing capacity to express their feelings in words and through bodily control.

Comment

A striking feature of this account, similar to that of the four girls in the special school, is the demand that the individual child makes for attention from the adults. If an adult fails to pay due attention to any one member, or conversely pays too much attention, it is at great cost to the work with the whole. The question of alliances, collusions, or exclusions with any child or children by the therapists is avoided in these discussions of group work.

The last account gave very little indication of any interaction with their peers, although they seem to learn how to tolerate the presence of one another. The therapist working with the children commented on their limited ability to communicate with one another. She described each changing group of children as different but stressed that the majority appear to be at the early 'parallel play' stage of development seen in pre-school children. (This factor may well have contributed to the lack of cohesion within the group of four girls described earlier in this chapter.) 'Once the children are confident of their ability to play and work in the presence of emotionally available adults, they move forward into social behaviour.'

The influence of the setting on group work is perhaps too obvious to need comment. The educational staff were members of the multi-disciplinary team, whereas the school staff's attitude to the two psychologists (who were also educational therapists) was ambivalent. It was not clear what the school staff expected, and we are left with the impression that the therapists remained outsiders whose contribution to the improved level of functioning of each child in the group was barely acknowledged.

Part V

THE PLACE OF PLAY FOR THE LEARNING-DISABLED CHILD

13

PLAY WITH LINDA, WHO IS 5
YEARS OLD

Our final chapter is devoted to an account of an educational therapist working with a very young child, Linda. We have included this to illustrate how essential it is for the therapist to be in touch with her own capacity to play and to demonstrate the importance of bringing a child into a 'state of play' as a requisite for scholastic learning.

Like the children described in Chapter 9, Linda had acquired no basic skills. In our opinion she epitomises an anxiously-attached child, having experienced repeated rejections, losses and separations in a short life full of traumatic transitions. In addition to the work of all the supporting professionals, Linda received individual help from an educational therapist during school terms over a period of three years. Together Linda and her therapist worked slowly and painfully through play, to a point where Linda could begin to consider the possibility of a future. The importance that the educational therapist placed upon maintaining her own professional boundaries and the way she handled the pressures to take on the role of psychotherapist are addressed.

The experience of playing safely in the presence of an adult allows children to reiterate and make sense of adult conversations and interactions, and to work through internal conflicts or confusions about their own perceptions and experiences. Even at a later stage of development, the knowledge of an adult's presence, at least within calling distance, can be an essential contribution to the activity. Play can become too threatening, exciting or harmful if an adult is not available to keep behaviour and feelings under control. But, because children feel that play belongs to them and is separate from the adult world, the adult is expected to wait until invited to intercede or even occasionally to join the child's play. An unwanted adult intervention can be destructive and may halt the flow of creativity and negotiating skills required in group play, and possibly bring about an unwanted abandonment of the activity. Children observed at play reveal the importance of their imaginative thinking during the preparation or creation of that play. When the 'goal' is achieved this may spark off an extension of the play, a sudden switch to a quite different adventure, or the dispersal of the group.

Throughout the account of educational therapy sessions with Linda the therapist was making links between the roles of mother and infant and teacher and schoolchild. Learning and play are significant components of the experience of childhood and to make a distinction between them is perhaps no longer thought to be necessary. In 1933 Waggoner made an interesting claim: 'Play is a way of development and learning is implicit in it.' In most reception classes in mainstream schools in Britain this statement can be seen in action, although entry into school is usually equated with the concept of 'work' rather than play. It is perhaps adults who have difficulty in accepting statements like Waggoner's; certainly members of the families with whom we work often consider play to be 'wasting my time', like Mr Sopwith in Chapter 11.

A general and simplistic view of school work is that it is task-oriented. Can he or she add 10 and 9, read or spell twenty words, or pass a test or qualifying examinations? Many parents have complained to us that there is too much play in school. If they have not experienced learning the value of numbers or the meaning of words through play for themselves, it is understandable that they may feel that their children's time is being wasted. Children who by force of circumstance have to become adults prematurely are often deprived of the experience of play as a resource for future hope. Although we are thinking here of children who have to survive extremes of poverty and hunger, we are thinking also of children from families where play is not valued. In his *History of Childhood* (1974) de Mause suggested that children over the centuries were rarely encouraged to play; play seems to have been an activity they shared with adults for the pleasure of the latter rather than their own.

Although as adults we occasionally play as distinct from playing games, play is quintessentially a part of childhood, a state of mind. A teacher reported that a group of learning-disabled 7- and 8-year-olds were happily engaged in playing Snakes and Ladders, Snap and other games in the classroom. When the school bell rang to signal a morning break, and all these activities came to an end, two of the children asked, 'Can we go out to play now?' This request implies a wish to engage in free imaginative play, either to interact with peers or to play quietly alone.

Winnicott suggested (1971) that the child's state of mind is preoccupied during play and that it is this 'preoccupation that characterises the playing of a young child', which he likens to the 'concentration of older children and adults'. A child's state of mind during play is creative, but also exploratory in the sense of thinking and taking action; a personal testing out of ideas and experiences which are an integral part of cognitive learning. The following account of educational therapy with Linda incorporates her capacity for work on her feelings and what is taking place in the interaction between her and the therapist. In his book *The Piggle* (1977) Winnicott's description of the first consultation with the parents and Gabrielle (called the Piggle) gives the readers a picture of the child. 'Gabrielle looked serious and it was evident to

236

me that she had come for work as soon as she put her head in the door.' Even quite young children understand what is meant by 'work' about feelings and trying to understand them, although adults may observe this as play.

'WILL YOU PLAY WITH ME?'

The therapist who worked with Linda asked us to retain her title ('Will you play with me?') because it is a request she often receives from deprived children. The work began when Linda was 5 years and 4 months old and ended soon after her eighth birthday.

Barr (1988):

'I am aware that the tradition, philosophy and theoretical stance of the clinic where I undertook this piece of work have become part of the inner reality and the external reality between which my "play" takes place and they help me to overlap with the play areas of my clients. I had discovered that the founder of this clinic, a member of a religious order, had been held in high esteem by John Bowlby and others for her work with emotionally disturbed children. Long before play therapy was officially recognised as a valuable technique for dealing with these children, she was strongly advocating the value of play in assessment and treatment. She saw play as children's most natural mode of expressing themselves and learning, and also as a means of communicating with them. She sometimes recorded her thoughts in the early days of the clinic. One example, "Situations fraught with anxiety in real life can be recreated in the play situation with consequent lessening of tension", I thought was reminiscent of Melanie Klein (1955). In another of her recordings her thinking seems closer to that of Erikson (1950): "to 'play it out' is the most natural self-healing measure childhood affords". Although her thoughts about the use of play as the major route of access to the child's unconscious or about the symbolism of play were never published, I believe that she would have agreed with Klein that a child dramatises his fantasies while playing, and in so doing elaborates them and can work through his conflicts.

'Another of her views was that inhibited play is a very important symptom that indicates an inhibited fantasy-life leading to a slowness in general development. She believed that each year of a child's life is marked not only by sensory and muscular growth as well as mental development, but also by a corresponding need for a new phase of play, which is the child's method of learning. If any stage is missed, opportunity should be given to supply the omission, even in adolescence. Unlike Klein she did not provide special toys for the analysis of children, but provided play settings containing a large walk-in play house, a tea room, a shop, sandpits and some gymnastic apparatus to help the child in all facets of his development.

'Erikson's view (1950) of the use of play in therapy "that a child made insecure by a secret hate against, or fear of, the natural protectors of his play in family and neighbourhood seems able to use the protective sanctions of an understanding adult to regain some play-peace", I think is echoed in the theory of play as described by Winnicott (1971) on which I have based much of the work with Linda.

'Deprived children are often notoriously restless and unable to play. The loss of capacity for play seems to be related to the loss of reliability on the mother-figure. This seems to have been Linda's experience. She did not seem to have lost the play area entirely but the "potential space" (Winnicott 1971) between her inner reality and her environment did seem full of persecutory material. This made it difficult for her to accept and respond to the help and care offered by her teachers, care staff and surrogate parents.

'Winnicott (1971) wrote about psychotherapy taking place in the overlap of the two areas of playing – that of the therapist and that of the child. The area of playing is defined as the space between inner reality (i.e. fantasy) and the external reality of the outside world. Linked with these statements about the initiation of playing and the location of cultural experience the concepts conjure up, for me, a whole dynamic, multi-dimensional theme of inter-relating which makes for a very complex process. Using my work with Linda I shall try to tease out the various elements of this process and relate them to Winnicott's theory. I have already referred to my own external reality. One of the most powerful aspects of this is that I am a member of a religious order and, as such, have taken a vow of celibacy – one of the consequences being that I will not marry or have children. The relevance of this will become apparent in later sessions with Linda, the little girl with whom I worked for three years. My inner reality is that I have ideas, beliefs, hopes, fears, and fantasies about my work with Linda and about her inner and external reality.'

LINDA

'Linda was an attractive-looking child who could be very beguiling; she could also behave like a fiend exhibiting severe temper tantrums. She was referred because of this behaviour but also for stealing. She was described as a restless sleeper, over-active, excitable, destructive, aggressive, craving food, attention-seeking, clumsy, untruthful and a slow learner. In spite of this catalogue she was also described as likeable and I certainly experienced this during the assessment period.

'Her father was not known. She was taken into care in infancy, placed in a children's home, fostered, then, following a breakdown of contact with her mother, was again returned to the children's home. In the interim periods when she returned to her mother Linda was often left in the care of relatives, friends or neighbours. At the time of the assessment and the first eighteen months of therapy Linda was back with her original foster parents. I shall make only brief reference to the numerous decisions made by professionals in whose care she was placed from time to time. Although some of these dramatically affected my work with Linda, I would like the focus to remain on Linda herself and the "use" she was able to make of me in her sessions.

'During the assessment Linda showed that she was of average intelligence. She could play, but her play was full of persecutory material (e.g. her food was always being stolen. Nobody liked her). She seemed to alternate between being a needy, immature child and a competent, demanding pseudo-adult. After I had completed my initial assessment of Linda in my role as educational psychologist, a case conference was held and a decision taken that she should be offered individual play therapy sessions with me. This decision was influenced by two factors: Linda had been referred by the school because of her lack of basic skills, and I was a clinically trained educational therapist. The other members of the team were a social worker working with the foster parents and another psychologist.

'I saw Linda once a week, except for school holidays, in a large, airy, bright playroom. During this time the changes in her home situation were reflected in the themes which recurred in different ways whenever there were changes in her environment. These themes were as follows.'

Trust

'At first Linda was wary of me but we gradually built up a trustful, therapeutic relationship. She showed her trust in me by giving me things to care for and to mend (e.g. a stuffed toy elephant). At each big change Linda tested out this trust in order to see if my care was "good enough" and could keep her safe.'

Bad/good

'Throughout the sessions Linda struggled with bad/good feelings and images of a bad/good mother. In the first phase she seemed to view herself as entirely bad, and no punishment was bad enough. She did not seem able to tolerate that there could be anything good about her. This took a long time to shift and at difficult points would revert to an all-bad image of herself. It was not until the last months of therapy that there were any signs that she was able to see that she could be good as well as "naughty".'

Control

'Linda had a great need to show that she was in control and independent. She did this by dictating the sessions, even to the extent of telling me when to stand up, sit down, etc. At first she found it intolerable to accept my help. Although this changed a little she never entirely lost this and I feel it was not totally inappropriate. However, she was able to allow herself to become dependent and to regress.'

Rejection

'She was playing out the many rejections she felt, for example, by her foster family and by her natural mother, and this most recurrent theme was hardly surprising given her life-experience. She worked through many, very painful, feelings of anger, sadness, etc.'

Self-concept

'Linda's struggle for a sense of her true self was illustrated by her difficulty in naming herself. While with her foster family she insisted on using their surname. For some time after the rejection she continued to call herself Linda .... Once settled in the children's home she refused to use any surname. (At this time there was a great sense of loss around her.) It was not until the last phase of therapy that she was able to accept and own the name on her birth certificate and the name by which she was known, Linda Brown (not her actual name).'

Destructive power

'She saw herself as so bad that she had the power to destroy adults. At other times she assumed magical powers, making herself a wicked fairy or a witch who cast spells which could destroy something or someone – usually me. Looking back over the therapy I can identify several distinct phases which in some ways corresponded to the stages of play described by Winnicott (1971).

'In the early sessions with Linda it seemed as if I was of no importance at all. Her attachment seemed to be to the room and the toys contained therein. Especially significant was a bean-bag frog called 'Froggy'. During these sessions I was ignored while she was engrossed in sifting sand through her fingers, burying toys, digging them up and moving about the room. Froggy was always much in evidence beside her. The only comments of mine which were tolerated were purely factual; any others were angrily rejected and I was told to "get on with my own work" or to "shut my eyes". If I remained attentive and refrained from commenting she would continue her play, at times fixing me with an intense look. I was allowed occasionally to respond to her needs by fetching water or something from a high shelf which she was unable to reach. At the end of sessions she left without reference to me, ignoring my remark about seeing her next week.

'I experienced these sessions as being long and difficult. It felt to me as though there was no shared space but only a huge void. On reflection I feel that this void was more the "neutral zone" or "potential space" (Winnicott 1971) where desultory, formless or rudimentary playing was being allowed to take place. Only by being able to tolerate this, without adding any unhelpful comments, and responding to those practical needs she expressed, was I able to gain her trust. "Playing can aid communication with self and others" (Winnicott 1971)). In this phase it seemed to me that she was communicating with herself and getting in touch with creative and motor sensory impulses which would become the stuff of her future playing. I wondered also if Froggy was in some way being used as a transitional object to bridge the gap of our acute separateness to one of overlap. Towards the end of this phase Froggy was silently given to me to look after until the next session.

'The second phase corresponded to Winnicott's (1971) stage of solitary play in the presence of an adult who is trusted and who is felt to reflect back what is happening in the play. Here I was almost being allowed to give a running commentary on what she was playing out. I was allowed to make comments about how the toys were feeling. Much of her play at this time was about stealing food, being hungry and getting sent away.

'The next phase corresponded to Winnicott's (1971) mutual play stage where the adult and child play together but the adult is careful to fit in with the child. In this phase Linda directly involved me in her play, always assigning me a role – usually the bad girl who was being punished. During these sessions she was extremely managing and controlling and could not tolerate my making even minute adjustments to her play. Much of her play at this time consisted of school games with school and home being presented as very persecuting and punishing experiences. If I did not comply with her requests she seemed to feel even more persecuted.

'During another phase Linda left me with the impression that she was exploring the "not me" described by Winnicott (1965) as the period when an infant is able to perceive the mother as separate from itself. During this brief period Linda seemed to want to do away with all differentiation between herself and me. The activities of these sessions were painting and drawing with felt pens on paper or with chalks on a board. She would start the activity and then direct me to do exactly as she did. Any deviation on my part was greeted with anger and distress. At the end of these sessions I sensed Linda's real feeling of satisfaction when these pictures had been completed. From this we moved into a new dimension of therapy, in terms both of how the sessions were conducted and of the play material produced.

'The final phase I identified corresponded with Winnicott's (1971) concept of mutual play when the child can accept ideas contributed by the adult. In this phase there really was an overlap of play areas corresponding with the shift in the therapeutic work alluded to above. I have identified several distinct phases, and it is worth noting that although there is a sense of progression from one to another we moved back and forth between these different phases; at times we moved through all the phases in one session. An example of this took place in one session on resuming after the long summer break, during which Linda's foster placement broke down. (Linda had been moved briefly to a temporary foster home and then placed in an excellent children's home with a committed staff in a town 20 miles from where she had been staying, thus necessitating a change of school. Some of the staff may have promoted a minimal feeling of continuity because they had remembered her from when she had been there as a toddler.) Linda would enter the room very purposefully, and there would be a period of very controlling managing play about school where I was the pupil and she a very angry, punitive teacher. I would be given very hard sums to do. After this she would go to the toilet and when she came back we would get down to the real business of the session. It was almost as if she had been physically getting rid of what was inside her before she could deal with the emotional conflicts, which were exacerbated by the reality of her environment.'

A session

'Linda presented as very babyish, whining and complaining of pains in her tummy. I acknowledged that she seemed an unhappy little girl today.

She said, "I don't remember this room."

Th: "You sound mixed-up ... look, here's Froggy."

L: "I don't remember Froggy."

'Linda then sat down at the narrow end of the sand-tray, sifting the sand through her fingers without speaking. I commented that she seemed mixed up because a lot of things had changed for her during the holiday ... that a lot of hard things had happened. She started battering toys in the sand-tray as I talked. When I acknowledged that it could be very frightening when a lot of things changed she hammered loudly on the sand-tray. I then commented that it was too hard for her to listen to these sad things and assured her that the therapy room was the same, that the toys were the same, that I was seeing her on the same day and at the same time. At this she stopped hammering and returned to battering the toys in the sand.

Th: "Maybe you are wondering if I am still the same ... or if I had forgotten you."

'Linda made no reply to this but left the sand-tray and moved to the blackboard, where she drew thick, heavy lines with the chalk and then rubbed them out. She repeated this activity several times in a rough, noisy, angry way.

Th: "The chalk and duster seem to be very angry today – they are making a lot of noise and being very rough. Maybe they're very angry with me for not being there when a lot of hard things were happening ... maybe they felt I had left them and forgotten all about them."

'While I was saying this the activity with the chalk and duster became quieter and Linda announced, "I'm going to paint!"

'She painted a black figure and I remarked that it looked very sad. She then wrote "Li" above the figure – at which I commented that perhaps she was trying to tell me that she was feeling very sad. She then fetched two jugs of water, four cups, the baby's feeding bottle, a knife, fork and spoon, and prepared for a feeding game. Having done this she went to the toilet. On her return she then took the role of a very angry mother, putting me in the role of the "bad" girl who was being punished by being put to bed after being given "bad" food. I was slapped for "waking up in the night". As I "slept" the mother had a conversation with the other children in the family telling them to slap me if I woke up in the night. She yelled and screamed angrily every time I opened my eyes and said, "I'll have to tell your daddy when he gets home. I'm fed up with this. I can't be bothered with this nonsense any more. I'll have to wake her up in the morning."

'After I had been wakened in the morning I was put back to bed and told to close my eyes. When I did this she said, "Now she's asleep. Her suitcase is going to be packed and she's leaving in the morning."

'She then "woke me up" and told me in a very angry tone that I was leaving ... being sent to a horrid place with rats, tigers, etc., which would eat me up.

While she was saying all this I was expressing fear, anger, sadness in my role as the little girl.

She went on, "You have to go 'cos I don't like you ... I don't want you!"

'At this the game became too much for her and she terminated it by saying she wanted to do a picture. I acknowledged that this game was making her remember things that were painful which made her feel sad, angry, and mixed up.

'She went to the window and stood, looking extremely sad as she gazed out. As I acknowledged her sadness she immediately regressed to being a very new baby just home from hospital. She made "crying" sounds like a hungry new baby and fed from the bottle. At other times she crawled, tried to get into the pram and then "slept" in the "cot", which was two chairs placed together. While all this was going on I verbalised her needs and her feelings of being unwanted and unloved. At the end of the session she reverted to being the 6-year-old she now was and became able to leave the "baby" in the playroom.

'From this session and through to about the eighteenth month of the therapy this theme of abandonment/rejection was played out over and over again. It seemed to me that she was successively recapitulating all the separation traumas she had experienced, right back to the original one from her natural mother. These sessions were extremely painful.

'When Linda had been in the children's home for about five months a child care review was held and the decision taken to start the search for a new foster family for Linda. Unfortunately one professional worker told Linda that they were going to find her a new Mummy and Daddy.'

A session

'On entering my room at the next session Linda made straight for the sand-tray and started sifting the sand. Suddenly she turned to me and asked why she was not going back to her Mum and Dad (her foster parents). I acknowledged her feelings and explained to her simply and honestly why the decisions had been made. After a while of sifting the sand she built a mound saying it was her Mum and Dad's house. She built the mound bigger and bigger saying that there *was* room in their house for her. At the same time I was trying to verbalise her feelings.

'She suddenly turned on me, saying, "It's your fault. It was your idea. You don't want me to go back. They told me it was just for a short holiday. It's all your fault!"

'I acknowledged her feelings of anger and gave her permission to be as angry with me as she liked. She started angrily burying things in the sand.

Th: "Maybe you would like to do that with me because you are so angry with me?"

L: "Yes .... It's your fault! Get into this tray."

'With this she started throwing the sand about the tray, then said, "You're too big for the tray."

Th: "Perhaps you could just bury my hand, then."

'She set about this with some relish. Once the hand was buried she dug it out and started on a series of games really meant to test out how much of her nastiness I could take by setting up games which I couldn't possibly win. She seemed relieved when I survived all this.

'By the time that I had been seeing Linda for eighteen months, further consideration was given to finding her a foster home. As is so often the case, she had sensitive antennae for detecting any change proposed for her. At this time in therapy the whole issue of mothering and feeding was brought into the sessions in a very direct way. In these sessions Linda alternated between being the good and the bad mother, while I was always cast as the bad girl. It was around this time that the roles were reversed to make Linda the bad daughter.

'Towards the end of one session she drew a figure which she told me was a man. She then proceeded to change this into a female figure by adding breasts and nipples and added a baby feeding at the breasts. It was also around this time that she began asking about my husband, babies, etc. I feel sure that the question of my ability to be a mother was around her, but any comments I made were rejected and I couldn't get near her fantasies about me. I found these sessions very difficult and, although I felt Linda's fantasies were about my becoming her mother, I found myself unable to raise the issue with her. On reflection I realised this was because of my own feelings about causing her more pain through my seeming to add another abandonment and rejection. I knew that they were not associated with any unresolved issues appertaining to my choice of celibacy. Another important factor at this time was that the clinic social worker who saw Linda's key worker was visibly pregnant and Linda often brought this knowledge into the sessions.

'Much of her play now consisted of playing with baby girl dolls which were often Sellotaped to me. I was exercised as to how I was going to deal with the mothering issue when the following session took place just before the long summer break.'

A session

'Linda was very quiet when she came into the room. I acknowledged that it was her last session before the holidays. She ignored my statements and told me that she was going to give me some hard "sums" to do. She proceeded to do this, dictating exactly how they had to be set out, etc. No matter how I tried, the sums were always wrong and I was berated for my dreadful work. I acknowledged the feelings of anger, etc., that were around. Linda did not deny these feelings, as she sometimes did when she was annoyed.

'After this the pattern changed and she began to play with water and sweets. We both had to drink the water which she said was whisky. She halved a few sweets and shared them with me. This was repeated several times and had a ritualistic feel about it. I remarked that she seemed to want us to be the same.

L: "Yes ... " (nodding her head).

Th: "Maybe you would like to be part of me like a little girl is part of her mummy."

L: "Mm ... "

Th: "Maybe you would like to be my little girl ... to have me as your mummy."

'At this Linda spilled some water and looked at me anxiously to see my reaction. I acknowledged this and assured her that, no matter how bad she felt, I would not send her away and would be seeing her after the holiday. She then said she needed to go to the toilet and that when she returned she would give me some more sums to do. On the way out she picked up and took along a toy telephone. Once in the toilet she dialled and I answered.

Th: "Hello, can I help you?"

L: "What kind of place is this?"

Th: "This is the XYZ Child Guidance Clinic."

L: "Do you know the ABC Home?"

Th: "Yes. This is the ABC Home. That's another name for the XYZ Clinic. Can I help you?"

L: "Who's speaking?"

I told her my name.

L repeated: "Is that the ABC Home?"

Th: "Yes. Who's speaking, please?"

L: "Say you're Troon."

This was said in a loud whisper and she then put down the phone and re-dialled.

Th: "Hello. This is Troon. Can I help you?"

L: "Is that XYZ House?"

Th: "Yes, this is Sister Martha speaking."

L: "Do you know a little girl called Linda?"

Th: "Oh yes, Linda Brown. I know her very well. She's a friend of mine."

L: "That's true."

Th: "Sometimes she is a very sad little girl because she would like me to be her mummy. But Sister Martha can't be her mummy and that's very hard for Linda."

L: "Good-bye."

With this Linda came out of the toilet and returned to the room where she set some more "very difficult" sums written faintly on the blackboard in red chalk so that I could hardly see them and, of course, could not get them right. Then there was the brief ritual of sharing sweets. The conversation continued:

L: "What would you do if I said I had magic powers?"

This took me unawares, so I was not sure how to respond. I reflected it back to her and continued.

Th: "I wonder what you would like me to do?"

L: "I'd get rid of you."

I again acknowledged her anger and assured her that she would never be able to do that because I was a very strong lady and she was a little girl who couldn't get rid of me no matter how bad she felt.

'The game was then set in a school where I was the child and Linda alternated between being the teacher and the mother. After a while the teacher (Linda) came to the door looking for Linda (me). At this point Linda switched the roles. I became the teacher while she became the mother as we pretended that Linda was hiding. We then had a long conversation about the child. This covered the areas of stealing, being bad, being powerful enough to get rid of grown-ups, and wanting her therapist to be her mummy.

'In the role of mother Linda was able to acknowledge all of this while I, in the role of the teacher, acknowledged the sad feelings and offered assurance that, no matter how bad the child felt, the therapist would remain her friend and helper and that she wouldn't get rid of Linda or send her away. Linda accepted that this was true by saying, "Sister Martha is not a mummy. That's the truth. It's not her job." We then acknowledged just how painful and sad this was to think about. The game continued with the mother wanting the teacher to be very angry with Linda. The teacher said that she could not be angry with her at this time because Linda was a very sad and unhappy little girl. At this she came out of role, gave me a big smile, and abruptly changed the game to snakes and ladders and then the alphabet soup game. She nodded agreement as I said that she had had a lot of extremely difficult things to manage and think about today. When told that she had just 5 minutes left Linda asserted that she was not leaving. I commented that she might be afraid that I would forget her during the school holidays, and I assured her that I would remember because I had memories of her in my mind which meant I could think of her when she was not here. I added that to show her I had not forgotten her I would send her a card each week. She responded: "I bet you don't, I bet you don't. I bet you won't do that." I felt that there was a question mark at the end of that assertion, and I acknowledged how difficult it was for her to believe me, repeating that I would send the cards. With this she was able to leave without remonstrations.

'This had been a harrowing session in that Linda was such an attractive and beguiling child and I was aware of having to keep a tight hold on what I was able to offer in her sessions and could keep on giving her. At times in this session I had the feeling that she was working hard to show me the beguiling child she could be so that I would not be able to resist being her mother.

'The following autumn term was a very unsettled period for Linda. The whole fostering issue was again raised and her key worker was ill and then on holiday. The composition of the home had changed with the admission of several teenagers whose behaviour was very disturbed. Their conversation was continually provocative, with unpleasant sexual overtones, accompanied by sexually suggestive behaviour towards the staff. At this unsettling time for Linda I was ill with 'flu, which meant that I had to cancel a session. There was a marked deterioration in Linda's behaviour, both at home and at school. Her manner became defiant and obstructive and there was an increase in her stealing and running away.

'In spite of her confused state of mind she maintained school progress as her reading and number work continued to improve. During this period her therapy sessions were full of troubled play. A great deal of anger was expressed and one of the main themes was the bad child who was so awful that no family, home or school could keep her and she always ended up in prison. All adults were portrayed as persecutory and punitive. This very much reflected the disagreement and conflict between the professionals involved with making decisions about Linda's future, and I began to fear that I, as one of the adults, would lose her trust. However, I felt that I did manage, well enough, to help her to contain her confused, frightened and often desperate feelings. At no time did she bring to me the reality of her difficult behaviour or talk about the "trouble" she was in at school or in the children's home. She seemed unable to bring these really "bad" bits to me in the session, perhaps for fear of being rejected by or of destroying me. Eventually we were able to work through this and enter a more stable phase.

'We struggled with the existence of good bits as well as bad bits in the next phase, but for Linda it had to be all good or all bad at any one time. There then began a gradual change where Linda was really getting in touch with her own bad feelings about herself. This was marked by various confessions she made to me about her actual "naughty" behaviour at home and at school. During this time she became quite provocative and rebellious during sessions: for example, she would start to throw things about, threaten to destroy things, and use sexually suggestive language. She seemed to be inviting me to reject her. At last she seemed to accept that I could tolerate the good and bad parts of her, that I was not destroyed by them and that I as the adult in control of the sessions could keep her safe and set limits for her when necessary. Gradually she was able to control her own behaviour, at home and also at school where she was beginning to be seen in a more positive light. Also, in this final phase of therapy she came to accept her own name and call herself Linda Brown.

'I hope this next session will illustrate some of the changes I observed in Linda's behaviour. After a brief period of the controlling, managing, school game Linda went to the sand-tray, which was very dry and dusty. She asked me to get a bucket of water to make the sand into a very wet, gooey mess. She did this with great relish and thoroughly enjoyed putting her hands through it. This was the first time that she had engaged herself in this type of messy play; she had previously avoided it. After some minutes I was invited to join in the play by putting my hands in the mess and to agree that it was great fun. She also splashed around a bit, trying to shower me with the dirty water to test out my tolerance of the mess. I reflected this back to her and this conversation followed.

L: "What does this remind you of?"

Th: "Remind me of?"

L: "Yes. What do you think this is like?"

Th: "Well, ... it reminds me of the seaside."

L: "Is that all? What else does it remind you of?"

Th: "Mmm ... well ... when I see such a dark mess like this it sometimes reminds me of jobbies [faeces].... What about you?"

L: "No ... it reminds me of tar ... black tar."

'This led to some discussion about how it could remind us of the dark, black, messy feelings we can have and the dark, black, messy things we can sometimes do. I wondered aloud if she was telling me about the difficult behaviour she sometimes showed me and about the messy feelings she sometimes had and whether she thought about whether I could bear such messiness. In answer to this she started to bury my hand and arm nearly up to the elbow in the mud. She then took my hand in hers and buried both. My hand and arm were then buried separately in the mud. All this she obviously found very enjoyable. She stopped about 10 minutes before the end of the session so that we could clean ourselves up. While washing she told me that she was very sad because her key worker's dog had died. This was the first time that Linda had directly told me something that she was feeling. The theme of loss was to recur during our next phase of working and playing together.

'There was a settled period after this session, when Linda's play was age-appropriate without any of the intense anger or confusion of previous sessions. Soon after this she moved from the children's home to her new foster parents, and she continued to attend the clinic for another three months. Our sessions had to end, because it became impracticable for her to continue attending once she had become settled in her foster home. After numerous hiccups and much testing-out her lifestyle changed. The social worker remained in touch with the foster parents, giving support and advice where necessary and appropriate. Linda was doing well at school and her behaviour was much less problematic. I felt that Linda was now free enough to make a creative use of cultural experiences. It had not been my task to be a substitute parent or to try to redress the wrongs of the past. I think that the work through play that Linda and I shared enabled her to accept and respond to the help and affection offered to her by her "new" surrogate parents. There was every indication that this would be the final move of her childhood.'

The educational therapist used the phrase 'final move' as a reference to the numerous and frequently painful changes Linda had experienced in her short life.

John Bowlby (1973) in his exploration of human sorrow posed the question as to why 'some individuals should recover largely or completely from experiences of separation and loss while others seem not to ...'. His ensuing discussion examined the range of responses that children reveal during separations from their attachment figures. From the information we had about Linda's recall of her early separation we became aware of the angry feelings that she had expressed during the course of the therapy. Later she revealed her feelings of sorrow – sorrow not only at the loss of her mother but also for the loss of a little of herself. However, her acknowledgement of this loss also revealed a certain resilience, and her memory of self interacting with another suggested that she had been able to retain an internal working model of a secure-enough attachment, which enabled her to accept, adapt and update her understanding of her subjective self and to make use of the educational therapist.

In Chapter 1 we began to think about first learning within the dyad of mother and infant, the source of learning in the widest sense. We suppose that Linda was in touch with this learning experience, however intermittently. The educational therapist was able to create a shared working and playing space within which Linda's second-chance learning could take place. The educational therapist's interaction with Linda epitomises for us the concept of an educational attachment figure. This concept has some similarity to Sroufe's (1983) 'specific attachment figure', but there are children like Linda who do not know how to make use of these figures, even when teachers try to show clearly that they are emotionally available. Their anxious behaviour precludes the possibility of their believing that a teacher can care for them when they believe that she cares more for others. Linda was able to explore her feelings within the security of her sessions, but many children continue to function and behave in a manner that becomes increasingly uncontainable for themselves and their teachers, and sometimes for their peers too.

We believe that the intervention of individual educational therapy for one hour a week offers a way of helping children such as Linda to develop emotionally and to learn scholastically.

CONCLUSION

'ENDINGS'

All through this book we have emphasised the importance of endings. Each ending means a new beginning, as Luke in Chapter 4 discovered. John Bowlby's theory of attachment and loss has enabled us to understand the circular effect that attachment behaviour can have throughout life. We have taken the experience of secure children as our starting point, and then focused on the crucial part that anxious attachment behaviour plays in perpetuating the problems of the children referred to us for help with their learning difficulties. With the use of vignettes and detailed accounts we have introduced educational therapy as an intervention that can address these difficulties and initiate change. The principles on which educational therapy is based are relevant to all who work with children. The clinically trained educational therapist combines her roles as teacher, as educational attachment figure, and as consultant to provide the opportunities that are necessary to allow change to occur.

We have examined those interactions between individuals within a dyad or as members of a group which influence their learning. The importance of having a secure base from which exploratory behaviour can take place and develop has been repeatedly stressed.

Children who are struggling with their learning frequently can be heard saying 'I can't get started' and 'teachers never give me time'. It is our task as educational therapists to help children to get started and to give them time to recover their lost capacity for playing and learning so that they can take their rightful places as full members of society.

APPENDIX

Educational therapy as an intervention was first introduced in Britain in the early 1960s by Irene Caspari, a principal educational psychologist working at the Tavistock Clinic, London. A component of her training course for teachers who wished to become educational psychologists was the remedial teaching of severely learning-disabled children, individually and in small groups. Through the supervision of this work Caspari recognised the importance of paying attention to the emotional disturbance of the children referred, and the influence the 'unconscious mechanisms' had on the interaction between child and trainee. Towards the end of her life she included working with families in this clinical training. This led her to develop a part-time evening course for teachers wishing to enhance their understanding of the teacher/learning-disabled child dynamic. Her work also led to the formation of the Forum for the Advancement of Educational Therapy (FAET).

After the death of Irene Caspari, Muriel Barrett, the Tavistock Clinic teacher, continued the evening course for a short period. In 1979 she introduced a post-graduate clinical training for fully qualified teachers, with a minimum of three years specialist or remedial teaching. The course was open also to overseas psychologists with a teaching qualification. It was continued until 1985, and included educational therapy with individual children, peer groups and families.

Since 1986 the Forum for the Advancement of Educational Therapy (FAET) and the National Association of Therapeutic Teaching (NATT) jointly organise a training in educational therapy at Regent's College, London. The course is open to experienced teachers and educational psychologists who are working in a variety of settings where they encounter individual children, or adults, with specific areas of learning disabilities. The training is of two academic years' duration, and members attend twice weekly evening seminars, and one day a week in a clinic placement, where trainees obtain practical experience of educational therapy.

The course is on the Department of Education and Science list of approved courses, and is a full member of the United Kingdom Standing Conference for Psychotherapy.

Further information is available from:

Mrs Mia Beaumont,
Hornsey Rise Child Guidance Unit,
Hornsey Rise Health Centre,
Hornsey Rise,
London N19 31U.

BIBLIOGRAPHY

Ainsworth, M.D.S. (1967) *Infancy in Uganda: Infant Care and the Growth of Attachment*, Baltimore: Johns Hopkins University Press.

—— (1973) 'The development of infant–mother attachment', in B.M. Caldwell and H.N. Ricciuti (eds) *Review of Child Development Research* 3, Chicago: Chicago University Press.

—— (1984) 'Adaptation and attachment', paper presented at the New York International Conference of Infant Studies.

—— (1985) 'Attachment across the lifespan', *Bulletin of the New York Academy of Medicine* 61(9): 792–812.

Ainsworth, M.D.S. and Wittig, B.A. (1969) 'Attachment and exploratory behaviour of 1-year-olds in a strange situation', in B.W. Foss (ed.) *Determinants of Infant Behaviour* IV, London: Methuen.

Ainsworth, M.D.S., Blehar, M.C., Waters, E., and Wall, S. (1978) *Patterns of Attachment: A Psychological Study of the Strange Situation*, Hillsdale, New Jersey: Lawrence Erlbaum Associates.

Alston, J. and Taylor, J. (1987) *Handwriting Theory, Research and Practice*, Beckenham: Croom Helm.

Apter, S.J. (1982) *Troubled Children Troubled Systems*, New York: Pergamon Press.

Barkley, R.A. (1981) 'Learning disabilities', in E.J. Mash and L.G. Terdal (eds) *Behavioral Assessment of Childhood Disorders*, New York, Chichester, Brisbane, and Toronto: Wiley.

Barr, J. (1988) 'Play therapy with a severely deprived girl aged five', *Journal of Educational Therapy* 2, 1: 57.

Barrett, M. (1985) 'Consultation to sub-systems', in E. Dawling and E. Osborne (eds) *The Family and the School: A Joint Systems Approach to Problems with Children*, London: Routledge and Kegan Paul.

Bateson, G. (ed.) (1973) *Steps to an Ecology of Mind*, St Albans: Paladin.

Bauer, D. (1980) 'Childhood fears in developmental perspective', in L.A. Hersov and I. Berg (eds) *Out of School: Modern Perspectives in Truancy and School Refusal*, Chichester: Wiley.

Bauer, J.R.G. (1972–3) 'The "Therapy" in educational therapy', *Academic Therapy* VIII, 2: 199–205.

Beaumont, M. (1988) 'The effect of loss on learning: the stillborn sibling', *Journal of Educational Therapy*, 2, 1: 33.

Belz, E. (1985) 'Educational therapy: a model for the treatment of functionally illiterate adults', *Adult Educational Quarterly* 35, 2: 96–104.

Berridge, D. (1985) *Children's Homes*, Oxford: Blackwell.

Berridge, D. and Cleaver, H. (1987) *Foster Home Breakdown*, Oxford: Blackwell.

Bettelheim, B. (1976) *The Uses of Enchantment: The Meaning and Importance of Fairy Tales*, London: Thames & Hudson.

Bettelheim, B. and Zelan, K. (1982) *On Learning to Read: The Child's Fascination with Meaning*, London: Thames &Hudson.

Bick, F. (1968) 'The experience of the skin in early object-relations', *International Journal of Psycho-analysis* 49: 484–6.

—— (1987) 'Notes on infant observation in psycho-analytic training' in M.H. Williams (ed.) *Collected Papers of Martha Harris and Esther Bick*, Strathtay, Perthshire: Clunie Press.

Bion, W.R. (1962) *Learning from Experience*, London: Heinemann Medical.

Blos, P. (1975) 'The concept of acting out in relation to the adolescent process', in A.H. Esman (ed.) *The Psychology of Adolescence: Essential Reading*, New York: International University Press.

—— (1979) *The Adolescent Process: Developmental Issues*, New York: International University Press.

Blyth, E. (1985) 'Mirrors on girls and maths', *Bulletin of The British Association of Psychotherapists*, London: Acorn Press, 73–98.

Boston, M. and Szur, R. (1983) *Psychotherapy with Severely Deprived Children*, London, Boston, Melbourne, and Henley: Routledge & Kegan Paul.

Bowlby, J. (1953) *Child Care and the Growth of Love*, Harmondsworth, London: Pelican Books.

—— (1969) 'Attachment' in *Attachment and Loss* 1, London: Hogarth Press and Institute of Psychoanalysis; New York: Basic Books.

—— (1973) 'Separation: anxiety and anger', in *Attachment and Loss* 2, London: Hogarth Press and Institute of Psychoanalysis; New York: Basic Books.

—— (1977) 'The making and breaking of affectional bonds', *British Journal of Psychiatry* 130: 200–10 and 421–31.

—— (1979) 'On knowing what you are not supposed to know and feeling what you are not supposed to feel', *Canadian Journal of Psychiatry* 24: 403–8.

—— (1980) 'Loss: sadness and depression', in *Attachment and Loss* 3, London: Hogarth Press and Institute of Psychoanalysis; New York: Basic Books.

—— (1982) 'Attachment and loss: retrospect and prospect', *American Journal of Orthopsychiatry* 52: 664-78.

—— (1988) *Secure Base*, London: Routledge & Kegan Paul.

Bretherton, I. (1985) 'Attachment theory: retrospect and prospect', in I. Bretherton and E. Walters (eds) *Growing Points of Attachment Theory and Research*, Chicago: Chicago University Press.

Bryan, T.H. (1977) 'Learning-disabled children's comprehension of non-verbal communication', *Journal of Learning Disabilities* 10: 501–6.

Bryan, T.H. and Bryan, J.H. (1976) 'Learning disorders', in H.E. Rie and E.D. Rie (eds) *Minimal Brain Damage*, New York, Chichester: Wiley.

Byng-Hall, J. (1973) 'Family myths used as a defence: conjoint family therapy', *British Journal of Medical Psychology* 46: 239.

Casimir, A. (1987) 'Angry feelings about learning', unpublished paper.

Caspari, I. (1974a) 'Educational therapy', in V. Varma (ed.) *Psychotherapy Today*, London: Constable.

—— (1974b) 'Parents as co-therapists: a family approach to the treatment of reading disability', London: Tavistock Clinic document EN 781.

Chambers's Twentieth Century Dictionary (1965 edn), W. Geddie (ed.) Edinburgh and London: W. and R. Chambers.

Chazan, M. (1970) *Reading Readiness*, Swansea: Faculty of Education, University College.

Clancier, A. and Kalmanovitch, J. (1986) *Winnicott and Paradox from Birth to Creation*, trans. A. Sheridan, London: Tavistock Publications.

Copley, B. and Forryan, B. (1987) *Therapeutic Work with Children and Young People*, London: Robert Royce.

Cowan, P. (1982) 'The relationship between emotional and cognitive development', *New Directions for Child Development* June, 16: 49–81.

Crittenden, P.M. and Ainsworth, M.D.S. (1981) 'Child maltreatment and attachment theory', in D. Cicchetti and D. Carlson (eds) *Child Maltreatment: theory and research in the causes and consequences of child abuse and neglect*, Cambridge: Cambridge University Press.

Dahl, R. (1961) *James and the Giant Peach*, Harmondsworth, New York, Victoria, Ontario and Auckland: Penguin Books.

da Vinci, Leonardo (1938) *The Notebooks of*, 1A, trans. E. MacCurdy, London: The Reprint Society.

Dowling, E. and Jones, H.V.R. (1978) 'Small children seen and heard in family therapy', *Journal of Child Psychotherapy* 4, 4: 87–96.

Dowling, E., Barrett, M., Taylor, D., and Golding, V. (1985) 'Patterns of interactions in families presenting a child with an educational problem: a clinical research development', in E. Dowling and E. Osborne (eds) *The Family and the School: A Joint Systems Approach to Problems with Children*, London, Boston, Melbourne, and Henley: Routledge & Kegan Paul.

Duhl, B. (1983) *From the Inside Out and Other Metaphors*, New York: Brunner Mazel.

Dunn, J. (1988) 'Normative life events as risk factors in childhood' in M. Rutter (ed.) *Studies of Psychosocial Risk: The Power of Longitudinal Data*, Cambridge: Cambridge University Press.

Duve, A.-M. (1965) *The A.M.S. Method, an assessment procedure*, Oslo: Oslo University Press.

Education Act (1981) Department of Education and Science, London: HMSO.

Education Reform Act (1988) Department of Education and Science, London: HMSO.

Elizur, J. (1986) 'The stress of school entry – parental coping behaviors and children's readjustment to school', *Journal of Child Psychology and Psychiatry* 27: 625–38.

Emanuel, R. (in press) 'Counter Transference – a spanner in the works or a tool for understanding', lecture given in 1990, London: Forum for the Advancement of Educational Therapy.

Erickson, M.F., Sroufe, L.A., and Egeland, B. (1985) 'The relationship between quality of attachment behavior problems in pre-school in a high risk sample', in I. Bretherton and E. Waters (eds) *Growing Points of Attachment Theory and Research*, Chicago: Chicago University Press.

Erikson, E.H. (1950) *Childhood and Society*, rev. edn, London: Hogarth Press.

—— (1965) 'Clinical observations of play disruption in young childen' in M.R. Haworth (ed.) *Child Psychotherapy Practice and Theory*, New York, London: Basic Books.

Estrada, P., Arsenio, W.F., Hess, R.D., and Holloway, S.D. (1987) 'Affective quality of the mother–child relationship: longitudinal consequences for children's school-relevant cognitive functioning', *Developmental-Psychology* March 23(2): 210–15.

Foulkes, S.H. and Anthony, E.J. (1957) *Group Psychotherapy – the Psychoanalytic Approach*, Harmondsworth, Baltimore and Victoria: Penguin.

Freud, S. (1915a) *The Dynamics of Transference* S.E., 2: 97–108. (Abbreviation 'S.E.' denotes the Standard Edition of *The Complete Psychological Works of Sigmund Freud*, published in 24 vols by Hogarth Press, London.)

—— (1915b) *Theory of Instinct* S.E., 14: 122.

—— (1915c) *The Unconscious* S.E., 14.

—— (1917) *Mourning and Melancholia* S.E., 14.

—— (1920) *Beyond the Pleasure Principle* S.E., 18.

—— (1921) *Group Psychology and the Analysis of the Ego* S.E., 18.

Freud, S. (1926) *Inhibitions Symptoms and Anxiety* S.E., 20.

Gardner, H. (1980) *Artful Scribbles*, London: Norman.

Goodenough, F.L. (1926) *Measurement of Intelligence by Drawings*, New York: Harcourt, Brace, and World.

Gottfried, A.W. (ed.) (1984) *Home Environment and Early Development*, Longitudinal Research, New York: Academic Press.

Gurman, A.S. (1970) 'The role of the family in under-achievement', *Journal of School Psychology* 8(1): 48–53.

Hanko, G. (1985) *Special Needs in Ordinary Classrooms: an approach to teacher support and teacher care in primary and secondary schools*, Oxford: Basil Blackwell.

Harris, C. (1978) *The Glen* (Fuzz Buzz Books), Oxford: Oxford University Press.

Heard, D.H. (1978) 'From object relations theory to attachment theory: a basis for family therapy', *British Journal of Medical Psychology* 51: 67–76.

Heard, D.H. and Barrett, M.C. (1977) 'Family learning', in *Irene Caspari: A Commemorative Symposium*, London: Tavistock Clinic: 14–19.

—— (1982) 'Attachment and the family relationships of children with specific reading disability', in C.M. Parkes and J. Stevenson-Hinde (eds) *The Place of Attachment in Human Behaviour*, London: Tavistock Publications.

Hopkins, J. (1983) 'Mastering the experience of hospitalization: the emotional task facing young children and their parents', *Nursing Times* 19 October.

Horowitz, M.J. (1979) *States of Mind; Analysis of Change in Psychotherapy*, New York and London: Plenum Press.

Howlin, P. (1985) 'Special education treatment', in M. Rutter and L. Hersov (eds) *Child and Adolescent Psychiatry: Modern Approaches*, 2nd edn, Oxford, London, Edinburgh, Boston, Palo Alto, Melbourne: Blackwell Scientific Publications.

Kellogg, R. (1970) *Analysing Children's Art*, Mountain View, Cal.: Mayfield Publishing Company.

Klein, M. (1930) *Contribution to Psychoanalysis*, London: Hogarth Press.

—— (1931) *The Theory of Intellectual Inhibition*, London: Hogarth Press.

—— (1955) 'The psycho-analytic play technique: its history and significance', *New Directions in Psychoanalysis*, London: Tavistock Publications.

Koppitz, E.M. (1968) *Psychological Evaluation of Children's Human Figure Drawings*, New York and London: Grune & Stratton.

—— (1971) *Children with Learning-disabilities: A Five year Follow-up Study*, New York: Grune & Stratton.

Lee, L. (1959) *Cider with Rosie*, London: Hogarth Press.

Lewis, E. (1976) 'Management of Stillbirth: Coping with an Unreality', *The Lancet* II, 7986: 619–20.

Lewis, E. and Page, A. (1978) 'Failure to mourn a stillbirth: or, an overlooked catastrophe', *British Journal of Medical Psychology* 51: 237–41.

Maher, P. (1987) *Child Abuse: The Educational Perspective*, Oxford: Basil Blackwell.

Main, M., Kaplan N., and Cassidy, J. (1985) 'Security in infancy, childhood, and adulthood: a move to the level of representation', in I. Bretherton and E. Waters (eds) *Growing Points of Attachment Theory and Research*, Chicago: Chicago University Press.

Matsuyama, K., Tanimura S., Shibata, C., and Ogawa, Y. (1975) 'Educational therapy for severely retarded children', *Japanese Journal of Child Psychiatry* 16, 5: 282–95.

Mattinson, J. and Sinclair, I. (1979) *Mate and Stalemate*, Oxford: Blackwell.

Maughan, B. (1988) 'School experiences as risk/protective factors', in M. Rutter (ed.) *Studies of Psychosocial Risk: The Power of Longitudinal Data*, Cambridge, New York, New Rochelle, Melbourne, and Sydney: Cambridge University Press.

Mause, L. de (ed.) (1974) *The History of Childhood: The evolution of parent-child relationships as a factor in history*, USA: The Psychohistory Press.

Miles, T.R. (1983) *Dyslexia: The Pattern of Difficulties*, London, Toronto, Sydney, New York: Granada.

Miller, D.R. and Westman, T.C. (1964) 'Reading disability as a condition of family stability', *Family Process* 3: 66–76.

Milner, M. (1955) 'The role of illusion in symbol formation', in M. Klein *et al.*, (eds) *New Directions in Psychoanalysis*, London: Tavistock Publications.

Nagera, V. (1967) *Van Gogh: A Psychological Study*, New York: International University Press.

Oram, H. (1982) *Angry Arthur*, London: Anderson.

Osborne, E. (1983) 'Teachers' relationships with pupils' families and teachers' relationships to other professional workers', in I. Wittenburg-Salzberger, G. Henry, and E. Osborne (eds) *The Emotional Experience of Learning and Teaching*, London: Routledge & Kegan Paul.

Osborne, E. and Barrett, M. (1985) 'The child, the family and the school: a clinical perspective', in E. Dowling and E. Osborne (eds) *The Family and the School: A Joint Systems Approach to Problems with Children*, London: Routledge & Kegan Paul.

Parinaud, A. (1977) *The Unspeakable Confessions of Salvador Dali*, London: Quarto Press.

Pauss, K. (1980) 'Psykhodynamiske synspunkter på Lesevansker' in K. Pauss, L.T. Leira Hangsjerd, and B. Urdal (eds) *Vanfker og Vekst hosBarn og Ungdom*, Oslo: Universitets Forlaget.

Perlmutter, M.S. and Ringler, D. (1986) 'Nuclear anxiety: social symptomatology and educational therapy', *Marriage and Family Review* June, 10(2): 59–84.

Pianta, R., Egeland, B., and Erickson, M.F. (1989) 'The antecedents of maltreatment: results of the Mother–Child Interaction Research Project', in D. Cicchetti and V. Carlson (eds) *Child Maltreatment: Theory and Research on the Causes and Consequences of Child Abuse and Neglect*, Cambridge: Cambridge University Press.

Pincus, L. (1976) *Death and the Family: The Importance of Mourning*, London: Faber & Faber.

Pincus, L. and Dare, C. (1978) *Secrets in the Family*, London and Boston: Faber & Faber.

Platt Report (1959) *The Welfare of Children in Hospital, the report of this committee*, Central Services Council, Ministry of Health, London: HMSO.

Poincaré, H. (1952) *Science and Hypothesis*, New York: Dover.

Pontielli, A. (1985) *Backwards in Time*, United Kingdom: Roland Harris Education Trust.

Pratley, R. (1988) *Spelling it Out*, London: BBC Books.

Quinton, D. and Rutter, M. (1988) *Parenting Breakdown: The making and breaking of inter-generational links*, Aldershot: Gower Publications.

Radecki, J. (1984) 'Educational therapy defined', *Journal of Learning Disability* 17, 1: January.

Rayner, E. (1988) *Human Development: An introduction to the psychodynamics of growth maturity and ageing*, 3rd edn, Boston and Sydney: Allen & Unwin.

Richardson, E. (1975) Selections from 'The Environment of Learning', in A.D. Colman and W.H. Bexton (eds) *Group Relations Reader*, 1st edn, Sausalito, Cal.: Grex.

Ricks, M.H. (1985) 'The social transmission of parental behavior: attachment across generations', in I. Bretherton and E. Waters (eds) *Growing Points of Attachment Theory and Research*, Chicago: Chicago University Press.

Robertson, J. and Robertson, J. (1967–75) *Young Children in Brief Separation*, film series (5), Ipswich: Concord Films.

Robinson, M. (1982) 'Reconstituted families: some implications for the family therapist', in A. Bentovim, G. Gorrell-Barnes, and A. Cooklin (eds) *Family Therapy vol. 2: Complementary Frameworks of Theory and Practice*, London: Academic Press; New York: Grune & Stratton.

Rothstein, A., Benjamin, L., Crosby, M., and Eisenstadt, K. (1988) *Learning Disorders*, Madison: International University Press.

Rutter, M. (1974) 'Emotional disorders and underachievement', *Arch. Dis. Childh.* 79: 249–56.

Rutter, M. and Yule, W. (1975) 'Concept of severe reading retardation', *Journal of Child Psychology and Psychiatry* 16: 181–97.

Rutter, M., Maughan, B., Mortimer, P., and Ouston, J. (1979) *Fifteen Thousand Hours: Secondary Schools and their Effects on Children*, London: Open Books.

Salmon, G. and Franco, A. (1989) 'An educational therapy group in a school setting', unpublished paper.

Sander, L.W. (1965) 'The longitudinal course of early mother–child interaction –

Cross-case comparison of mother–child pairs', in B.M. Foss (ed.) *Determinants of Infant Behaviour* IV, London: Methuen.

Sandler, I. (1980) 'Dimensional analysis of children's stressful life events', *American Journal of Community Psychology* 8, 3: 285–302.

Segal, H. (1973) *An Introduction to the Work of Melanie Klein*, London: Hogarth Press.

Shaffer, D. and Dunn, J. (1980) *First Year of Life*, Chichester and New York: Wiley.

Sroufe, A. (1983) 'Infant caregiver attachment and patterns of adaptations in pre-schoolers: the roots of maladaptation and competence', M. Perlmutter (ed.) *Minnesota Symposium in Child Psychology* 16, Hillsdale, New Jersey: Erlbaum.

Steig, W. (1972) *Amos and Boris*, Great Britain: Hamish Hamilton.

Stern, D. (1985) *The Interpersonal World of the Infant*, New York: Basic Books.

Strachey, J. (1930) 'Some unconscious factors in reading', *International Journal of Psychoanalysis* 11: 322.

Symington, N. (1986) *The Analytic Experience*, London: Free Association Books.

Taylor, D. (1982) 'Family consultation in a school setting', *Journal of Adolescence* 5: 367–77.

Tinbergen, N. and Tinbergen, E.A. (1973) *Autistic Children – New Hope for a Cure*, London: Allen & Unwin.

Torgesen, J.K. and Wong, B.Y.L. (1986) *Psychological and Educational Perspectives on Learning Disabilities*, San Diego, New York, Berkeley, Boston, London, Sydney and Toronto: Academic Press.

Trevitt, J. (1989) 'Educational therapy with a 10-year-old boy: the possibility of a story being a transitional object within the working space', *Journal of Educational Therapy* 2, 3: 18–38.

Ungeleidder, D.F. (1986) *Reading Writing and Rage: The Terrible Price Paid by Victims of School Failure*, Rolling Hills Estates, Cal.: Jalmer Press.

Varley, S. (1984) *Badger's Parting Gifts*, London: Anderson Press.

Wagenheim, L. (1960) 'First memories of accidents and reading difficulties', *American Journal of Orthopsychiatry* 30: 191–5.

Waggoner, L.C. (1933) *The Development of Learning in Young Children*, New York: McGraw-Hill.

Warnock, M. (1978) *Special Educational Needs: The Report of the Enquiry into the Education of Handicapped Children and Young People*, London: HMSO Cmnd 7212.

Watt, H. (1978) 'Processes in educational therapy', paper delivered to the Forum for the Advancement of Educational Therapy, sup. 11.

Weiss, R.S. (1982) 'Attachment in adult life', in C. Murray-Parkes and J. Stevenson-Hinde (eds) *The Place of Attachment in Human Behaviour*, London and New York: Tavistock Publications.

Weschler Intelligence Scale for Children (Revised) (1976), Slough: National Foundation for Educational Research.

White, E.B. (1952) *Charlotte's Web*, London: Hamish Hamilton.

Winnicott, D.W. (1965) *The Maturational Processes and the Facilitating Environment*, London: Hogarth Press; Toronto: Clarke, Irwin.

—— (1971) *Playing and Reality*, London: Tavistock Publications.

—— (1977 pub. posthumously) *The Piggle*, London: Hogarth Press.

—— (1986 pub. posthumously) *Home is Where We Start From*, London: W.W. Norton.

Wittenburg-Salzberger, I., Henry, G., and Osborne E. (eds) (1983) *The Emotional Experience of Learning and Teaching*, London: Routledge & Kegan Paul.

Wohl, A. and Kauffman, B. (1985) *Silent Screams and Hidden Cries*, New York: Brunner Mazel.

Yule, B. and Rutter, M. (1985) 'Scholastic skills', in M. Rutter and L. Hersov (eds) *Child and Adolescent Psychiatry: Modern Approaches*, Oxford, London, Edinburgh, Boston, Palo Alto, and Melbourne: Blackwell Scientific Publications.

INDEX

abuse 24, 37, 109, 132, 133
adolescence 117–84, 194–7
affective attunement 186
affective relationship 10
Ainsworth, M. 27, 54, 78, 144–8 *passim*, 170, 171
Ainsworth, M. & Wittig 11, 32, 57, 143, 144
Alston, J. & Taylor 131
Amos and Boris (Steig) 105–6, 169, 189, 190
anger 20, 27, 31, 96, 100, 114, 119, 127, 134, 160, 163, 185
Angry Arthur (Oram) 163
animals 91, 105–6, 118–20, 125, 160–7, 172, 208, 216
anxious attachment behaviour *see* attachment behaviour; Main *et al.*
assessment 217
attachment behaviour 11, 26, 35, 41–2, 58, 59, 61, 148; anxious 11–13, 32, 36, 61, 99, 143, 144–5, 190; anxious avoidant 144; anxious ambivalent 144; anxious disorientated/ disorganised 144; non-assuaged 171; secure 10, 29, 40–54, 143
'attachment dynamic' 35
'attachment organisation' 30
attachment figures 14, 18–19, 29–30, 77, 99, 148, 185, 249; *see also* educational attachment figures; specific attachment person
attachment theory 26–31; *Attachment and Loss see* Bowlby

backdating 32, 190
Badger's Parting Gifts (Varley) 159

Barkley, R. 1
Barr, J. 237–49
Barrett, M. 18, 36, 76, 78, 91, 251; *see also* working space
Bateson, G. 38
Bauer, D. 195
Beaumont, M. 149–58, 252
beginnings 64, 65, 69, 73, 218
behaviour 95; aggressive 20, 21, 37, 79, 238; anxious 19–20; attention-seeking 11, 24, 170, 171, 204, 238; clowning 191, 192; disorganised 191; disruptive 190, 204; proximity-seeking 27, 44, 148, 170–1; punitive 191; violent 24; withdrawal 2, 12, 20, 23–4, 37, 96, 114–15, 136, 204; *see also* attachment behaviour; exploratory behaviour; goal-seeking behaviour
behavioural system 27, 44; *see also* Bowlby
Berridge, D. 17, 123
Bettelheim, B. 103–4
Bettelheim, B. & Zelan 84
Bick, E. 41
Bion, W. 124, 214
Blos, P. 184
Blyth, B. 127, 128
books 69, 70, 72, 74, 89–90, 92, 106, 174
Bowlby, J. 1, 8, 26–45 *passim*, 77, 81, 100, 122, 144, 148, 185, 190, 192–2, 237, 249, 250
box 63, 80, 91–3, 159–60, 162, 167, 188–9, 195–7
breaks in therapy 99, 162, 164, 175, 183, 197, 212, 218, 247
Bretherton, I. & Waters 30
Byng-Hall, J. 149

259